VALUEGENESIS

TEN
YEARS
LATER

A STUDY OF TWO GENERATIONS

By *V. Bailey Gillespie, Ph.D.*
with
Michael J. Donahue, Ph.D.
&
Barry Gane, D.Min. and Ed Boyatt, Ed.D.

VALUEGENESIS

TEN YEARS LATER
A STUDY OF TWO GENERATIONS

An exploration into the responses from the
Valuegenesis[1] and Valuegenesis[2] research
on faith, values, and commitments in
Seventh-day Adventist young people

EXPERIENCE BY EXPERIENCE

We normally think of adolescence as one challenge after another, tensions and good times, experience by experience—almost as if growth were nothing more than all the narratives of human pain and family joy assembled in sequence. And surely this is, often enough, an adequate description of growing up in contemporary society. But growing up Christian is unique. It is also the narratives of grace, the recountings of those blessed, and inexplicable moments when someone did something for someone else, said the right thing, bestowed a gift, gave something beyond what was required by circumstances, or simply shared the love and compassion of the God they serve. One cannot help but be awed by the phenomenon of growth and maturity. It is the genius of creation expressed in each and every child and young person who explores life.

In a way, this book in the *Valuegenesis* series of publications from the North American Division of Seventh-day Adventists and the John Hancock Center for Youth and Family Ministry, School of Religion at La Sierra University, explores this emerging young person as he or she comes face to face with the realities of church, family, and school. In it I mean to retell the story of the emerging Christian young persons and their responses to the gift-givers in families, local churches and schools, those youth entrusted to our keeping, our singular treasure maturing in faith and loyalty to the institution of the church, our church, that we love and which we want to see reflect the Kingdom of God's grace.

— V. BAILEY GILLESPIE, PH.D.

VALUEGENESIS

TEN
YEARS
LATER

A Study of Two Generations

( )

V. BAILEY GILLESPIE

WITH

MICHAEL J. DONAHUE

&

Barry Gane • *Ed Boyatt*

Hancock Center Publication

Riverside, California

PUBLISHED BY HANCOCK CENTER PUBLICATIONS
LA SIERRA UNIVERSITY
4700 Pierce St., Riverside, CA 92515

Hancock Center Publications is a part of the ministry of the
John Hancock Center for Youth and Family Ministry at the
School of Religion, La Sierra University in Riverside, California

Valuegenesis Series Editor: V. Bailey Gillespie
Book and cover design by V. Bailey Gillespie
Statistical Analysis by Michael J. Donahue
Preprint design by: John Anthony
Proofing: Sharon Churches

Cataloging-in-Publication Data
Gillespie, V. Bailey. Donahue, Michael J.
VALUEGENESIS—Ten Years Later:
A Study of Two Generations
Includes index.
ISBN 0-9748531-0-0

To Bailey Jessica,
Hannah Jane,
& Emma Grace

(Generation "Z")

Unless there is a new mind, there cannot be a new line; the old will go on repeating itself with recurring deadliness. Without invention nothing truly changes

—Adapted from William Carlos Williams

SPONSORING SEVENTH-DAY ADVENTIST UNIONS

Atlantic Union

Columbia Union

Lake Union

Mid-America Union

North Pacific Union

Pacific Union

Seventh-day Adventist Church in Canada

Southern Union

Southwestern Union

SPONSORING SEVENTH-DAY ADVENTIST CONFERENCES

Alberta
Allegheny East
Arkansas-Louisiana
Arizona
Bermuda
British Columbia
Carolina
Central California
Central States
Florida
Georgia-Cumberland
Greater New York
Gulf States
Hawaii
Idaho
Illinois
Indiana
Kansas-Nebraska
Kentucky-Tennessee
Lake Region
Michigan

Minnesota
Mountain View
Nevada-Utah
New Jersey
New York
Nevada-Utah
Northeastern
Northern California
Northern New England
Ohio
Ontario
Oregon
Pennsylvania
Potomac
Rocky Mountain
South Central
Southeastern California
Southern California
Southern New England
Texas
Upper Columbia
Washington

Contents

( ) INTRODUCTION
Ten Years later 13

1 FOCUSING ON TEENS
So we're focusing on teens because most people aren't 27

2 THE MORE THINGS CHANGE
Let's highlight the good news first 47

3 WE ARE THE CHURCH
What's the flip side? 93

4 A FAITH THAT ENDURES
Valuegenesis and the journey of faith 127

5 FASHION ME A PEOPLE
Loyalty and the content of faith 151

6   NOW I LAY ME DOWN TO SLEEP
Personal piety and the quest for spiritual life   175

7   SPIRIT MADE FLESH
How to build a Kingdom   195

8   DANCING, MOVIES, AND OTHER SINS
Challenges and choices   221

9   THE MOST PERDURING FACTOR
Nurturing spiritual families   255

10   YES, YOUTH MINISTRY IS IMPORTANT
Making a difference   277

11   SCHOOL DAYS, SCHOOL DAZE
Valuegenesis and Adventist schools   297

12   THE SUM OF THE MATTER
Discovering positive influences   317

13   STARSHIP BEYOND
The way to the future   339

14   FROM THE STATISTICIAN'S DESK
What do the numbers say?   373

( )   APPENDIX
Scales and other indices   393

( )   HOW DO I FIND THAT?
Valuegenesis² index   411

INTRODUCTION

()

THE GENERATIONS OF FAITH
Ten years later

INTRODUCTION

THE GENERATIONS OF FAITH

Now—here is my secret: I tell it to you with an openness of heart that I doubt I shall ever achieve again, so I pray that you are in a quiet room as you hear these words. My secret is that I need God—that I am sick and can no longer make it alone. I need God to help me give, because I no longer seem to be capable of giving—to help me be kind, as I no longer seem capable of kindness; to help me love, as I seem beyond being able to love.

— *Douglas Coupland*

Young people started it all—and by "it," I mean so many of the things we care about, the underlying values that make all of us, old and young, pastors and teachers, administrators and lay-persons, tick. Without young people, we would see the world through different eyes, hear with different ears, even feel with different feelings. And not only would our sensorium, the screen through which we receive the world, be different, but also we would think with a different mind, interpret all our experience differently, draw different conclusions from the things that befall us. And we would have set a different course for our lives. Young people, you see, were at the very beginnings of our church—organizing, visioning, administrating, creating, changing, and challenging. They were the ones that formed the "Great Advent Movement." They were in the first band of believers who envisioned the Missionary Volunteers blossoming into the youth ministries organization with

Pathfinders, Adventist Youth, Storm Co., community service, Sabbath Schools, worship services, schools, colleges, universities, and all of the myriad other entities of our denominational life.

Young people were the ones who asked the first questions, studied the first texts, and made the first changes in a system of religious life that was perceived as going nowhere. They saw their home somewhere else. They were the true pilgrims of our church. And as they challenged, doubted, changed their lives, history turned the inevitable wheel, and they were challenged themselves by the creative minds of their own children. This, then, is a study of generations.

As Henri-Charles Puech says of Greek thought in his seminal *Man and Time:* "No event is unique, nothing is enacted but once. . . ; every event has been enacted, is enacted, and will be enacted perpetually; the same individuals have appeared, appear, and will appear at every turn of the circle." Young people are like that. Their generations come, rolling by like the waves of summer. They are given names by the scholars—the Silent Generation, Boomers, Generation X, and now the next generation, Y. Some even now talk of the next generation in preschool as Z. These millennial kids, as they are called, carry on the task of repetition and innovation with care. Their task: taking what is almost sacred and making it real in a world that doesn't often recognize traditions as having real strength and values. They are caught in this cycle of their own

A GENERATIONAL MODEL	
Silent	1925-1942
Boomers	1943-1960
13th/Xers	1961-1979
Generation Y	1980-1994

personal change, and they struggle to see out of the cyclone created by their own feelings, identity quest, culture, and faith concerns. Their doubt will eventually turn into hope. Most research shares that, but during the midst of the storm, eternity has new meaning and reality. And when on the receiving end of these struggles for life itself, parents often become frustrated, administrators feel inadequate, and pastors pray for power and rescue while this generation keeps on going and growing through it all.

MAKING A DIFFERENCE

This book is about making a difference. In the '90s, amidst the challenge of a culture caring less for others, big business models impacting higher education, and growing tuition costs, the Seventh-day Adventist church looked carefully at their educational system to see what was working and what needed fixing. Project Affirmation it was called. Affirming faith, values, and commitments; affirming the centrality of the second largest private educational system in the United States; affirming quality and Christianity. Out of this the *Valuegenesis* research was born.

It was the first of a kind for us. This research, nurtured by scholars and local church leaders, was one of the largest research projects the Seventh-day Adventist church had ever funded. It was a milestone of sorts. The road it wandered became a freeway of information shared by public events, ministerial meetings, church publications, Vision-to-Action focus groups, some fifteen books, doctoral dissertations, and myriad PowerPoint presentations, each with one purpose in mind—helping local church leaders, educators, pastors, and parents understand their children and make the necessary changes that might, just might make a real difference.

While traveling in the Zulu-Natal region of South Africa, after sharing with local churches and young adults the challenges of building climate-oriented, grace-targeted ministry, I was introduced to my driver back to the airport in Johannesburg. My wife, Judy, and I watched the magnificent plains and rolling green meadows of the hinterland of South Africa and listened as this local church youth director/computer store owner shared the challenges of his youth ministry. He told of the problems he had had with his own sons and how his local congregation was not youth-friendly and growing older in spirit and distant every year. He was frustrated, as his boys were disengaging with the denomination and beginning to attend a more "with it" church in the city.

As he shared his story he said, "Then one day I heard a General Conference officer who was visiting our church talk about a study the North American Division had completed. One that targeted some of the reasons why youth felt disenfranchised with local congregations, outdated standards approaches, and generally unfriendly congregations." He said he ordered a copy of the research and began to read. The book was *Faith in the Balance* by Roger Dudley with V. Bailey Gillespie. It was *Valuegenesis*[1] research and our attempt to clarify the issues and point the readers to a new model of home, church, and school.

Then came the punch line of the story. He said that he began to apply the lessons he had learned from the *Valuegenesis* research and committed himself to not let any of the negative observations sorted out in the book happen at his church any longer. He began a youth ministry, involved his own boys, and now, he said he and his sons were the local leaders shepherding over 45 young people each week towards worship, study, small group prayer, and accomplishing personal challenges. I then knew all of the sermons, presentations, discussions, publications had been worth it if just one church had become a vibrant, faithful, grace-oriented sanctuary for youth and young adults.

I believe this is why it is crucial to compare these generations and to continue this research. Things have changed over the ensuing years. This generation is an exciting one. Wendy Murray Zoba writes in *Christianity Today*, "These millennial teenagers are forcing the church to rethink youth ministry."[1]

HEARING GEN Y

American youth born between 1979 and 1994 have been labeled by marketers and demographers as Generation Y, since they followed Generation X. They are seen as some 78 million strong and are more numerous than Generation X, rivaling Baby Boomers in size and spending power.[2]

While it may appear that im-

GENERATION Y & MONEY

() Teens spend $63 billion per year.

() Teenage girls spend an average of $44 per week.

() Teenage boys spend an average of $34 per week.

() Generation Y accounts for 46% of adult spending on audio equipment.

() Generation Y accounts for 48% of adult spending on athletic shoes.

() Nearly 60% of United States households of children under the age of seven have personal computers.[3]

age is everything for Generation Y, being "cool" is crucial. "Cool isn't just an adjective, it's a comprehensive set of life-guiding concepts. 'Cool' is shorthand for all the qualities necessary for a teen's social survival: acceptance, popularity, fun, and success. In the brutally simple world of adolescents, being thought of as uncool by the social group to which you aspire is not simply a matter of not making the grade or even being rejected; it is the mark of The Loser."[4]

And since identity is so crucial, and acceptance an unspoken goal of most adolescents in this generation, this research is especially significant. Local churches, homes, and Christian schools need to realize that understanding the generation to which they minister will enhance the practical nature of that ministry and make the Gospel story sink into the very core of their lives. As young people continue to grow up, this assumption has direct implications for local congregational resources, pastoral support, and resource needs. Of equal importance, the homes from which these youth come will find increasing pressure from this culturally aware group to become "cool" or to use an older expression, "with it" as they try to rear their children in the way of the Lord as Scripture recommends.

THE RESEARCH TEAM

While I am the sole author of the core of this book, the study which it reports was a joint project involving a number of people. The field research was conducted by the John Hancock Center for Youth and Family Ministry of La Sierra University, Riverside, California, under the guidance of a *Valuegenesis* coordinating committee consisting of V. Bailey Gillespie, Ph.D., Professor of Theology and Christian Personality and director of the Hancock Center in the School of Religion, the chief researcher in this project; Michael J. Donahue, Ph.D., Coauthor and currently is an independent researcher and data analyst in Azusa, California, and the chief statistician for both *Valuegenesis*[1] and *Valuegenesis*[2] research who wrote the chapter in this book entitled, "From the Statistician's Desk"; Charles T. Smith, Ph.D., of La Sierra University and the original overall coordinator of Project Affirmation and the *Valuegenesis*[1] project; Barry Gane, D.Min., of Andrews University Theological Seminary and researcher for the South Pacific Division *Valuegenesis* research who was the author of our chapter exploring the impact of youth ministry.

This team was advised in matters of research design, questionnaire construction, and preparation of materials by a Consultation Committee consisting of Ed Boyatt, Ed.D., from La Sierra University who took a close look at Adventist schools and wrote the chapter entitled, "School Days, School Daze"; Janet Mallery, Ed.D., of La Sierra University; Ella Simmons, Ph.D., Provost of La Sierra University; Edwin Hernandez, Ph.D., of Notre Dame University; Gail Rice, Ed.D. and Richard Rice, Ph.D. of Loma Linda University; Jerry Lee, Ph.D., of Loma Linda University; Won Kil Yoon from La Sierra University; and Jane Thayer, Ph.D., from Andrews University.

The entire team is responsible for this research study and its voluminous findings and insights. And like Roger Dudley in the study of *Valuegenesis* in *Faith in the Balance,* I have borrowed language from Search Institute, Minneapolis, Minnesota, which did *Valuegenesis*[1] and helped formulate the original questionnaire, along with the many publications which were the by-products of that research over the past years, as well as from scores of publications over the past decade produced from the data of earlier research.

Research is only as good as its application. Research contains myriad concepts, ratios, aspects, and correlations that only become clear as we try to make significant application from the portraits that the brush strokes of this research paints. Many view Generation Y through a stereotypical lens—seeing apathetic, unmotivated and primarily self-interested young people. However, we saw a much different picture and a much more optimistic one when we looked at these students in Seventh-day Adventist schools, grades 6 through 12, as they prepare for graduation and their entrance into the "real world." They could easily be described as a "very connected, very education-minded and spiritual" group.

The findings reported here are based on over 16,000 respondents of Seventh-day Adventist youth in Seventh-day Adventist schools throughout the North American Division during the 2000 school year. As we continue the *Valuegenesis* research, we will in other publications, focus on college and university students and Adventist students in non-Adventist or public education at some later date. But now there is so much to be learned by studying this group we just couldn't wait any longer to share what we have discovered. But before we begin in earnest, we want to thank a number of people that have made this research both viable and possible.

KUDOS

I would like to thank the North American Division of Seventh-day Adventists for the grant that made it possible for me to spend time on this project and La Sierra University for allowing the necessary release time. I want to thank my wife, Judith, a busy businesswoman and court reporter, who assisted me in the editing of this manuscript and listening by the hour to interpretations of the data in hundreds of presentations over the past years. And, in addition, a special thanks must go to the Unions and local conference organizations that have supported this project with both funding and encouragement.[5] Special kudos go to the Office of Education in the North American Division who fully sponsored this research and coordinated its funding. I can't forget Roger L. Dudley's work on the first *Valuegenesis* book, *Faith in the Balance,* which provided the basic outline for this follow-up. He deserves kudos too.

Understanding *Valuegenesis* insights is only possible because of the time-consuming endeavor of those that have worked on the various reports already available to the sponsoring Unions. This would only be possible because of the efforts of John Anthony, actor, artist, musician, information technician, webmaster, church worker, youth minister and all-around Man Friday to the John Hancock Center for Youth and Family Ministry at La Sierra University. As a free-lance assistant, his work is always important. His coordination with the eNewsletter, *UPDATE* and the servicing of the web site where these updates can be downloaded is truly appreciated.[6]

In addition, Dr. John Jones, the dean of the School of Religion, through his commitment to good scholarship and administrative expertise understood the time it takes to provide both public presentations, regular newsletters, union reports, and book-length manuscripts for publication by the Hancock Center and the North American Division. He deserves credit for his behind-the-scenes help in allowing me to work with a reduced load during various quarters at La Sierra University, even while nurturing our new fledgling M.Div. graduate degree at the university. And one final thank you is in order. Stuart Tyner, former Director of the John Hancock Center for Youth and Family Ministry and Associate Pastor of the La Sierra University Church provided clear editing and insight into the Orthodoxy II Scale in this research. Building on our earlier work, his additional and clear statements of belief helped us understand the theology of the Adventist church, and more importantly, helped youth to clarify what it is that our church believes.

What motivates research of this kind? It is a deep conviction that the youth of the church are the church of today. We can't wait for them to be the church of the future because that future is being built now by their commitment, love for God's grace, and careful, thoughtful choices to help build the Kingdom of God here, now. And churches can't wait either. Youth culture is changing almost as fast as the children's song suggests, "The wheels of the bus go round and round, round and round, round and round." Things just continue to go on and churches and schools, not to mention the families that grow them, can't be ignorant of the things that truly make a difference.

We hope that anything you discover in reading this work will help youth and young adults in your church, school, and family come closer to the God of love that we hope is disclosed in this research. *Ten Years Later: A Study of Two Generations* is committed to just such a contribution.

REFERENCES

1. Shared from Wendy Murray Zoba, *Christianity Today* (February 3, 1997), Vol. 41, No. 2, 18.
2. Choonghoon Lim, Douglas Michele Turco, "The Cyber-Journal of Sport Marketing," http://www.cjsm.com/vol3/lim34.htm, 1.
3. N. Rosenthal. "The Boom Tube," *Media Week,* 8 (20), 44-52; M. Beck, "The Next Big Population Bulge: Generation Y Shows its Might," *The Wall Street Journal.* (February 3, 1997).
4. S. Reese, "The Quality of Cool." *Marketing Tools,* 3 (6), 27.
5. The unions and conferences that supported financially the *Valuegenesis²* research are listed as follows: *Sponsoring Unions*—Atlantic Union, Columbia Union, Lake Union, Mid-America Union, North Pacific Union, Pacific Union, Seventh-day Adventist Church in Canada, Southern Union, Southwestern Union. *Sponsoring Conferences*—Alberta, Allegheny East, Arkansas-Louisiana, Arizona, Bermuda, British Columbia, Carolina, Central California, Central States, Florida, Georgia-Cumberland, Greater New York, Gulf States, Hawaii, Idaho, Illinois, Indiana, Kansas-Nebraska, Kentucky-Tennessee, Lake Region, Michigan, Minnesota, Mountain View, Nevada-Utah, New Jersey, New York, Nevada-Utah, Northeastern, Northern California, Northern New England, Ohio, Ontario, Oregon, Pennsylvania, Potomac, Rocky Mountain, South Central, Southeastern California, Southern California, Southern New England, Texas, Upper Columbia, Washington.
6. If you would like to receive our free eNewsletter *UPDATE*, just send us your e-mail address and we will make sure you get on the mailing list. We would love to hear from you and have you share your stories of successful children, youth, young adult, and family ministry. Contact us at: <hcyfm@lasierra.edu>.

This generation's pulse runs fast. Bombarded by frequent images, they are in need of continual "hits." The remote control symbolizes their reality: change is constant; focus is fragmented. They've eaten from the tree of knowledge. They live for now. They are jaded, having a "been there/done that" attitude, nothing shocks them. They take consumerism for granted. They are a cyber-suckled community. They process information in narrative images (like Nike commercials). They've had everything handed to them. They don't trust adults. They care about God.

— Wendy Murray Zoba,
Adapted from Christianity Today

CHAPTER 1

( )

FOCUSING ON TEENS
So we're focusing on teens because most people aren't

1

FOCUSING ON TEENS

*So we're focusing on teens because
most people aren't*

*What is the relationship to the ultimate which is symbolized in these
[cultural] symbols?* —Paul Tillich

*There is a whole generation that the church has lost. MTV has captured
them, but the church hasn't. So we're focusing on teens because most people aren't.*
—Ed Basler

I f you believe the critics, you might come to the conclusion that young people today are superficial, often distracted, aimless, inscrutable, self-absorbed, unfocused, pathetic, often confused. If you believe their parents they might add to this list irresponsible, lazy, undisciplined, egotistic, and materialistic. Talk to many youth pastors, and they might conclude they are disorganized, stressed, and frenetic. One ponders, what is youth's relationship to the Ultimate? And, of course, we wonder how pastors, teachers, and parents cope with them over the long haul.

While the generation dubbed X—young people born in the '60s and '70s who are currently pushing their life cycle predecessors, the overanalyzed "Baby Boomers," off the center of the podium—were, during the last decade, the center of attention. Now viewing the horizon, we see this new one, the Y Generation,

Millennial kids, as they like to be called, not the "lost generation" of the Xers. But for most youth workers, educators, pastors, and parents, they are a true, new challenge. They are the ones at center stage, and knowing about them will help us understand our role as parents, teachers, and pastors. We focus on them in this book because most people aren't.

A CHALLENGE AHEAD

How do you tap into the core of their lives? How can we understand their spirituality? What makes them tick? What is it that makes this new generation, Generation Y, stand out? It is even riskier to try to *understand* their spiritual life and not just to *observe* it.

Generation X was hard enough to understand, and people are still talking about their impact on culture. Of them, the theologian Harvey Cox said, "If their [Generation X] ever-shifting tastes in consumer commodities—Patagonia jackets, Macs and PCs, Tevas, rock music on compact discs, and movies about aliens—have well been charted, at least for the moment, their religious proclivities have remained a mystery, almost as inscrutable as that of the Holy Trinity."[2]

It is no wonder that many youth workers throw up their hands in

GENERATIONS X AND Y

"Gen Xers lived to hear the words, "We don't have a lot of rules here." They tended to be individuals who value work-life balance. Generation Y, however, grew up in a time of economic expansion and until recently, never experienced an economic downturn. They tend to be more optimistic than Gen Xers and expect success early in their lives."[1]

frustration whenever they are asked to classify their ministry generation. One wonders if Harvey Cox is correct when he adds, "Or are they merely conspiring to bamboozle anyone who tries to put them in a pigeonhole?"[3]

For three decades now, I have been teaching courses on religion at La Sierra University. I have seen classes come and go, modulate, and reverse themselves again and again. What we see is not altogether new. Even Socrates (470-399 BC) groused about what young people were like: "Children today are tyrants. They contradict their parents, gobble their food, and tyrannize their teachers."

WERE ADAM AND EVE EVER TEENAGERS?

While we don't really know whether Adam and Eve were ever teenagers, after they began to have children, there have always been persons that were chronologically the age of adolescents or teenagers. As we look at their stories in Scripture, we can identify persons who must have been teenagers and/or who acted much like what corresponds to our modern view of adolescents. Daniel Aleshire saw some of these precocious biblical youth and chronicles their stories. He identifies David and Samson as typical teens.[4] Of David he suggests that the interchange between David and his brothers is not unlike one that you may have heard in your own home. Especially notice the last two sentences.

> David asked the men standing near him, "What will be done for the man who kills this Philistine and removes this disgrace from Israel? Who is this uncircumcised Philistine that he should defy the armies of the living God?" They repeated to him what they had been saying and told him,

"This is what will be done to the man who kills him." When Eliab, David's oldest brother, heard him speaking with the men, he burned with anger at him and asked, "Why have you come down here? And with whom did you leave those few sheep in the desert? I know how conceited you are and how wicked your heart is; you came down only to watch the battle." "Now what have I done?" said David. "Can't I even speak?"[5]

In addition, one can't forget the great warrior Sampson known for his adolescent hormonal rages and teenage reactions in his relationships with family and friends, and, we might add Mary, the mother of Jesus. She was, it seems, a teen when she was committed to marry Joseph.

One glaring story in the New Testament about Jesus stands out. Remember, He was in the temple in Jerusalem. Like a classic teen, He challenges the authorities and clarifies His identity in spite of his parent's request to travel. His classic response, *"Why were you searching for me?"* he asked. *"Didn't you know I had to be in my Father's house?"*[6] shines as a clear testimony to adolescent identity questing even though we don't hear anything from him from ages 12 to 30.

There are many more illustrations that we can cite. If you run a concordance check on passages in the wisdom literature of the Bible, the Psalms and Proverbs, looking at those texts that refer to youth and growing up, you are astounded at their number and quality.[7] The counsel provided by Psalm 119:9 still makes sense today: *"How can a young man keep his way pure? By living according to your word."*

Of course we "older" ones don't like to admit we simply don't understand our children. We figure we grew up; they will too. And while this is a truism regarding physicality, it very well may not be the case spiritually and emotionally. We often think we are contemporary, never truly out of touch with the next generation. But in truth, your modern teenager is not about to listen to advice from an older person, defined by writer Dave Berry as a person who remembers when there was no Velcro. Their peers are influential and have power well beyond their wisdom at giving advice and capturing attitudes. Being older doesn't always mean wiser either. But I am getting ahead of myself. We will save the detailed discussion about the influences that impact youth in our schools to another chapter later on in this book.

YES, WE SUPPORT CHRISTIAN EDUCATION

As Roger Dudley said in *Faith in the Balance,* "When it comes to Christian education, the Seventh-day Adventist church can hardly stand accused of not having put enough into it."[8]

Our own family is committed to Christian education. Both our children, Tim and Shannon, attended all their elementary, junior high, and high school in Adventist education. Both Judy, my wife, and I are graduates of Adventist elementary and secondary schools. Everyone in our family has graduated from Adventist colleges or universities, and three of our family have advanced degrees from Adventist higher education. And our first granddaughter, Bailey Jessica just started second grade at Loma Linda Elementary School. Not only has Christian education captured our tuition dollars, it has captured our hearts. I simply love it.

I remember when I first became a Christian and asked my parents to go to a private school and transfer from my public schooling. My sister was already in a private school. My father, who was not an active Christian, didn't hesitate. In fact, he encouraged me to go and challenged me to make the most of my education—an education that not many of my friends from public school would ever experience. I'll never forget the positive influence Mr. Davis our math teacher, Mr. Olmstead our biologist and Mrs. Smith's English class, and the leadership of Miss Fouts. All of them contributed to my choices to work for the church and to continue in higher education.

In a recent session of the Trans-European Division quinquennial conference on education, Humberto Rasi, recently retired General Conference superintendent of Education, Dr. Rasi, in response to a question of the importance of Adventist education said, "No Adventist education. No future!" His sentiments reflect hundreds of appreciative graduates of our schooling system.

Ten Years Ago—1990

() More than 50,000 students were in K-8 classrooms.
() Another 16,000 were in Adventist secondary schools.
() There were 1,100 elementary schools and junior academies.
() There were 93 senior academies.
() Nearly 17,000 additional students attended the Division's twelve colleges and universities.
() 7,150 teachers and administrators
() Primary school fixed assets were estimated at $668,000,000.[9]

While sharing my positive childhood experience about Adventist education with my wife's mother, Ottilia Bietz Walcker, she told of how hard it was to get a Christian education in North Dakota when she grew up. And since her parents were 100 percent behind Christian education, both her mother and father were united in sending all nine of their children to an Adventist Christian school.

Then the family read some significant statements from the *Testimonies* by Ellen G. White relative to sending children to a Christian school. Statements she remembered as, "It is no longer safe to send our children to public schools," or something of that nature. She shared how her mother and father hitched a team of horses to the buggy and searched for available land near the closest Adventist church.

Since homesteading was not available in that area, the problem was solved after they found 160 acres for sale one mile west of the church. As the story is told,

> *In a few days, two monster steam-propelled engines were hitched to the house and things were ready for the nine-mile trip. The move was made in May after the April showers and there was still soft areas which were difficult to negotiate or avoid. . . .Only one mile from the goal, both the engine and the house were extracted from the sinking soil and the move continued. In a few days the house was resting on the new foundation only one mile from the school.*[10]

Thus a new Adventist school was launched with a full enrollment. If the school couldn't come to the family, the family would move to the school!

TEN YEARS LATER

The decade past *Valuegenesis[1]* has shown some changes in Adventist Christian education, but not its centrality in Adventism in general. During the 1999-2000 school year in the North American Division, more than 48,384 students were enrolled in kindergarten through grade eight and another 14,530 at the high school level.

These students attended nearly 941 elementary schools and junior academies and 113 Adventist high schools. Over 20,500 additional students attended the Division's fifteen colleges or universities.

The denomination spends an inordinate amount of money to support the second-largest private school system in the country. In the most recent years, educational institutions in the North American Division employed over 6,900 teachers and administrators. In addition, think of the operating costs to run so many schools. Imagine the support personnel such as maintenance workers, cooks, bus drivers, secretaries, grounds people and janitors needed to keep the schools up and actually running. So add to this the cost of building upkeep, equipment upgrading, libraries, utilities, insurance, cafeteria food and you can see that the costs for this endeavor are staggering. It is actually hard to determine the actual costs of this activity. Ten years ago costs for the educational ministry of the church were estimated to be "between five hundred million and one billion dollars."[11] Just think what it might be now if it could be calculated.

Who pays the bills? This is the question. The majority of the expenses are borne by local parents and churches. Tuition drives our schools and often is from 65% to as much as 90% of the total costs of operating. But schools could not exist if they were not heavily subsidized by the denomination. Education costs a great deal of money. If you could determine the amount of money put into our system by local congregations, generous donors, caring corporations who want to assist educational technology, perhaps the subsidy could be considered even larger. Most of the rest of the money comes from local conference, union, division, and General Conference appropriations.

There are grants that some schools are eligible to receive from local government and private funds; and some still come from school industries; however, this is a decreasing source of income for Christian education. The total fixed asset value of all our educational institutions in North America was conservatively estimated in the year 1997 at over $866,000,000. Overall in the world field of the Seventh-day Adventist church, educational assets amount to over $1,728,000,000. We have made quite an investment in Christian education. What Joseph Addison (1672-1719) said is true: "What sculpture is to a block of marble, education is to the soul." Adventists have seen and continue to see Christian education as a cornerstone of moral teaching and training for the children of the church.

There is no question that Adventist education is important. We could point out the percentage of medical workers per capita among Adventists, the number of pastors, and teachers, youth workers, administrators, and local church leaders that have been trained and equipped through the educational ministry of the church. Add to this the number of baptisms, evangelistic contacts, service projects coordinated through the educational system, student missionaries sent from our colleges and universities, and you have an amazing commitment to church growth and evangelism from the educators and individual schools within the Seventh-day Adventist school system.

One young person e-mailed me

ELLEN G. WHITE WROTE

Schools of the prophets, founded by the prophet Samuel in ancient Israel, "were intended to serve as a barrier against the wide-spreading corruption, to provide for the mental and spiritual welfare of the youth, and to promote the prosperity of the nation by furnishing it with men [women] qualified to act in the fear of God as leaders and counselors."[12]

about her experience in an Adventist school after she had spent a number of years in public education. "My life is totally different now. My classmates pray for me, my teachers care about the problems I face, and my pastor is available during the school day whenever I need to have some encouraging."

We continue to face, however, serious realities regarding the costs, enrollment, demand for quality education, declining percentage of denominational funds for education, and increasing student choice in educational options. And we face a critical opportunity when it comes to involving our workers' children in Christian education. It seems as if many who have little background in Adventist education themselves don't see the significance of their own children being trained in Adventist schools. This is a growing challenge.

And in spite of these lingering challenges, Adventist education continues to provide a quality, value-added education for thousands of young people in the Adventist church. And in addition, it continues to bring an evangelistic fervor to its ministry with children, youth, and young adults. It amazes me why only a little over a third of Seventh-day Adventist parents take advantage of the Christian education our church has and its positive influence over time.

Adventist educators continue to be committed to the same three educational and eternal issues that Ellen White once wrote about: creating a barrier against corruption, building mental and spiritual strength, and training men and women in the fear of God. We still have a multitude of reasons to be in the education business in our church. And if any one of these little ones find Jesus in their lives, the immense expense is well worth it.

THERE ARE SCHOOLS AND THERE ARE SCHOOLS

No one is hinting that problems don't still exist. We have always been faced with problems, expectations, and challenges. The new age of technology presents additional opportunities and unbelievable cost expenditures or upgrades to our systems. As the generational bulge has moved through the grades, schools have had to adjust: fewer primary schools, more junior high and senior schools. College and university expansions are necessary as increasing class size and population growth in this age category continues in the new century.

Fine high schools have closed and others have been saved only by creative funding by local congregations, while at the same time eighth-grade primary schools have needed to expand to junior academies and finally senior high schools in order to satisfy the demand for quality Christian education by parents who refuse to send their children off to boarding schools.

Public education has its draw. You can send your children to secular school for a fraction of the cost. Some say, "It is a lot of money to pay for a Bible class!" But of course, that answer simply doesn't explore the multifaceted impact that a Christian environment can have on the development of values and lifestyle practice. We see that Adventist education provides a much safer environment, indeed, more costly, but significantly safer than any public, secular experience could ever have. And one must weigh that value in order to make a clear decision.

In some conferences our research indicates that as high as 70% of the school-age students attend public education rather than choosing an Adventist Christian school. There are a myriad of reasons for this—financial considerations, location, perceived quality, and access—but since we have such a financial commitment to education as a denomination, it is crucial to understand the benefits and challenges working with the Millennial generation if we are to solve and explore the options for the future.

In many ways, this generation in our study represents most young people of this age. In public school or out, they have many of the same values, interests, attitudes towards their church and family. *Valuegenesis[2]* proposes to explore these issues and provide some clear direction for change for families, schools and churches.

This book deals with one specific project targeted at understanding Adventist youth who responded to our surveys in grades 6 through 12 in Seventh-day Adventist Christian schools. It was no doubt, one of the most ambitious and expensive project our church has undertaken in its history. The research has spanned now over ten years. Beginning in 1989 the North American Division Office of Education began research to provide a picture of the value systems of Adventist youth in our schools and to try to see just what factors in Adventist homes, schools, and churches best nurture the values and faith that we love.

WE CALL IT *VALUEGENESIS*

Valuegenesis research was the term coined for this project. It is research about values, and it was the first of its kind, and thus, the name *Valuegenesis* was born. In 1990 the study was conducted for the Division Board of Education by Search Institute of Minneapolis in consultation with researchers at Andrews, and La Sierra universities, and a few selected educators outside of the Adventist system in order to collect the needed information. Special "Adventist" research instruments were developed, checked by Adventist theologians, and used in the original comprehensive instrument. Over 500 questions were in the *Valuegenesis[1]* survey. The first research project consisted of a census of over 16,000 individuals with some 11,000 in the original study for publication. This time around the survey was distributed to over 21,000 students and this book is reporting on over 10,000 respondents during the 2000-2001 school year in Adventist schools in the entire North American Division of the Seventh-day Adventist church.

Our goals for this book have not changed since our first publication of *Faith in the Balance* in 1992. Then the major purpose of the book was to present the "most pertinent findings of the *Valuegenesis* study to the Adventist church in North America and to draw implications both for our educational system in particular and for youth ministry in general through the channels of our homes, churches, and schools."[13]

Valuegenesis[2] is a richer study in many ways than the first one. Revisions were made in a number of scales, new issues were addressed, and more timely questions emerged as the study was prepared. Included in this round was a more extensive set of questions about grace, along with a clearer exploration into the challenge of works in the life of the Christian young person. Family scales were included in the latest research in order to get a clearer picture of family styles and their impact on discipline, lifestyle choices, and loyalty to the church. The section about at-risk behaviors was enlarged. Adventist standards and Biblical doctrines were explored and examined in a more complete way. So there is much that is new in this volume. And while this book lays no claim to be exhaustive in understanding the multiple ways to look at the responses of the young people in grades 6 through 12 of the Adventist school system in North America, it does try to get at many possible relationships and has created numerous new scales that shed light on the young people under the microscope of research.

Over the past ten years the John Hancock Center for Youth and Family Ministry at La Sierra University has been responsible for publishing parenting, youth, and congregational resources based on the original study. In addition, over ninety-one separate studies were completed during those years in schools and local churches and conferences all around the world by the Hancock Center staff. The information goes on and on, and the insights gleaned from this exploration have impacted the mindsets of young Adventists and created a wellspring of information that has informed churches, schools and families. This book is the first major report, "a skimming of the cream" as Roger Dudley said of the study.[14] It, too, represents only the highlights of the research. We tried to pick information that was not only interesting but helpful in building clear ministry, supporting strong families, and helping value-added Christian educational institutions. Much still remains to be uncovered. There is still much to do if we are to fully understand the spiritual lives of the youth of the church.

The Hancock Center staff is committed to sharing with church boards, leaders, pastors, youth workers, and church members the wealth hidden here in hopes that things will be different as we understand correctly and take steps to change.

The data sets are stored at La Sierra, Loma Linda, Azusa Pacific, and Andrews universities, where they are available to responsible scholars who wish to mine this information in the coming years. We hope many will take up the challenge to enrich the church with their results. All in all, over 27 separate publications, books, and scores of articles in church papers, scholarly journals, and dissertations grew from the original research. We hope more will come from new data.

I am reminded of a number of Norman Rockwell paintings used for the covers of magazines in the past: pictures of families preparing to send their children off to college; boys sitting with their dads, hanging on the running board of the family pickup while waiting for the coming bus to take them away for the first time; or another painting of a boy balancing precariously on, trying not to tumble off, surrounded by family showing faces of anticipation and hope; or another of a typical family, an intelligent, bespectacled young boy with diploma in hand getting the pats of praise from his teachers and close family. Each time I see these pictures I am reminded of my own stable childhood and of my wife's family's friendship and love during those challenging and often mysterious years of schooling.

I've always wondered if Norman Rockwell were alive today what would he paint of the typical American family. Would he paint the family kitchen with only a few sitting together to eat, with one teen running off to catch his friend at the mall, ear-phoned, iPoded, and MP3ed? Would a child be pictured arriving home from school leaving the yellow bus to go to an unsupervised house with unlimited TV viewing and video games galore. Or the graduation picture would show a family loaded down with debt and student loans, looking forlorn? We can only wonder what it might look like. At the same time, we can hope for a better future because we are attempting to understand families, children and teens. Better now because we focused on them for a short while and then made the important, necessary changes that truly would make a difference.

REFERENCES

1. Joanne Sujansky, "The Private Sector: Energetic Generation Y bores easily, needs coaching," *Post Gazette, Business News* (November 20, 2001). http://www.post-gazette.com/businessnews/20011120forumsujansky1120bnp5.asp.

2. Harvey Cox in Tom Beaudoin, *Virtual Faith: The Irreverent Spiritual Quest of Generation X* (San Francisco, CA: Jossey-Bass Publishers, 1998), ix.

3. Tom Beaudoin, *Virtual Faith*, x.

4. Daniel O. Aleshire, *Understanding Today's Youth* (Nashville, TN: Convention Press, 1982), 11-13.

5. I Samuel 17:26-29 (NIV).

6. Luke 2:49 (NIV).

7. Some of the passages relating to youth growth in scripture include: Psalm 25:7; 71:5,17; 88:15; 89:45; 103:5; 110:3; 119:9; 127:4; 129:1-2; 144:12; Proverbs 1:4; 2:17; 5:18.

8. Roger L. Dudley with V. Bailey Gillespie, *Valuegenesis: Faith in the Balance* (Riverside, CA: La Sierra University Press, 1992), 2.

9. This total reflects 1990 and 1997 fixed assets reports for primary schools. Reports for the year 2000 are not available in financial statements.

10. Reinhold Reinhardt Bietz, *Happy Home Farm: An Expression of the Faith and Fun in a Christian Home* (Brushton, NY: Teach Services, Inc., 1994), 43.

11. Roger L. Dudley with V. Bailey Gillespie, *Faith in the Balance*, 5.

12. Ellen G. White, *Education* (Haggerstown, MD: Review and Herald Publishing Association, 1903), 46.

13. Roger L. Dudley with V. Bailey Gillespie, *Faith in the Balance*, 15.

14. Roger L. Dudley with V. Bailey Gillespie, *Faith in the Balance*, 16.

Could I climb to the highest place in Athens, I would lift my voice and proclaim, "Fellow citizens, why do you turn and scrape every stone to gather wealth and take so little care of your children to whom one day you must relinquish it all."

The child is not a vessel to be filled but a flame to be kindled.

Children nowadays love luxury, have bad manners, contempt for authority, disrespect for elders.

Children today are tyrants. They contradict their parents, gobble their food, and tyrannize their teachers.
—Socrates (470-399 BC)

I see no hope for the future of our people if they are dependent on the frivolous youth of today, for certainly all youth are reckless beyond words . . . . When I was young, we were taught to be discreet and respectful of elders, but the present youth are exceedingly wise and impatient of restraint.
— Hesiod (800 BC)

CHAPTER 2

()

THE MORE THINGS CHANGE
Let's highlight the good news first

2

THE MORE THINGS CHANGE
Let's highlight the good news first

The more things change, the more they remain the same. —*French Proverb*

O ne pastor lamented not too long ago, "I just don't relate well to today's teens." As any speaker knows, youth are a tough crowd, and even harder to reach. Believing that the young are so negative about everything, especially towards adults and what the church stands for, paints such a discouraging picture many churches and ministry leaders in local congregations figure if you just leave them alone, somehow they will grow up and eventually be just like us. As George Barna, researcher and youth specialist, says, that attitude may be "the sign that [you] are getting too old to do relevant ministry."[1]

Things haven't changed that much either. Hesiod, the Greek poet in 800 BC proclaimed, "I see no hope for the future of our people if they are dependent on the frivolous youth of today, for certainly all youth are reckless beyond words . . . . When I was young, we were taught to be discreet and respectful of elders, but the present youth are exceedingly wise and impatient of restraint."[2]

There have been articles in the New York Times devoted to

teens asking the question, "Who are these people, anyway?" In fact, such topics have become a popular content for national debate. One teenager who wrote to us said, "I don't know what I want, I only know I don't want what everyone else wants." One father wrote, "Probably the best snapshot of kids these days is the statistic about youth suicide. The rate is higher than it has ever been. I think that reflects where they're coming from and their sense of the meaninglessness and emptiness." This father had just recently given up coaching his son's baseball team because of his frustration with their attitudes.

The mass media is filled with images, labels, and stereotypes about America's teenagers. Here is what some youth experts say about today's youth:

() They've eaten from the tree of knowledge.
() They process information in narrative images.
() They don't trust adults.
() Their focus is fragmented.
() They've had everything handed to them.
() They are jaded.
() They have a "been there, done that" attitude.[3]

In contrast to these responses, here is what teens say about themselves:

() The word *teenager* is synonymous with, like, headache.[4]
() No one has any sense of honor anymore.
() We have no one to look up to; we have nothing stable to grasp.
() We worry all the time.

( ) We're just coasting.

( ) We're not standing for anything.

( ) We desperately need to be standing for something.

( ) Teens want God; they will look for Him.[5]

Lists like these, short and punctilious, often provide a caricature of youth rather than paint a complete portrait of young people. And while they may be correct in some respect, they seldom provide much help in making decisions, planning discipline, or building family faith. Instead, *Valuegenesis* research tries to process as complete a picture portrait as possible. A portrait that includes a careful look inside the lives of Adventist early teens and young people.

Many religious educators say that teens are religious beings. After all, you can't be making decisions about life, future, relationships, values, and identity without considering those essential values that manifest themselves in religion itself. Adventist youth are no different. They too must make those masterful decisions that frame their future, but at the same time be true to the times and culture in which they grow.

No matter who you are parent, teacher, pastor, religious worker, youth pastor, lay leader, uncle, aunt, or sibling your young people may not always present themselves as particularly spiritual with a deep,

THE SENIOR CLASS OF 2000

( ) They consider themselves to be in the vanguard of a new generation.

( ) As a name for their generation, they vastly prefer the "Millennials" over Generation Y" 55% to 14%.

( ) They think their parents' generation expects them to meet a higher standard of personal behavior than their parents apply to themselves. 60% felt this way."[6]

vertical relationship to God. They may seem religious in the sense that they choose behaviors, ideas, choices, and values that have God at their core. But as young people work through these major values choices in their growing-up years, you can be sure that they are processing religious issues and values. After all, we have as Christian parents, "trained them in the way they should go," and we must trust that they "will not depart from it," as the Scripture shares.

"Nothing helps us understand youth more than living with one through their teen years." This truism is implicit in *Valuegenesis* research. The longer we look at the youth of the church, the better we get to know them. When we get truly close to these young people, over a longer period of time we can see glimpses that share deep emotions, attitudes, and visions for the future. We learn more than when we meet them at the mall or after church in the parking lot. And as we learn, we are often surprised by what we find.

Adult expectations often color what we hope to see. Parents are often unaware of what their youth's true feelings are all about. The local youth leader who shares Christ once a week doesn't know the deep feelings of frustration with the church that stem from alienation and climates that are uncaring, with members that have often forgotten what it was like to be young themselves. We just might be surprised at what is really going on in the heads and minds of youth.

VALUEGENESIS²

We have completed for the second time in ten years a comprehensive look into the lives of Seventh-day Adventist young people. More than 21,000 surveys were sent, with 16,000 who completed the sixteen-page questionnaire composed of 396 items. After cleaning the data and removing those non-Adventist students in our school, we looked closely at over 10,000 respondents. Again we can take a look at the portrait of Adventist youth in Adventist schools and see what changes have happened over the ensuing years since *Valuegenesis[1]* in 1990.

We know we will find challenges in this research. Some of them will be specifically reflective of homes, others of the schools these students attend. Still others will find challenges in their own local congregations. These concerns, serious as they may seem, are proleptic in nature. They call us forward, never backwards. They move us towards better goals and more precise practice. They call us to change and are the core reasons for this research. But let's get right to the point and answer your overarching question as to the worth of this research. Have we found out anything that is positive? Are the results of this research encouraging to families, schools and churches? As the old Nike commercials say, "Let's just do it!"

WHO ARE THESE PEOPLE?

If most church members are not very hopeful about today's rising generation, it is because so many of them figure that history generally moves in straight lines. They might even assume that the next batch of youth will follow just as blindly along all the life-cycle trends initiated some thirty or forty years ago by the Boomers, which were confirmed about ten to twenty years ago by the Gen Xers.

One observer has concluded,

"These trends point to more selflessness in personal manner, more splintering in public purpose, more profanity in culture and daily discourse, more risk-taking with sex and drugs, more apathy about politics, and more crime, violence, and social decay."[7]

Our survey size included the following demographics:

TOTAL *VALUEGENESIS* [2] —NORTH AMERICAN DIVISION

	Male	*Female*	*% of Census*
6th grade	48%	52%	17%
7th grade	45%	55%	19%
8th grade	47%	53%	20%
9th grade	47%	53%	14%
10th grade	48%	52%	10%
11th grade	46%	54%	8%
12th grade	45%	45%	12%

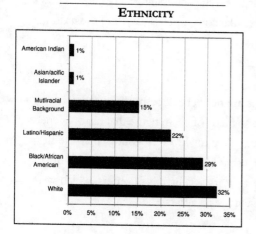

ETHNICITY

80% come from two-parent families while 20% are from one-parent families. Another 20% from divorced parents. Of the total sample of students surveyed in Seventh-day Adventist schools, 77% of the fathers are members of the church; 92.5% of the mothers represent the Adventist faith.

47% of the census for *Valuegenesis²* were male, with 53% female. The average age for baptism of the students in Adventist education was 11.6 years of age, with only 14% of the total group over 13 years of age. And as you look carefully at this percentage it is interesting to note that 22% were not baptized at all, and 42% were baptized before the age of 12.

And as you can see by the chart of ethnicity there is a balance among the races represented in this study as well. 68% of the census size represented ethnic communities other than white and included 15% who saw themselves as multiracial.

REASONS TO REJOICE

We can say without reservation that there is good news—and plenty of it. In spite of the challenges we will find illustrated in the following pages, there is much that bears exploration. And like our first book, *Faith in the Balance,* there are many reasons to celebrate. This chapter wants to highlight them right away lest anyone says it was not worth it to take this close a look at our children.

So let's enter into this story together. Hold off your criticism and conclusions until the last chapter. Take this journey with us as we try to understand the youth of the

TEN YEARS AGO AND TODAY
1990-2000

() 88% believe their mothers feel comfortable talking with others about matters of faith (1990).

() *91% believe their mothers feel comfortable (2000).*

() 31% of high school seniors report having family devotions once a week or more (1990).

() *40% of high school seniors report having family devotions now (2000).*

church and what we can do to make a difference and challenge our children to take the journey together with Christ. After all, as Eugene Peterson says,

> *We are invited into becoming full participants in the story of Jesus and show others how to become such participants. We are not simply told that Jesus is the Son of God; we not only become beneficiaries of his atonement; we are invited to die his death and live his life with the freedom and dignity of participants. And here is the marvelous thing: we enter the center of the story without becoming the center of the story.*[8]

We feel the same way and want Jesus Christ to be glorified in all of this data and analysis. After all, God's children are worth it.

THE IMPORTANCE OF FAITH

Spirituality is not a minor story with today's adolescents. The spiritual dimension influences all dimensions of their growth. Some writers call us to remember the "big four" of adolescent development. The spiritual dimension influences all of them. In Luke 2:52, we have the description of Jesus' development which models all our growth. We are told, *"Jesus grew in wisdom and stature, and in favor with God and men."* Typically biblical scholars, youth pastors and preachers have explained this text this way: *Wisdom* equals our mental development; *Stature* involves physical development; *Favor with God*—our spiritual development; *Favor with men*—targets our social and emotional development. These are the "big four."

Personal religion plays a major role in the lives of many of our young people. We asked the question, "How important is religious faith in your life?" While ten years ago about half (50%) responded positively to this question, now ten years later more than half, some 58%, gave the same testimony. Only 2% said that religion was not an important influence in their lives at all.

In earlier research by Search Institute, information on the mainline Protestant churches (United Methodist, United Church of Christ, Christian Church/Disciples of Christ, Presbyterian Church of the USA, and Evangelical Lutheran Church in America) less than 30% of the youth reported that religious faith was either the most important or a very important influence in their lives.[???] In comparison, these Adventist young people report to be nearly two times as likely to emphasize the importance of religious faith as are those in mainline Protestantism.

When we look at their commitment to the person of Jesus Christ in their lives, we find an even more sizable majority. 90% of the young people in grades 6 through 12 in Seventh-day Adventist Schools claim commitment to Jesus, either at a specific moment or gradually in the course of their lives. And this is not their only commitment.

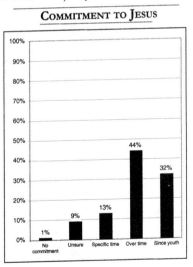

COMMITMENT TO JESUS

They pray. When we asked whether, "It is important to me to spend time in private thought and prayer," that simple question received a 74% positive response. And when we probed the practice of prayer in their personal devotions by asking how often they practice the discipline of prayer or meditation, other than in church or before meals, more than 73% prayed at least once a day, and 91% prayed privately on at least a weekly basis. Only 2% of the Adventist youth never prayed at all.

Compare this with ten years ago where (53%) prayed at least once a day and only two-thirds prayed privately on a weekly basis. To say that this generation is more "spiritual," no matter how you define this term, is an understatement.

REACHING OUT — EVANGELISM

In the *Valuegenesis²* survey form there are questions about evangelism. Just how comfortable are you with sharing your own faith? This is not an easy part of the Christian life to put into practice because we all have some fear of sharing and many don't have the skills needed to do so. But our young people responded positively even to this challenging activity. 59% had tried directly to encourage someone to believe in Jesus Christ during the past year, two-thirds of the study group had shared with others about the work of God in their lives, and 40% had encouraged someone to join the Adventist church. And like ten years ago, most of the sharing was only one to two times during the year. Still, youth feel free to bear their testimony about their religious commitments. I wonder what the numbers would be for adults sharing their faith in the church? Surely this picture of sharing is more positive than negative, but upon close observation, they find it easier to share God or Christ than to talk about the Seventh-day Adventist Church. Later, when we discuss the Seventh-day Adventist Attitude Scale, the reasons for this might become clear.

SAVED BY GRACE

One critical area in *Valuegenesis¹* research was regarding the process of salvation. Are we saved by grace or through our works? While this discussion is clear in Adventist theology—like the reformers, we are strong advocates of salvation through grace by faith—we noticed that over two-thirds (67%) of young people in our first study were confused as to this process. What is the place of works in the Christian life? Do works contribute to our standing before God? What does it mean to be saved by grace?

These concerns were further explored and clarified in our newest research. A number of additional questions were included to clarify this confusion. In addition, we identified a "Love of God" scale in our earlier work that is evident now in *Valuegenesis².*

Our youth demonstrate a clear understanding of God's rich love given by grace to humanity. They have a clear love orientation (which emphasizes the consistent, unconditional love of God in spite of our waywardness). And they now understand in a clearer way now the role of obedience and works as a response to God's gift of life. We will discuss this in greater detail in a later chapter, but for now it is significant to understand the clarity with which our youth understand God's love.

LOVE SCALE QUESTIONS AND PERCENTAGES

I know that God loves me no matter what I do.

	Total%	6th	7th-8th	9th-10th	11th-12th
Not sure	3%	2%	3%	3%	3%
Tend to agree	7%	5%	7%	7%	7%
Definitely agree	90%	92%	90%	89%	89%

I am loved by God even when I sin.

	Total%	6th	7th-8th	9th-10th	11th-12th
Not sure	3%	3%	3%	4%	3%
Tend to agree	8%	7%	8%	9%	8%
Definitely agree	88%	89%	88%	86%	88%

WHAT ABOUT GRACE?

With regard to understanding God's rich and ever-present grace, our teenagers also share a clear understanding of salvation by grace through faith alone. In our 1990 research, there was concern that the questions in the survey did not clearly reflect our position on God's grace and salvation. Some said that there simply were not enough questions to get a clear picture. When students responded with two-thirds confused about how they were saved, there was concern from the coordinating team.

Valuegenesis² provides a number of more focused questions on a new Grace Scale that show that rather than the early 2/3rds (67%), now slightly over 50% share that confusion about grace, a decrease over ten years of more than 17%. While this is encouraging, 50% confusion is not a particularly good statistic, but in this area, any improvement is welcome. And we are now moving in the right direction.

We learn more with a closer look at the Grace and Love Scale. Our new Love Scale (part of the former Grace Scale), the mean of two items scored from 1 to 5, averaged 4.83 (trivially higher than the *Valuegenesis[1]* value of 4.75), indicating a solid grasp of Gospel principles. One item is: "I know that God loves me no matter what I do." Here, about 95% agreed at all grade levels. It should be noted that the original score was so high (4.75; already 95% of the highest it could possibly be, which would mean that every single student chose "strongly agree") that little increase was possible (a situation known in statistics as a "ceiling effect").

In contrast to love orientation on our original study, law orientation has declined considerably since *Valuegenesis[1]*. Earlier, 60% had agreed with the statement: "The way to be accepted by God is to try sincerely to live a good life." In *Valuegenesis[2]*, that had dropped to 45%. Further, the average on the Law Scale declined from 3.59 for 6th graders to 2.67 for 12th graders, in contrast to the earlier corresponding scores of 3.90 to 3.40.

Thus, in *Valuegenesis[2]*, not only did 12th graders start at a lower level than that observed in the original study, but they showed nearly twice as great a decline across grades. This indicates that our youth, in addition to affirming a grace orientation, increasingly reject a law orientation. Students understand how we are saved through God's actions and correctly place their response in the area of obedience and worship rather than thinking that they somehow contribute to what Jesus did at the cross. And it is clear now, as you will see in the chapter that targets God's grace, that as students get older they become more grace-oriented.

STAYING CONNECTED TO GOD

We identified a number of activities that help young people stay connected to God. I am reminded of a unique illustration given to me during my seminary days. We were discussing God's activity in salvation and our response. One student was completely confused. This young pastor was sure that an acceptance of salvation by grace through faith would cause a once-saved-always-saved mentality. The professor tried to assure him that this just wasn't the case if one correctly understood the power of God's grace.

He shared two graphic illustrations. He drew on the chalkboard a battery and a trolley car. He said that one could look at the process of salvation in these two ways. A battery gets charged up and then functions on its own, an obvious metaphor for salvation through one's own works. Even if God first initiated the charge, one ran on the battery's power rather than through the power source.

On the other hand, however, the trolley car was particularly unique. It could only run when connected to the power lines. When it was disconnected, it couldn't move an inch. "Salvation is like that," he said, "When we stay connected through our choices and commitments, we can watch the power of God flow through us and our life is successful." Staying connected is one challenge.

That's where one's personal piety comes in. The young people in our study were interested in learning about spiritual life. They were given a choice and asked to make a commitment on how interested they would be in learning more about each one at school or at church. The topics in *Valuegenesis²* included: sexuality, drugs and alcohol, Adventism, the Bible, gaining a deeper relationship with Christ, other cultures and ethnic groups, how to talk with parents, how to talk to a friend about faith.

Ten years later it is interesting to see the responses. I'll put the *Valuegenesis[1]* percentages in parenthesis throughout this book so you can make a comparison. Some of the questions were not asked the first time around, so there won't be comparisons in every category. The topic "gaining a deeper relationship with God" was easily the leader with 81% (76%) indicating "interested" and "very interested." The next highest topic ten years later was the Bible 67% (65%). "How to talk to my friends about faith" was a close third 61%, while talking about being an Adventist scored 50%. These scores are another indication of the increased spirituality of this generation. Such being the case, it would seem that the church must find relevant ways to teach about the church, its mission, and message. If it does not do a good job of this, this generation will probably find it somewhere else.

THE IMPORTANCE OF BEING ADVENTIST

A common question as I have shared this research are shared across the denomination is: "How many youth drop out of the Adventist church?" I wish there were a clear answer to this probing question. Roger Dudley, in his landmark longitudinal study of Adventists over ten years, indicated that about 48% of those who began the study remained active in the church after time. The people that can answer this question the best are, of course, those that have left the denomination. The problem is obvious: How do you find this group? And if you found them, asking them why they left probably isn't the appropriate first contact to make, especially since often the reason they have become distant is that they simply were not loved as carefully as they should have been by the local congregation.

We can say some positive things about church loyalty, however. We celebrate that youth are loyal to the Seventh-day Adventist movement. And when they were asked how important it was for them to attend a church of their own denomination, 71% (75%) said it was important or extremely important. A much higher number claimed that it was not important 26% (9%) compared with our first research. This is another indication that these youth see themselves as committed Christians; however, their specific denominational loyalty seems to be on the wane.

While the importance of being Adventist seems to be changing, when asked if they would join an Adventist church if they moved to another location where they could choose from any number of denominations, a startling at 88% (90%) said they would.. They don't seem to see themselves switching faith communities particularly, but they are slightly less committed to its importance than our earlier respondents in 1990. In discussions about this concern with pastors and teachers, we tried to explore why this is the case. Some argued that Adventism, with its Seventh-day Sabbath creates a different kind of commitment to a church. It seems it is difficult to make the switch in the day to worship.

How often do you attend worship at a church?

	Total%	6th	7th-8th	9th-10th	11th-12th
Never	2%	2%	2%	2%	1%
Less than 1x/month	4%	5%	4%	4%	4%
Once a month	4%	5%	3%	3%	4%
Two to three times a month	11%	11%	11%	11%	10%
Once a week	62%	56%	62%	63%	64%
Several times a week	18%	20%	17%	17%	17%

Loyalty can be measured in contrast to other denominations. And other research in our church seems to indicate that those who drop out of active participation in the Adventist faith community, probably don't join another denomination. This however, may change if there is a continual decline regarding unique loyalty to the church.

Another important question on our survey had to do with perceptions of future loyalty. In *Valuegenesis[1]* (72%) replied that there was a "good" or "excellent" chance that they would be Adventist at age 40. Only (2%) saw no chance, with another (7%) foreseeing a small chance.[11] The *Valuegenesis[2]* information for Generation Y is to the right of this paragraph.

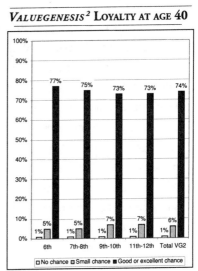

VALUEGENESIS[2] LOYALTY AT AGE 40

ATTENDANCE PATTERNS

What were the attendance patterns for youth in the church? Are they active participants or passive observers? We know that youth participation in religious activities helps children and youth learn ideas and values that are not as easily understood if they are passive learners. This is referred to as religious socialization, "the process by which the child learns the values, beliefs, and traditions of a religion, and ultimately becomes a fully participating member of that religion."[9] And we know that church attendance is strongly related to the religious behavior of a youth's parents. In fact, the principal determinant for church attendance is parental attendance and parental religious values.

In addition there are indicators in major research that if you want better grades, go to church.

A number of years ago, Reggie Benson was so full of rage his mother was unable to control him, but today things have changed. On a recent weekend, this ninth-grader was in church according to Amber Anderson, reporter for *Christianity Today*. He took his seat beside other boys in the congregation in this small Pasadena church on a Sunday evening, Saturday afternoon, or weekday at 6 a.m. He was eager to learn. His grades have jumped from C's to A's, and he is a leader now among the younger youth in his church. He has been mentored by the associate director of this church's family ministry. Reggie, whose name is fictitious, "comes from a community in which racism, poverty, and drug abuse deplete the neighborhood's natural resources. The church can be the path for kids like him to find a future, both spiritually and academically."[10]

In a recent study, researchers Mark Regnerus and Glen Elder, Jr., demonstrated that when youth from low-income neighborhoods attend church, their academic performance improves.[11] And in this unique research, improving academic performance seems to flow more from "doing" church than from merely believing. It seems that the church's social life had powerful influences that make a difference.

72% of our youth attend worship services once a week to several times a week. And that figure does not drop as the students pass through the higher grades. This will have a significant influence on their positive outlook towards church and as a by-product, might improve their academic performance. With such significant attendance patterns, you can see why it is important to "do" church right!

Other research provides insight into the factors that influence religious participation. Researchers have seen a number of elements that may influence participation in religious activities:

() Church attendance is strongly related to the religious behavior of a youth's parents. In fact, the principal determinant for church attendance is parental attendance and parental religious values.

() Youth's attitudes towards church depend on past religious education, types of leaders, and beliefs.

() Children and youth need opportunities to be involved as active participants and leaders in the life of the congregation.

() Youth need ways to participate that are meaningful to them and help them relate their religious education and practice to everyday life. For example, children can serve as leaders of worship, greet worshipers, and offer prayers. Also, they can be involved in mission projects in the church and community.[12]

According to nationwide surveys released by the Barna Research Group, church attendance by adults has rapidly declined for the fifth consecutive year; in fact, it has hit an 11-year low. While more than four out of five Americans call themselves Christians, less than half, 37%, attend church services in a given week. And the biggest decline is in the baby boomers age group between 30 and 50. So it is rewarding to see these patterns of church attendance in the youth of our church, and we are aware that, "participation and involvement are significant ways in which faith and commitment are nurtured."[13]

But there is much more to be excited about in this research. We have still to discuss orthodoxy, life-affirming choices, Adventist standards, families, faith maturity, Adventist schools, attitudes, at-risk behaviors, and a myriad other topics that make a difference in the lives of youth.

COMMITMENT TO ADVENTIST BELIEFS

Webster's defines the word "orthodox" as "conforming to established doctrine especially in religion." So how do the youth of the church feel about what Adventists believe? In our first research project, *Valuegenesis¹*, we had only ten questions in what we called our Orthodoxy Scale. In our recent research we added another fifteen questions so all of our doctrines could be explored.

Since a more sophisticated belief system is one of the products of faith development during these growing years. It is crucial to see what kind of commitment young people have regarding their own theological system. The best news is that Adventist youth continue to prize the Adventist theological heritage; they accept its beliefs and values.

In the original *Valugenesis¹* Orthodoxy Scale, there were ten statements with six possible responses starting with "I have never heard of this, " and "I definitely do not believe this," to "I definitely believe this." (Remember, the *Valuegenesis¹* percentages are in parenthesis following the *Valuegenesis²* information). The percentage of those who definitely believed ranged from 27% to 91% (45%-91%) with only three doctrines below 35% (65%). Very few students ever choose "I definitely do not believe this." And for most of the doctrines fewer than 1% (1%) were definite unbelievers. These first ten doctrines explored basic beliefs like the Sabbath, the second coming, the importance of the Ten Commandments, state of the dead, and the literal creation week. Only three uniquely Adventist beliefs—the remnant doctrine, Ellen G. White's prophetic role, and the 1844 sanctuary message—were significantly low in the percentages. We'll look more closely at this serious challenge in chapter five entitled, "Fashion Me a People."

In looking at the additional doctrinal questions in our new research, we continue to be impressed with theological commitment of our youth. For example, in scoring at a three-level approach (1.

"Never heard of this," 2. "Belief is neutral, or they disbelieve the doctrine, and 3. "I definitely believe it"), we see some interesting insights.

Summarizing the additional fifteen questions on doctrine, the average "definitely believe" score was 71%. The range of scores was between 39% and 91% in most of the doctrines. Two of the doctrines, "Marriage should only be for those who share a common faith" and "The Millennium begins with the Parousia and ends with destruction of wicked," were low with 39% and 53% respectively in the "definitely believe" category. One, the question about our beliefs on marriage, showed more who were disbelievers or neutral on this doctrine. Some 59%, of those youth shared that sentiment.

We will look in detail and explore these beliefs in a more careful way later in this book, but for now, it is interesting as well to note that orthodoxy increases as students grow older and most of the doctrines are strongly held.

An orthodoxy scale was created by combining all of the original orthodoxy items and scoring them from 1 to 5 with the "Never heard of this" response scored the same as "I am uncertain whether or not to believe this." What is revealed

---

NEW SURVEY QUESTIONS

Orthodoxy II Scale Questions target the followin doctrines in the Seventh-day Adventist Church.

() The Trinity—Father, Son, Holy Spirit
() The Great Controversy between Christ and Satan
() The Church
() Baptism
() Communion
() Spiritual gifts
() Stewardship
() Marriage
() Millennium

is the average score. Remember, we now have now two series of questions available to explore what we call orthodoxy. We call them the Ortho I and Ortho II Scales, to refer to the short list of ten questions and the longer list with the additional fifteen questions. The research findings share the strength of the knowledge of belief. For example:

() Ortho I. The original *Valuegenesis[1]* scale: 4.48 at 6th grade; 4.59 at 12th grade.

() Ortho II: *Valuegenesis[2]* on this original scale: 4.23 at 6th grade, 4.44 at 12th grade level.

According to our statistician, the number of students involved in the two *Valuegenesis* surveys were so large that almost ay difference is statistically significant. (Like a very powerful microscope that can see particles that are real, but are so small they don't matter). Instead, we should concentrate on differences large enough to have practical influence. In the case of a 5-point scale, you would want to look at a difference of .50 or more to project significant changes. And as you can see, the scores are well within the that range. *Valuegenesis[2]* indicates, again, strong adherence to the core of Adventist beliefs. We will spend more time later looking at specific doctrines and scan the additional questions we used this time. The results are interesting.

It seems clear that as students get older, they are more able to understand some of the more complex doctrinal statements of the church. For example, the question that explores the Millennium moves from 40% "definitely believe" in 6th graders to 64% in 12th grade students.

Uniquely Adventist identity doctrines such as the Investigative Judgment is only 40% "definitely believed" in the 12th grade, but begins at 14% in the 6th grade. Only two doctrines decrease in belief status as students age. The statement that Ellen White fulfilled predictions of prophesy in the last days actually decreased from 46% to 42% as students progressed through the grades. And the belief that the Adventists as remnant church decreased, from 53% to 43% "definitely" believing this statement.

Belief in the humanity and divinity of Jesus increased as students grew older. Was Jesus fully human? The percent who "definitely believe" rose from 54% to 81%. Was he fully divine? Movement here was from 74% to 83% in the 12th grade. And an encouraging belief in regards to support for the church was the question about tithing. It moved from 59% in 6th grade up to 71% definitely believing this statement by the end of high school. Of course we don't truly know just how committed youth are to these doctrines other than their statements of belief.

Once, while I was working in an Adventist school teaching high school religion, my student, who was a janitor, worked to clean the room after six periods of active students destroying it each day. We were near a public college and often students would drift by our school and ask questions. This day my student was sweeping outside of the classroom on the front street as a young man from college stopped and asked, "What is this place?" My student, who was usually opposed to much of what we tried to teach, gave a personal testimony that would make any educator in a Christian setting proud. He told of his belief in the Sabbath, church, and Christian education. Who would have thought he was that committed to our beliefs, when in his personal life he was a bit off the mark from an administrative perspective.

Youth develop their ideology and theology as they grow. And as their identity becomes more stable and their lives reflect their goals and vision, it is good to see that Adventist young people have a clearer view of what they believe. And since building a Christian ideology is an important identity function of growing teens, you can easily see the church's role in that development. Those beliefs that are on the low end need some clear focus and expert analysis to make them as relevant to today's youth as possible.

WE'VE GOT GOOD KIDS

Anyone in a position of leadership or pastoral ministry knows that at some point and at some time the discussion of Adventist lifestyle standards will come up. The Hancock Center published a book on this very topic by Steve Case of *Piece of the Pie Ministries* called *Shall We Dance: Rediscovering Christ-Centered Standards.* Written with a number of other writers, it provides a look at some of the biblical guidelines for ten standards and challenges parents and youth to explore the meaning of good lifestyle choices using an open discussion approach to clarifying these issues. Still these questions come up no matter where you are in Adventism.

While working with youth in Norway, Australia, South Africa, or France someone will eventually say, "Pastor, what do you think about movies?" or "When do you think the church will approve dancing?" These always create tension and debate. Let's look at what Adventist youth say about this issue.

Later on in this book we will detail the research about specific Adventist standards, but right now we want to look at first the good news. We learned a number of years ago that one of the best ways of talking about Adventist standards is to look at them as life-affirming choices as opposed to life-denying choices. In this context, they don't sound like hard and fast rules. Yet they are framed in a positive way that invites discussion and nudges us toward positive life-affirming choices.

While it is true that the Seventh-day Adventist church encourages good choices, some of these so-called standards of the church are products of time, place, and culture, while on the other hand, some are based in more clear biblical principles and conservative church traditions. We always advocate clear, high biblical standards. However, youth in the church have decided to look at traditional standards in their own way. Our organization of these lifestyle choices reflects their priorities.

We have discovered three types of standards, all based on biblical values. The first type are those that are called *Substance Abuse Standards* or "temperance" issues. The percentage in agreement that one should not use illegal drugs is 91% (91%) who "tend to," or "definitely agree"; not use tobacco, 80% (91%); not drink beer or liquor, 84% (87%); not drink wine, 72% (72%); and should exercise daily, 82% (85%).

Another category of standards are identified as *Adventist Way-of-Life Standards*. These provide another look at youth's behaviors and commitments. Most agreed that one should observe the Sabbath, 90% (88%); and again the majority agreed with the position that sex should only occur in marriage, 77% (68%), and the need to wear modest clothes, 60% (65%).

When we asked if "Adventist rules and standards don't make sense," only 18% (18%) felt this way. But when asked, "Adventists are loaded down with too many restrictions," a total of 29% felt this was "often," "almost always" and "always" true.

There is a difference between how young people feel about standards and their actual practice. Information about standards and life-denying behaviors often isn't enough to change youth's involvement in these activities.

What is clear, however, is that the third category of standards—we have labeled them *Popular Cultural Standards*—continues to be a challenge for parents and leadership in schools and churches. We will have a lot more to say about this category of standards later, but what we can say in this summary of positive research is that this particular area of obedience is the weakest and most vague regarding overall support.

WHAT ABOUT AT-RISK BEHAVIORS?

Our research also talked to youth about their at-risk behaviors such as using alcohol, marijuana and cocaine, binge drinking (five drinks in a row), cheating, fighting, stealing, getting into trouble at school, and eating disorders. On a seven-point scale, youth were asked to share how many times they had done each of these things in the past year. They could choose between zero times up to 40 or more times. What follows are the responses in our most recent research.

AT-RISK BEHAVIORS

Drink alcohol alone/with friend	Total %	6th	7th-8th	9th-10th	11th-12th
Never in the last year	77%	93%	86%	72%	65%
At least once in last year	23%	7%	14%	28%	35%

Use marijuana	Total %	6th	7th-8th	9th-10th	11th-12th
Never in the last year	90%	98%	96%	88%	84%
At least once in last year	10%	2%	4%	12%	16%

Use cocaine	Total %	6th	7th-8th	9th-10th	11th-12th
Never in the last year	98%	98%	98%	98%	98%
At least once in last year	2%	2%	2%	2%	2%

5+ drinks in a row	Total %	6th	7th-8th	9th-10th	11th-12th
Not in 12 months	88%	96%	94%	87%	81%
At least once in 12 months	12%	4%	6%	13%	19%

Hit or beat someone	Total %	6th	7th-8th	9th-10th	11th-12th
Never in the last year	56%	52%	47%	55%	70%
At least once in last year	44%	48%	53%	45%	30%

Shoplift	Total %	6th	7th-8th	9th-10th	11th-12th
Never in the last year	83%	88%	83%	81%	81%
At least once in last year	17%	12%	17%	19%	19%

Use Tobacco	Total %	6th	7th-8th	9th-10th	11th-12th
Never	88%	97%	93%	85%	80%
Once or more times	18%	32%	7%	15%	20%

Eating disorder	Total %	6th	7th-8th	9th-10th	11th-12th
Never	76%	68%	76%	78%	78%
One or more times	24%	32%	24%	22%	22%

As you can see, every item selected in this At-Risk Scale shows that the majority of young people have never engaged in these practices and only a small percentages have *ever* engaged in chemical substances use. These figures are much smaller than any public school statistics revealed by national research. We can be proud of our youth for their behaviors. Adventist schools provide clear protective care for young people, just one more very clear reason to support and promote Adventist Christian education.

THE INFLUENCE OF A LOVING HOME

The Bible advocates that we love one another. That kind of love is described as self-emptying, self-denying, and self-sacrificing. And God's love to us is expressed in Scripture as something worth imitating. I John 4:10-21 suggests an imitation of the self-denying love of Jesus by saying, *"This is love: not that we love God, but that he loved us and sent his Son as an atoning sacrifice for our sins. Dear friends, since God so loved us, we also ought to love one another. . ."*

How then does this principle of self-denying neighbor-love apply to Christian families? Researcher George Barna says, "Family is a big deal to teenagers, regardless of how they act or what they say. It is the rare teenager who believes he or she can lead a fulfilling life without complete acceptance and support from their families."[13]

We know of no influence as great as early family life. It is often the most perduring variable in life itself. In this day and age we know how stressed families can become. Every family knows things don't always go as smoothly as we would have hoped. We are not immune to the pressures of this world and surrounding culture. Seventh-day Adventist families suffer from the same issues that challenge families in the world at large.

Valuegenesis² has good news about the family. It provides insight into young people's attitudes about their homes. Notice over 73% (72%) see their family life as happy, and 81% (77%) report to seeing lots of love in their homes, a very positive response that has only increased over the study period between research projects. Here are some significant findings regarding family attitudes.

FAMILY ATTITUDES

My family life is happy.

	Total %	6th	7th-8th	9th-10th	11th-12th
Definitely disagree	5%	4%	5%	6%	4%
Tend to disagree	10%	5%	10%	11%	11%
Not sure	12%	10%	13%	13%	10%
Tend to agree	41%	35%	38%	42%	44%
Definitely agree	32%	47%	34%	27%	31%

There is a lot of love in my family.

	Total %	6th	7th-8th	9th-10th	11th-12th
Definitely disagree	3%	3%	3%	4%	2%
Tend to disagree	6%	3%	7%	7%	6%
Not sure	10%	8%	11%	12%	8%
Tend to agree	31%	22%	27%	34%	34%
Definitely agree	50%	64%	53%	44%	49%

I get along well with my parents.

	Total %	6th	7th-8th	9th-10th	11th-12th
Definitely disagree	5%	3%	5%	6%	4%
Tend to disagree	9%	6%	10%	11%	9%
Not sure	10%	8%	12%	12%	8%
Tend to agree	38%	34%	36%	40%	41%
Definitely agree	37%	50%	38%	31%	39%

My parents give me help and support when I need it.

	Total %	6th	7th-8th	9th-10th	11th-12th
Definitely disagree	3%	1%	3%	3%	2%
Tend to disagree	6%	2%	6%	7%	6%
Not sure	8%	5%	8%	10%	8%
Tend to agree	28%	21%	26%	31%	30%
Definitely agree	55%	71%	57%	48%	54%

My parents often tell me they love me.

	Total %	6th	7th-8th	9th-10th	11th-12th
Definitely disagree	4%	2%	3%	5%	4%
Tend to disagree	6%	3%	4%	7%	7%
Not sure	6%	3%	6%	8%	6%
Tend to agree	25%	14%	23%	27%	29%
Definitely agree	60%	77%	64%	53%	54%

If I break rules, I get punished.

	Total %	6th	7th-8th	9th-10th	11th-12th
Definitely disagree	4%	5%	3%	4%	5%
Tend to disagree	12%	7%	10%	12%	15%
Not sure	12%	9%	11%	13%	14%
Tend to agree	38%	32%	36%	39%	41%
Definitely agree	34%	47%	40%	32%	25%

As you can see, 75% of the students "tend to agree" or 'definitely agree" that they get along well with their parents, while 83% note that their parents give them help and support whenever it is needed. 85% of the study group say, "My parents often tell me they love me." Strong families always make for stronger youth.

In other studies about the family there are the same positive responses. And in spite of the endless negative coverage in the media about the state of the family these days, it seems that most of the teens surveyed are proud of their families. In another national study, some nine out of ten (90%) consider their families to be healthy and functional. This is a very high figure since in this particular study the youth interviewed were living in either a blended or broken home—that is a home situation in which they are not living with both of their natural parents.[14]

In a 1997 study of Adventist families, it was found that faith in Christ is very strong among Adventists and has remained consistent since it was first measured in surveys over twenty years ago. More than two-thirds of the respondents to this survey, some 69%, indicate that they have an intimate relationship with Jesus Christ.[15]

LET'S LEARN TO TALK ABOUT FAITH

We learned in our earlier research about the power of faith-talk. This is when parent and child spend time sharing about their own religious experience. A number of questions on our survey focused on this issue. When we asked, "How many times in the last month have you had a good talk with one of your parents that lasted 10 minutes or more?" A surprising 53% (57%) of the total group from grades 6 through 12 responded they did take time to talk to their parents four or more times per month. As the young people progressed into 11th and 12th grades, that percentage rose to 61% who had four or more such conversations with their parents. What is more interesting, the percentage reporting this frequency tended to increase with age, rising from 49% (39%) in the 6th grade to 61% (51%) in the 12th. In *Valuegenesis²* only 8% (10%) reported no substantive talks with their parents within the last month, only a slight decrease from our research ten years ago.

Again, family worship is experienced by about 48% of the households surveyed. They reported on worships of more than one per week at this level. And while this is not as high as we would have hoped, those having more regular worship continue to tell us that it is both meaningful and important. Very few claim it is a waste of time. Quality worship in the family became a predictor in our first research for a host of other desirable attitudes and behaviors, according to Roger Dudley.

HOW MATURE IS YOUR FAITH?

A significant change has occurred in the faith maturity scores from our first research. For example, as we balanced the vertical faith (prayer, personal religion, meditation, Bible study, etc.) with the horizontal faith experience (sharing, caring, witnessing, etc.) we learned that 1/5th or 22% of the young people surveyed could be said to have a high faith maturity. We compared ourselves with the Southern Baptist church at that time where some 28% of the youth of that denomination us-

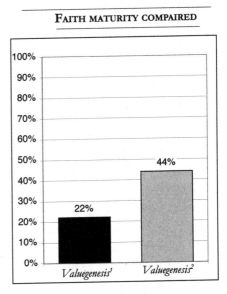

FAITH MATURITY COMPAIRED

100%
90%
80%
70%
60%
50%
40%   44%
30%
22%
20%
10%
0%
Valuegenesis¹   *Valuegenesis²*

ing the same scales as we had were said to be mature in faith. While we had one in five, they had one in four.

We were asked, "What was the problem?" We attributed this decrease of faith maturity to such things as the possible lack of youth ministry in local churches and even the climates in local congregations that did not seem as "user" friendly to youth as they might be.

But there is certainly better news now in regards to this part of the study. Over the past years there has been a 100% increase in mature faith. That means that something significant has happened over the ensuing years since our first report. As we continue to explore the insights from *Valuegenesis²*, we will try to understand the encouraging changes in the religious lives of the youth of the church.

INTRINSIC AND EXTRINSIC RELIGION

Like the Faith Maturity Index which measures particular qualities of the religious life, a new scale for our research was introduced during this second phase of our study. It was called the Intrinsic and Extrinsic Religious Scale.

Gordon Allport, a Harvard psychologist, first distinguished between intrinsic and extrinsic forms of religious commitment in his writings on healthy personality. He described that the extrinsically religious person uses religion as a means of obtaining status or personal security, for self-justification and for sociability, thus making religion more utilitarian and self-oriented. In contrast, the intrinsically religious person internalizes beliefs and lives by them regardless of outside or extrinsic social pressure or other possible personal consequences.

We had a scale of fourteen questions that explored these aspects of religion. We were excited to find that 44% of the youth in our census were intrinsic in their motivation while only 6% held the more distant extrinsic view. Our chapter on intrinsic and extrinsic religion helps clarify this information, but again this is good news.

WHAT ABOUT OUR SCHOOLS

The moving force behind the *Valuegenesis* research has always been the Office of Education of the North American Division. The implications of this research have resulted in books, numerous articles, hundreds of public presentations, planned change in schools and churches, and new prioritizing of family values. But the heart of this research is targeted at Adventist schools. The research census is from Adventist students in Adventist schools. Students are positive about the interest that their teachers take in their personal lives. As you can see by the next charts, the percentages begin high and remain throughout their academic life in their Adventist schools.

It would seem that in addition, they see the teaching as good. This is a positive sign that students feel good about their schools. In addition, when students were queried about whether or not their teachers praise them when they work hard on their homework, 70% agreed with this statement. And in a parallel question, when asked if they simply "liked" their school, again 70% said enthusiastically, yes!

Positive school climate is just one aspect of building a strong 'intrinsic" faith experience. For now, remember that when teachers are interesting, when discipline is fair, when teaching is considered good, and when teachers both praise and listen to students, the more intrinsic the religious experience becomes. Conversely, the more negative these scores are, the more they impact against intrinsic religious experience. This shows the importance of building a positive climate in schools.

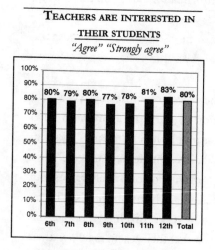

TEACHERS ARE INTERESTED IN THEIR STUDENTS
"Agree" "Strongly agree"

We can't go wrong when we help schools become emotionally warm and when we challenge students through teaching essential critical thinking skills.

A POSITIVE COMPARISON

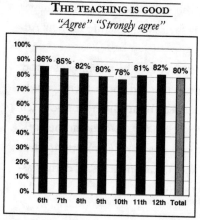

THE TEACHING IS GOOD
"Agree" "Strongly agree"

It is clear that Adventist schools have fewer of the type of behavior problems that disturb the learning process in public schools. We mentioned these before in our first book, *Valuegenesis: Faith in the Balance.* These include: student absenteeism, students cutting class, verbal abuse of teachers, vandalism of school property, and especially, student use of alcohol and other drugs.[19] In fact, when you look at the traditional behaviors (standards) of Adventism in the area of substance abuse (tobacco, alcohol, illegal drugs) it is clear that only a small minority of students are involved. If you look at the national averages in these same areas, you realize that public education is not nearly as safe an environment and the pressure to become involved in these at-risk activities is substantial.

The youth of the church are supportive of their Adventist schools. For example, about 67% (70%) agreed that Adventist schools should be a top priority among Adventist leaders. Support increased slightly to 74% in the 12th grade.

In a new scale in our research we contrasted positive versus negative feelings about Adventist schools. Most of the results were salutary. For example, when asked, "Is your school exciting or dull?" 48% of the students responded positively, while only 22% saw their school as dull. In a similar "bipolar" question, 54% versus 16% saw schools as warm rather than cold.

An important characteristic of Christian education is the inclusiveness and fairness exhibited in this environment. 46% of Students saw their schools in this positive light while only 17% were critical about its exclusiveness.

All in all, students are happy with their education and they see their school as "better" than public education. This is a positive sign when it comes to promoting Christian education and building positive memories during the school years.

Comparing Adventist education with that of secular types or even other denominational experiences, Adventist students excel. As Roger Dudley shared in our book ten years ago, a higher proportion of Adventist students enter four-year colleges or universities than either Catholic or public high school students. In addition, student educational aspirations are very high. To clarify this interest, *Valuegenesis²* asked, "How far will you go in school?" While this is a measure of aspiration rather than achievement, 64% of the students in Adventist education responded they wanted a baccalaureate degree before they ended their educational experience.

It seems appropriate to share a personal experience here. When I first got interested in Christianity, it was because of my meeting and sharing with new friends who invited me to church and to attend an Adventist school. My association with other Christian friends made the real difference in my life. I would not trade my Adventist school experience for public education—and I had good public school teachers too. In a Christian environment I was able to explore my religious commitments. And during a time when my mother was very sick and visits to the hospital replaced family outings, knowing I had committed teachers praying for me and my family, and Christian classmates who always took this into consideration in their plans with me is an unforgettable positive experience.

REJOICING ABOUT YOUTH MINISTRY

What about ministry to our youth? It is true that our church does not have a clear ecclesiology of youth ministry. This may be because in the New Testament the word for *church* is given to a number of situations that range from small groups to house churches (See Romans 16:5; 1 Corinthians 16:19). Often adults in local congregations do not see the importance of specific youth ministry because of other needs within their specific churches. But since we believe that young people are full members in the Body of Christ, it is gratifying to see positive changes in the types of ministry and the things that impact the local congregations of our denomination.[16]

We can rejoice that there has been an improvement in the perception of young people regarding the focus of the religious educational activities in a local congregation. When asked if programs at my church are interesting, 37% (31%) responded positively. That is only a slight 6% increase over the years, but any improvement in this area is important. Couple this with the attitude of students regarding their church teachers or adult leaders and how well they feel they are known, again there is an increase from (40%) to 46% over time. Are they warm and friendly? Remember church climate is a crucial factor in feelings of acceptance and support for one's local church. Again there is an increase from (56%) to 60% in this response.

What was particularly interesting, however, was the perception of youth ministry in local churches by these students in Adventist education. 60% of the students said there was a youth pastor at their home church. And 67% claimed that youth and young adults regularly take a leading role in the worship services at their church. This research shows that 18% of the students say that there is "never" a youth ministry in their local church.

Take a look at their responses below regarding the reality of a ministry for young people in their local congregations. When we asked, "Is there a youth ministry program at your church?"

Is THERE A YOUTH MINISTRY PROGRAM AT YOUR CHURCH?	
	Total Valuegenesis[2] Percentage
Never	18%
Once a month	29%
Every two weeks	11%
Every week	33%
More than once a week	10%

When you contrast the responses of the youth's understanding of youth ministry in the school with that of the church's, we can see some weaknesses in early teen ministry and some marginal success in high school ministry.

Church	School
6th-8th grades = 42%	6th-8th grades = 24%
9th-12th grades = 42%	9th-12th grades = 41%

In the chapter by Barry Gane, Professor of Youth Ministry at Andrews University that targets youth ministry, we'll discover the details of this focus on youth ministry and some of its practical rewards, but for now it is sufficient to say that youth are perceiving ministry as happening in their schools and churches, And to the degree that it is perceived, there is a concomitant increase in positive responses to the church and school. This research clearly shows the importance of having some kind of regular ministry to the young people of in our churches. Without such, youth often feel alienated and unloved.

We have many challenges when it comes to youth and pre-teen ministry: local church commitment, budget considerations, worship innovation and leadership training. Given the reality of the power and influence of ministry to young people and the transformation that can occur when done consistently and with a mission focus, we often feel paralyzed asking, "What can I do in my little church?" Jim Burns, a successful youth minister, responds to this challenge by talking about the feeling of the Israelites when they encountered the Philistines and met Goliath on the plain that long afternoon.

> *The Israelites were paralyzed with fear. The young shepherd boy David came out to the battle, at his father's request, to bring supplies to his older brothers. When David observed Goliath mocking the people of Israel and the living God, he decided to do something about it. Armed with five smooth stones, a sling, and his faith in the love of God, he killed the giant Goliath. While everyone else's philosophy was, 'He is so big I can't win,' David's belief was, 'My God is so big I can't miss!'[17]*

So as we look at ministry for young people, don't get discouraged, but trust in God's ability to guide us past the challenges into the light of clear, purposeful ministry that works. As we identify our priorities in this type of ministry we would do well to reflect on three top priorities discovered in research about building a youth ministry that transforms. Merton Strommen, Karen Jones, and Dave Rahn worked together to determine what is most often needed in our ministry to young people. They suggest the following:

◇ Develop a clearly stated mission statement

◇ Focus on the spiritual development of youth

◇ Assist in the training of volunteer leaders who love and care for young people.[19]

But of course, I'm way ahead of myself here. There is so much more to look at and we are just beginning. We'll spend time looking at the many reasons to celebrate in the forthcoming chapters, but in the midst of rejoicing there is often reflection. Reflection gives pause for change. So let's take our celebration to the next step now and see just what we can learn from a close exploration of the *Valuegenesis²* research and what conclusions we can draw that will impact the power for change in our homes, schools, and churches.

REFERENCES

1. George Barna, *Third Millennium Teens* (Ventura, CA: Barna Research Group, 1999), 4.
2. Quotations from Hesiod can be found at the following website: http://www.brainyquote.com/quotes/quotes/h/q126221.html.
3. Quoted in Wendy Murray Zoba, *Generation 2K: What Parents & Others Need to Know About the Millennials* (Downers Grove, IL: InterVarsity Press, 1999), 24. The list is from an article by Diana West, "Treat Your Children Well," *Wall Street Journal*, April 22, 1998, Section A, 20.
4. Evan Thomas, "Hooray for Hypocrisy," *Newsweek*, January 9, 1996, 61.
5. Randall Sullivan, "Lynching in Malibu," *Rolling Stone*, September 4, 1997, 58.
6. From a review of their book "Millennial Surveys," about Neil Howe and William Strauss, *Millennials Rising: The Next Great Generation* (New York, NY: Vintage Books, 2000) which can be found on the web at this address: (http://www.millennialsrising.com/survey.shtml).
7. Excerpt from Chapter 1 of Neil Howe and William Strauss, *Millennials Rising*.

Complete information can be found at the book website: http://www.millennialrising.com/aboutbook.shtml.

8. Eugene Peterson, "What's Wrong with Spirituality?" *Christianity Today,* July 13, 1998. Vol. 42, No. 8, 51.

9. Robin Kimbrough-Melton. (June 2000). *Children's Participation in Faith-based Organizations.* Paper presented at a symposium sponsored by Childwatch International and UNESCO on the topic of Children's Participation in Community Settings, Oslo, Norway, 8.

10. Amber Anderson Johnson, "Want Better Grades? Go to Church," *Christianity Today* (May 21, 2002), 60.

11. This research comes from sociologist Mark Regnerus who did the study with Glen Elder Jr. of the University of North Carolina-Chapel Hill in a study entitled, "Staying on Track in School: Religious Influence in High and Low Risk Settings. (Chapel-Hill, NC: Carolina Population Center, 2001).

12. Robin Kimbrough-Melton, "Youth Participation in Religious Activities," *Clemson University Institute on Family and Neighborhood Life Fact Sheet,* December 2001, 1.

13. A report from the Church of Christ at Cherryvale on their website: (www.churchofchrist.pair.com/cherryvale/text/attendance.htm).

14. George Barna, *Third Millennium Teens,* 16.

15. George Barna, *Third Millennium Teens,* 18.

16. Monte and Norma Sahlin, *A New Generation of Adventist Families* (Portland, OR: Center for Creative Ministry, 1997), 6.

17. Mark Senter, Wesley Black, Chap Clark, Malan Nel, *Four Views of Youth Ministry and the Church* (Grand Rapids, MI: Zondervan, 2001), xi.

18. Jim Burns and Mike DeVries, *The Youth Builder: Today's Resource for Relational Youth Ministry* (Ventura, CA: Gospel Light, 2001), 53.

19. Merton Strommen, Karen E. Jones, Dave Rahn, *Youth Ministry That Transforms* (Grand Rapids, MI: Zondervan, 2001), 119.

These young people of ours, so wed to their computers, are still growing up in a world where human beings are both a greater threat and a greater hope than any machine. And this is why we are important—you and I. Not because we can teach our young people about the wired world (indeed, we have to learn these skills from them), not because we must wean them away from it (we couldn't if we tried), but because we are the church and we have a story to tell. We are people who tell a particular story about the Creator and Judge. Our story tells us that we were created in the image, the very likeness of that Creator who has made all things beautiful in their time and that Judge whose loving kindness toward weak and wayward humankind (who are both the threat and the promise in that magnificent universe) endures forever.

— Katherine Paterson

CHAPTER 3

WE ARE THE CHURCH
What's the flip side?

3

WE ARE THE CHURCH
What's the flip side?

There is a tri-lemma, I told my new friend. "Upon examining the claims of Christ," I boldly said, "we must declare him either the Lord, a liar, or a lunatic." "Well, I believe he is Lord for you," came the response. "I must not have explained myself," I said. "He claimed not just to be Lord for Tony but for all humanity—in fact, for all creation." "That's fine. I believe that for you, he is Lord of all creation." "But he claims to be Lord of all creation for everyone." "Okay, for you he's Lord of all creation for everyone."

— *Tony Jones*

When the teenage prophet Ezekiel was trying to represent God and the Babylonians were creeping close to surrounding Jerusalem and nobody seemed to want to listen, he began to experiment with some truly bizarre behaviors. He went on a journey which ended up inside his house (Ezekiel 4); after a brief shave where his hair was formed into three stacks and weighed, this teenaged bald prophet tried to show what would happen when the Babylonians would finally capture their city (Ezekiel 5); and he prepares a dinner that actually burns up and the people don't get to share in Ezekiel's gourmet lamb snack (Ezekiel 24).

Ezekiel is full of illustrations of how God wanted to tell them the whole story, but the people just wouldn't listen. They had their own agenda, and like the postmodern response Q & A above, he faced the challenge of being both relevant *and* true. In fact, the people he spoke to heard so little, they were actually worshipping the sun in the east right on the front doorstep of the temple. (Ezekiel 8). Finally, God comes to Ezekiel one more time—now troubled by the people's lack of response to the love of God—and shares a metaphor about a marriage to the people of God. Perhaps now they would hear! He talks of a wedding ceremony where the people are cared for by God and finally they actually become his own. *"And you became mine."* The text says.[1] Would they ever learn? Do we ever learn?

THERE IS ALWAYS A FLIP SIDE OF THE STORY

With teens this truism is experienced almost every day and in most conversations with them. Teen perceptions are slightly different from their adult counterparts' reality. "Is your room clean?" a mom asks her growing adolescent. "Yeah," comes the reply. But upon entering the youth's private world, what becomes most evident is the dissonance in perception between parent and child. In some ways this same dilemma is evident in the way the church sees or perceives the role of young people in the church, much like the people in Ezekiel's time misunderstood God's vision for their future.

"I just wish Christians were nice." These words came from responses during *Valuegenesis*[2] focus groups in Adventist schools. The bottom line for many youth is simply wanting to be accepted and loved by a church that clearly shows that they are wanted, needed, and important. This is the "other side of the story" for concerned teens.

"Adventists don't seem to have any fun. They are always concerned about behavior and sin, it seems." These words from a teenage girl in the Midwest express frustration with the system of Adventism. Somehow we've missed it if youth in general feel this way.

"It is logical that Christians, too, should be happy." This phrase showed up in a journal in my freshman religion class at the university last quarter. Religion expressed in negative terms just doesn't represent the joy found in understanding God's saving grace. What makes this young woman feel her religion has no exit into happiness? What makes her see only the "other side of the story?"

It may be a popular perception that because of teens' wish for a happier, nicer religious experience, reflect spiritual values. However, secular researchers find a "remarkable convergence of opinion" among religious leaders, seminary presidents, writers, and social commentators who concur that American is going through a particular time of "individual and social reassessment, renewal, and redirection." This desire is very focused in much of the teen population, as seen in a modern survey taken by the Princeton Religion Research Center. Spiritual questions about the existence of God or about one's future or life after death command the attention of a majority of teens.[2]

George Barna from the Barna Research Group in Pasadena, Cali-

WHAT INFLUENCES TEENS[3]		
	a lot	*none*
◦ Your parents	78%	3%
◦ Your friends	51%	4%
◦ Christian faith	48%	17%
◦ The Bible	44%	15%
◦ Brothers/sisters	40%	11%
◦ Your teachers	34%	12%
◦ Church pastors	27%	17%
◦ Music	25%	21%
◦ Television	13%	24%

fornia, shares some things that influence youth. These percentages show an increase in religious concerns and their related influence in their lives. *Valuegenesis* research noticed the same kind of deepening concern. We mentioned it in the last chapter; however, "the other side of the story" is particularly interesting as well, and it centers on what we have come to call "mature faith."

Ten years ago we explored this issue in detail. Faith, a rich and growing faith, reflected what Ellen G. White said in her book, *Christ Object Lessons.*

> *At every stage of development our life may be perfect; yet if God's purpose for us is fulfilled, there will be continual advancement. Sanctification is the work of a lifetime. As our opportunities multiply, our experience will enlarge, and our knowledge increase. We shall become strong to bear responsibility, and our maturity will be in proportion to our privileges.*[4]

What is implied by this statement is a "wholehearted commitment" as Roger Dudley and I clearly indicated in our first book on this subject.[5]

The prophet Jeremiah wished for a people that would be keepers of the renewed covenant, a people that would put His law in their minds and *"write it on their hearts."* He wanted to be their God.[6] These desires by God for His own imply a close relationship, what we call a mature faith—one motivated by an inner desire to be close and to follow God. Both dimensions of faith are exhibited here—vertical and horizontal—in his expression and desire for God's people. Our wish is no less than this too. Of course the challenge is to internalize God's will in our lives.

WHAT IS FAITH MATURITY?

It is a very complex term. In Isaiah 22 we see implied a "surety" and understanding of God's power in the life. The prophet shares that God wants to be like a stake in the desert *"fastened securely"* in the sand. This allusion to God's desire for his people suggests again a deep, rich, and personal relationship with God and a sense of surety we need to appreciate.

Teens especially understand this meaning, even if their adult counterparts don't. For many adults a faith that is mature is one that "believes" correctly. And while this is certainly a part of one's faith experience, there is also another dimension that is equally significant: the spiritual side. This vertical relationship is mentioned earlier in this book. A classic sentence that defines it is, "a vibrant, life-transforming experience marked by both a deep, personal relationship to a loving God and a consistent devotion to serving others."[6] Faith describes the way we feel about God.

Since ten years ago when we used a rather innovative approach to faith maturity, it was important to ask some of the same questions the second time around so there could be some comparison between these two generations. The scale originally used was developed by Search Institute for its national study of adults and youth in six Protes-

TEN YEARS AGO TODAY—1990-2000

() 88% believe their mothers feel comfortable talking with others about matters of faith. (1990)

() *91% believe their mothers feel comfortable. (2000)*

() 31% of high school seniors report having family devotions once a week or more. (1990)

() *40% of high school seniors report having family devotions now. (2000)*

tant denominations. A large group of Adventist theologians assessed this index and decided it was worthwhile as a guide to understanding the religious experiences of youth in the Adventist church. There were seven responses possible in the original set of questions: "never true," "rarely true," "true once in a while," "sometimes true," "often true," "almost always true," and "always true." There were some thirty-eight questions on the original *Valuegenesis* questionnaire. Statistical analysis, however, indicated that we could measure the same concept using only 12 of the items, and with a simpler, 5-point response format.

The Faith Maturity Index (FMI) embodies an approach that includes not only a set of right beliefs, but is conceived more as a way of life, a world view like James Fowler's faith-stage theory, or a set of priorities and dispositions which mature in behaviors which evidence that faith is deep, vibrant, and life-changing.

There are eight core dimensions which define faith in this scale. And a portrait of a faithful person looks like this:

() Trusts in God's saving grace and believes firmly in the humanity and divinity of Jesus

() Experiences a sense of personal well-being, security, and peace

() Integrates faith and life, seeing work, family, social relationships, and political choices as part of one's religious life

() Seeks spiritual growth through study, reflection, prayer, and discussion with others

() Seeks to be a part of a community of believers in which

people give witness to their faith which supports and nourishes one another

() Holds life-affirming values, including commitment to racial and gender equality

() Advocates social and global change to bring about greater social justice

() Serves humanity, consistently and passionately, through acts of love and justice.[7]

What is apparent is that the two overarching themes—*vertical* faith and *horizontal* faith—build a balanced, mature approach to God. The *vertical* theme, which is expressed in one's relationship with God, and the *horizontal* theme, which shares one's devotion to helping and serving others, is seen through the youth's responses to the questions in the new survey. Since 1990 we have had the opportunity to build a very reliable scale which gives us comparison percentages by using only twelve questions. Observing it we can build a new faith-maturity percentage ten years later.

In addition, when redoing this research, the organizing team decided that the questions could be presented in a more significant and personal way. For example, we tried to be consistent this time by saying "I feel," "I help," "I apply," and so forth.

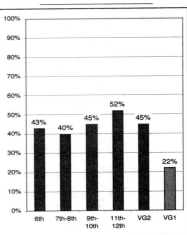

FAITH-MATURITY PERCENTAGES

This being the case, the format was slightly different, but probably does not represent a significant difference in the response percentages so comparison is possible.

The questions and their percentages follow. (Remember, the *Valuegenesis¹* percentages are enclosed in parentheses for contrast.) To simplify a picture of the faith maturity of our Adventist youth, we list the percentages of those who chose either "often true," 'almost always true," and "always true" for *Valuegenesis¹* and "often" and "sometimes" for *Valuegenesis².*

- () I help others with their religious questions and struggles. 40% (30%)
- () I seek out opportunities to help me grow spiritually. 55% (41%)
- () I feel a deep sense of responsibility for reducing pain and suffering in the world. 40% (45%)
- () I give significant portions of time and money to help other people. 26% (18%)
- () I feel God's presence in my relationships with other people. 56% (47%)
- () I feel my life is filled with meaning and purpose. 70% (66%)
- () I show that I care a great deal about reducing poverty in my country and throughout the world. 28% (50%)
- () I apply my faith to political and social issues. 42% (31%)
- () The things I do reflect a commitment to Jesus Christ. 61% (75%)
- () I talk with other people about my faith. 49% (42%)
- () I have a real sense that God is guiding me. 66% (60%)
- () I am spiritually moved by the beauty of God's creation. 75% (75%)

And as you can see by the chart on the earlier page, ten years ago the average high faith-maturity score was some 22% of our youth, while ten years later it is at 45%. That's a 100% increase in faith maturity. Something has happened. Let's look closer at this data and see if we can determine why.

On any item in the Faith Maturity Index (FMI) a youth could receive a score of between 1 to 5. Responses to the 12 items were averaged, giving for each person a mature faith score that could range from 1 to 5. In order to provide comparability with the scoring of the previous Faith Maturity Scale ten years ago, the scores were then multiplied by 7/5ths in order to transform the 5-point scale to a 7-item scale. A score between 1 and 2.99 indicates low faith maturity, a score between 3.00 and 4.99 indicates moderate faith maturity, and a score of 5.00 or above evidences high faith maturity.

The average faith-maturity score for all Adventist youth in Adventist schools was 4.8 (4.77), which is in the high-moderate range. Its value was basically at or near the value of 6th to 10th graders, and then rose in the 11th grade to 4.89 and in the 12th grade to 5.97, which is in the high range. About 45% of the sample were in the high faith-maturity category then, with the highest proportion in grade 12—some 53%— and the lowest faith-maturity scores were in grade 7 at 39%.

We also can look at faith maturity in a more complex way, which gives us a bit more information about the maturity of the faith of the youth in the church. On the basis of their faith-maturity scores, these young people were grouped into four natural groupings: undeveloped faith, vertical faith, horizontal faith, and integrated faith.

TYPES OF FAITH

The faith-maturity portion of our survey finds two distinct themes reflected by a number of questions in the index. There is a vertical theme having to do with a deep, personal relationship with a living God and a horizontal theme, which stresses commitment as seen in acts of loving kindness, mercy, and justice toward others. Looking at these themes we can construct two subthemes.

58% of our sample had a high vertical-faith while 42% showed low personal faith. 54% scored high on the Horizontal-Faith Scale with 46% in the lowest categories. But this scale could be explored even more carefully. For example, each person's faith could be classified into one of four distinct types of faith as follows:

() *Undeveloped faith*—Low on both the Vertical and Horizontal Faith Scales—28% (43%).

() *Vertical faith*—High on the vertical aspect, but low on the horizontal faith experience—18% (8%).

() *Horizontal faith*—A faith high on horizontal, but low on vertical faith experience—14% (24%)

() *Integrated faith*—High on both vertical and the Horizontal Faith Scales—40% (25%) of the students in *Valuegenesis* research.

Roger Dudley suggests these types of faith be understood in the following way:

> *This typology might be viewed in a developmental framework in which faith begins basically undeveloped. Then initial interest in things spiritual leads to a vertical faith. After establishing a relationship with God, one turns outward, expressing a horizontal faith, sometimes to the detriment of the personal relationship with God that characterized "first love." Finally, as the person matures, both vertical and horizontal faith are present in an integrated faith orientation.*[8]

Faith development theory would argue that these stages could be found at any age, by anyone who is learning commitment to God and the mission of the Kingdom of God for the first time, and over the lifecycle of an individual, they could be seen with some clarity moving to a final integrated faith, seen in the older and more religiously involved teens. The research validates this understanding, for as students grow older, their faith is more integrated. And it is encouraging to see that this maturity in faith has increased over the intervening years between research studies in a significant way with over 15% increase in integrated faith during this time.

Ten years ago, comparing our research with five mainline Protestant denominations whose undeveloped faith percentages ranged from (56%) to (68%) which were slightly higher than the Southern Baptists whose undeveloped faith score was (40%), we scored only (43%). However, now our undeveloped faith score is only 28%, again emphasizing the newly found spirituality and maturity along with concern for religion in the life of Generation Y among Adventist youth in Adventist schools. Now only a little over one in five of our youth exhibit undeveloped faith, while four out of ten show a strong integrated faith. We still must be concerned about the percentage of youth that do not have a strong vertical or horizontal faith. But since those with an undeveloped faith are often prone to slip into lifelong church inactivity, according to Dudley, we can rejoice in the growth seen in almost all aspects of these faith types ten years later.

Adventist youth understand grace better now. Their scores on this area of Christian life continue to increase. There is no doubt that the church has begun to place a crucial emphasis on God's actions in salvation. And much has happened over the ensuing years that we can be pleased about: For example, our new GraceLink children's curriculum and the emphasis on God's goodness in many of our publications, and the adoption of a curriculum that includes a special focus on grace, worship, community, and service in the General Conference Curriculum Committee's actions.

My son Timothy at this writing is the Chaplain of Loma Linda Academy. They have labeled their school "the grace place." They try in all of their actions to reflect this caring and accepting attitude God has for them in their actions and attitudes towards students, while at the same time attempting to show love in the context of responsibility and response to grace through obedience and good choices. This is always encouraging news.

Still, on the flip side, some students are identified as having an orientation towards understanding works as the method of salvation, although there are significant improvements in this perspective.

A. 64% (83%) now agree with the statement, "I know that to be saved I have to live by God's rules."

B. Now only 26% (58%) disagreed that "There is nothing I can do to earn salvation."

C. When asked, "The more I follow Adventist standards and

practices, the more likely it is that I will be saved," only 23% now, in contrast to (47%) ten years ago, understood their salvation in terms of their contribution through behavior.

D. In addition, while (44%) before believed that "The main emphasis of the gospel is on God's rules for right living," now some 36% felt that way in our survey.

Notice on the chart how A through D look in the darker scale when compared to our earlier research noted to the right in gray. See how acceptance of righteousness by grace through faith is stronger than ever before, but there is still room for clarification and certainty in our students' religious walk. And of course, we must still continue to clarify the proper

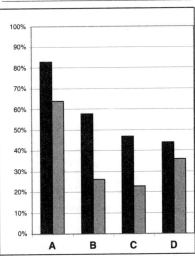

SALVATION BY GRACE THROUGH FAITH

place for actions and works in the life of the Christian as aspects of true worship and love for God. We'll spend time looking closer at this in a subsequent chapter and at the same time look again at the challenge we have as we assist youth to grow towards a faithful Christian life through understanding God's role in their lives. After all, we make the best changes when we are motivated by the grandest goals and purposes. And nothing is more central than God's rich grace.

WHAT EVER HAPPENED TO PERSONAL PIETY?

What continues to be a concern for Christian families is the religiousness or spirituality of their children. In more academic terms, we are concerned as parents about their piety.

I remember a long discussion with a professor once when we worked on a clarification of the term "spiritual." We found it hard to define. And in somewhat mystical terms, we understood it to be a description of a world view or attitude. We could add to this confusion the definitions of the term "religion." Both terms are almost vague and somewhat nondescript. When we talk about *religion,* the etymology of the word may be revealing. It is related to the Latin word *legare,* "to bind together," thus, re-legare (religion) is to "re-bind." The English word *ligament,* which comes from the same root, means connection. "Religion," then, refers somehow to the process of rebinding or reconnecting.[9] So the question of how we could become connected to God comes to the forefront. This theme should be clear to Adventists as we explore the meaning of the Great Controversy and our return to God through grace.

When we talk about *spirituality,* we understand it to reflect behaviors that link us with God, His will and purpose. These activities—Bible study, religious reading, Christian music, prayer, church attendance—all reflect the way one organizes the important things in life. It can put one against the stream, so to speak. The world doesn't know much about this. However, we are citizens of the Kingdom of God, and not of the world. And so Christian behaviors have a direct connection illustrating commitment to God. These activities become another way we worship. By looking at these activities (piety), we get a glimpse into one's involvement in personal spirituality and consistent religious life. Of course, it does not guarantee spirituality, but it does demonstrate its possibility.

There is no doubt that one of the most interesting insights of the *Valuegenesis*[2] research is about personal faith and one's relationship with God. We have already seen the improvement in what we might call spirituality in the life of youth of the church. And like most research, there is both very good news and some that brings concern. This area targets the vertical relationship with God, those devotional practices that often express one's commitment.

Recent research about this millennial generation argues that:

() Teens are less sanguine about their future now.

() Youth are more self-confident than those of the prior generations.

() This generation of youth and young adults tends to listen to mostly alternative rock music, both religious and secular types.

() They are often more cynical than their GenX counterparts and often feel abandoned by most of the culture they experience around them.

() The older they are, the more likely they are to be searching for meaning and some purpose in life.

() The older they are, the more likely they are to call themselves religious.[10]

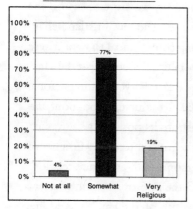

How religious are you?

Certainly, these suppositions are true in the *Valuegenesis* research as well. The next graph summarizes the responses on the survey that asked, "How religious do you consider yourself to be?" Note that 96% see themselves as very or somewhat religious while only 4% answered the question, "Not at all!"

Loyalty to the beliefs of Adventism is always a concern for parents and church leaders. So it was most interesting to look at this aspect of commitment on our survey. When we asked Seventh-day Adventist students about how committed they were to the teaching of the church, they responded positively again. 36% agreed "very much." An additional 51% agreed "somewhat." And only 14% "disagreed somewhat," "very much" or had "no opinion" at all. So commitment to their church does not seem to be the problem here. 87% can agree that they are definitely committed to the teachings of the Seventh-day Adventist church. Students in Adventist schools are loyal to their church. That is good news, and a percentage that all Adventist can be happy about.

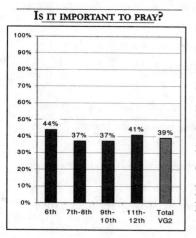

Is it important to pray?

PRAYER

New anchor Tom Brokaw tells the story of meeting a young New York City fireman a week after September 11. The fireman had participated in a memorial service for some of his fallen firefighters, and the two of them began to talk about the tragedy. "As I said good-bye," Mr. Brokaw recalled, "he grabbed my arm and his expression took on a tone of utter determination as he said, 'Mr. Brokaw, watch my generation now, just watch us.'" As the author of the acclaimed *The Greatest Generation,* the story of the World War II cohort that saved America from Nazism, Mr. Brokaw said he knew just what the man was saying: "This is our turn to be a greatest generation." With such commitment to the vision of the church, the youth of this generation have declared their desire to be an integral part of it.[11]

When you look closely and carefully at what makes a rich and growing faith—one that we identify as mature—we notice that an important predictor of this type of faith is personal piety. As students involve themselves in religious practices, their faith is strengthened and their faith maturity grows. Encouraging personal religious practice seems, then, like a mandate for Christian educators and pastoral leaders.

In the *Valuegenesis* research project we looked closely at a number of these issues. We were interested in the frequency with which Adventist youth engage in the following five devotional practices, and these we identified as our "Piety Scale."

() Prayer

() Watching or listening to religious programming (music is

included in this understanding)

() Reading the Bible.

() Reading the writings of Ellen G. White.

() Reading other religious literature.

We can contrast both *Valuegenesis* studies in these areas and get a picture of this generation's involvement in these religious practices. In doing so, we discover that there are some significant changes in this generation, another side of the coin, in keeping with our chapter's theme. Look at the statistics in this scale.

First we asked whether, "It is important to me to spend time in prayer." The students had five different responses to this question from which they could choose: "definitely disagree," "tend to disagree," "not sure," "tend to agree," and "definitely agree." Their responses represent only the "definitely agree" choice on the survey. In addition, for the North American Division some 35% of the study group marked "tend to agree." If you total both those that tend to and those that definitely see prayer as important, a full three-fourths of the total group surveyed see prayer as important to them.

Another question in this scale has to do with insight into their prayer life. For example, we asked if "Prayers alone are as important as church prayers." This gets to the personal nature of prayer and one's commitment to that practice. The percentages parallel the question explored above. 38% of the total students definitely agreed with this statement and another 28% tended to agree.

Of course, asking the more personal question as to their own private prayer life showed how central prayer is to the religious experience of Seventh-day Adventist youth.

Notice the next chart. We asked, "Do you pray other than at church or before meals?" We wanted these students to commit to disclosing how often they participated in this religious practice. Was it less than one time a month, once a month, or about two times a month? Then the questions get more targeted at regular prayer. Is it once a week, less than one time a week, or perhaps once a day or more than that? This chart reflects their

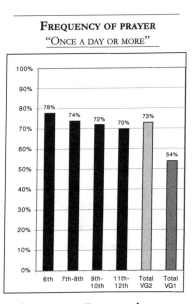

FREQUENCY OF PRAYER
"ONCE A DAY OR MORE"

comments regarding the frequency of prayer at "once a day or more." It is encouraging to see the growth over the past years in this behavior so central to Christian life and growth.

BIBLE READING

Another question on our Piety Scale was that of involvement in reading their Bibles. Adventists have a theological position that includes belief in the authority of Scripture. This objective revelation is central to Protestantism as well. Adventists early on in their history made the pulpit and the Bible central to even the design of houses of worship.

I grew up in a church where in front of the pulpit, where our preacher expounded, was a large family Bible sitting clearly on a table. Everyone's eyes were always focused on the pulpit and just below that our large red-lettered Bible. It was the center of our attention and directed our gaze in a symbolic way to the primacy of God's word. The Bible, this objective revelation, must be understood through study and exploration. So any drop in the study of Scripture poses a unique threat to how we develop our belief system in Adventism.

The answers to the question about how often they "Read their Bibles on their own" are revealing and probably reflective of the distance many in this generation are from reading when the options in media are so myriad and exciting. This chart begs us to ask the question if our students are reading everything less or just Scriptures. While we can't answer this question definitively, we are aware that interest in reading the Bible once a day or more is waning. We believe this presents serious challenges to a number of dimensions in spiritual life.

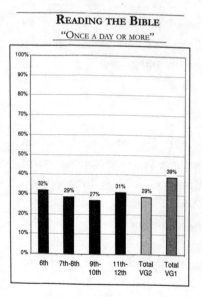

READING THE BIBLE
"ONCE A DAY OR MORE"

If you were fortunate enough to grow up in a family where reading was crucial, you have been richly blessed. You recognized that reading was a way of life, so to speak. And in your home you were challenged with history, literature, and Scripture.

In our family, reading was always a choice our children made, it evidenced itself in their university majors. Each took English as their focus along with education and ministry. It is gratifying to see our granddaughter, now in second grade, reading often. We hope this will have positive implications as to her own Bible reading.

READING ELLEN WHITE

Another related religious practice for Seventh-day Adventist youth is their regular exposure to the writings of Ellen G. White.

In *Valuegenesis*[1] research, we explored a number of issues relating to Ellen G. White, considering the wide influence that she played in the founding and growth of the early Adventist church and the part she continues to play through her writings. It is important that the new generation should not only believe in her, but also understand her place it the Advent movement.

In our early research we asked questions that paralleled the ones we asked on the inspiration of the Bible. We did not ask those questions in the second round of surveys; however, we continue to notice a trend that is troubling to many of the researchers involved in this study. Here is a recap of the earlier research, with positive responses noted.

() Ellen White's writings contain no more truth or wisdom than do the religious works written by leaders of other denominations. (3%)

() Ellen White was an individual who created stories of supernatural guidance in order to explain the mysteries of life. Her writings contain a great deal of wisdom about the human experience. (4%)

() Ellen White genuinely loved God and wrote in order to share her understanding of God's activity in the world. (19%)

() Ellen White was inspired by God and presented God's message in terms of her own place and time. (61%)

() Ellen White copied what God told her word for word, and wrote without being influenced by her own place and time. (13%)[12]

Roger Dudley explained that the first two views discount any divine inspiration in Ellen White's work, while the third is more sympathetic, yet humanistic. The fifth accepts the dictation theory of inspiration. The distributions of percentages were parallel to that of the questions we asked about the Bible's inspiration. (61%) held the more orthodox position, and he noted that "those in Adventist schools were significantly more likely to hold the orthodox view than those in public schools."[13]

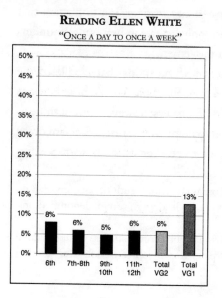

READING ELLEN WHITE
"Once a day to once a week"

The frequency of reading Ellen White is significantly down from our earlier study. When asked if they read "once a week or more," they responded merely at 6% (13%). The percentage in our research was never very good, as evidenced by the *Valuegenesis[1]* numbers. If this is one indication of commitment to the unique practices of Adventism, we are woefully lacking in this area. Of course, it may be simply a factor of the lowering of general reading skills among young people of this generation, or it may relate to the lack of emphasis on this particular Adventist religious practice. Whatever the cause, it concerns us. Our church has been clear on its position regarding the relevance of the messages Ellen White provided to the early Adventist church and to our continuing understanding of contemporary life. Those that don't read may not understand some of the basic tenants of Adventist belief nor ever gain the benefit of her perspective on these issues and her insights into possible answers to these questions.

MEDIA EXPERIENCE

While what one considers as media exposure in religion has changed over the past decade, Adventist students spend about a quarter of their time watching religious television or, more likely, listening to religious radio (probably Christian music). Over the past years the access to religious music has changed dramatically. The influence of the mass media upon the minds and hearts of America's youth cannot be overestimated. Secular research argues that teens spend an average of "four to six hours per day" interacting with the mass media in various forms. For instance, the Barna group discovered that:

() 94% listen to the radio
() 91% play audiocassettes or compact discs
() 89% watch television
() 69% read a magazine

() 58% read part of a book in a typical day

() 52% use the Internet

() 79% use a computer during a typical day

() Most teens use the telephone for additional communication.[14]

Most researchers who have studied the teen years recognize that the most underestimated influence on their lives is their music. In a unique sense it becomes a kind of private language that people over 30 just can't translate.[15] And it is a well-known fact that music is much more than mere entertainment or a diversion from the stress of daily life, chores, or worries about the end of time. For millions of young people, music produces a life philosophy for them to consider and follow, and it helps develop cultural heroes and role models that mentor their lifestyles on a regular, almost heart-pounding basis. That is why music is crucial to talk about.

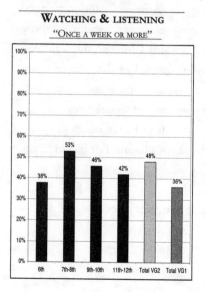

WATCHING & LISTENING
"ONCE A WEEK OR MORE"

While we did not ask in this survey about musical styles and preferences, Barna's research is helpful again. In 1997 his research showed that teens' favorite genres of music were alternative rock (listed by 27 percent as their favorite), rap/hip-hop (22%) and R&B (10%). No other genres were named by one out of ten teens. But by 2000 the research had changed. The list noted that alternative rock dropped out of favor and was replaced by traditional rock. Rap/ hip-hop maintained its core following and actually "became the most popular sound among teens. R&B retained favor, while pop jumped into the upper tier of styles. Christian music experienced a slight dip in popularity."[16] We believe that Adventist youth in Adventist schools are listening and watching more. Here are the results of our survey when asked if they did so "once a week or more." This growth is consistent with the times.

BLURRING THE EDGES

It is interesting to note that there is not as much difference between 15- and 16-year-olds who are technically from the Mosaic (GenY) generation, and youth who are 17 and 18 years old, who represent the tail end of the GenX cohort. George Barna says that this is to be expected for several reasons:

Remember that this notion of generations is a tool created by social scientists to help track and interpret social change. No one can definitively say when one generations starts and another stops. It's all determined by the analyst whose work you are exploring.[17]

One clear example of the blurred-edges phenomenon between the two generations who compose our research population is that of Adventist standards. The power of the world's influence are a force to be aware of and to plan some kind of response. We have already shared two types of standards: substance abuse and Adventist way-of-life. Later we will look at popular cultural standards and at-risk behaviors in context and see how the times have influenced the behaviors of the youth in the church.

NORTH AMERICAN DIVISION ADVENTIST STANDARDS

Grades	6th	7th-8th	9th-10th	11th-12th	Total VG^2
Endorse standards concerning "Substance abuse."	89%	85%	81%	81%	83%
Endorse standards concerning "the Adventist way-of life."	74%	74%	76%	79%	76%
Endorse standards concerning "Popular culture."	23%	17%	15%	16%	17%

() *Substance Abuse Standards*—relate to tobacco, alcohol, and illicit drugs.

() *Adventist Way-of-Life Standards*—relate to Sabbath observance, diet, exercise, modesty in dress, and nonmarital sexual behavior.

() *Popular Cultural Standards*—relate to caffeinated drinks, rock music, dancing, movies, competitive sports, jewelry, wedding rings, violent video games.

We've seen distinct parallels among these types of standards with only slight changes over time. However, in the final category of standards, those of the popular culture type, there continues to be a distinct erosion in practice and belief. And while we will explore this area in depth in a later chapter, it is important to notice how these three standard types are supported. Notice the following regarding endorsement of the various types of standards. Compared to data in our earlier study, we notice that support for Substance Abuse standards is down 5%. At the same time, endorsement for Adventist Way-of-Life standards is up 6%. It is difficult to compare the Popular Cultural standards as a group since our recent study added a number of "new" issues that deserve study, such as Internet usage and video game playing. While the first two categories of standards are at the highest percentages, those in the last category of standards reflect the growing influence of the 21st century. What people *do* often tells us how they define their values.

Consider what we have just revealed about the daily experiences and perspectives of young people as they relate to the church. The result of this review of teen reality is we begin to realize that while family and friends and personal achievements are important, experiences are what rule their lives. On a more philosophical level, it is these experiences that in reality determine what is of value and constant in their experience. As students participate more and more in the popular cultural experiences of behaviors, one can see how the church needs to provide more and more events that personally engage youth in the life of the church rather than simply condemn behavior without balance on the more positive activities of the Kingdom of God.

Teenagers, raised in the fast-paced world of videos and the interactive, personalized, and limitless world of the Internet and media, are challenging adults to provide experiences equally exciting in the development of values and priorities.

If we take this brief summary of endorsement of standards seriously, we might see at the core of youth's faith journey experience-driven reality that raises challenges as to how we might make their spiritual journey a positive, creative, and inspiring one. Youth are at the stage of life where their decisions can ultimately determine their future. In a sense, they are what they are becoming! As

() 60% (47%) felt sad or depressed during the last month.

() 17% (16%) have been physically abused by an adult to the extent that they sustained scars, black and blue marks, etc.

() 20% have been sexually abused one or more times.

() 15% (13%) had made multiple attempts at suicide.

() 11% (17%) have had one or more experiences of sexual intercourse ("gone all the way," "made love").

adults wishing to see true spiritual and personal transformation in the lives of our youth, we cannot afford to ignore the implications of poor choices, especially if these are not life-affirming ones. We must be realistic about what youth are doing and what they see as important and central to their understanding of Adventism.

In a unique way, this data reflects our observation that young people in the Seventh-day Adventist church are spiritual, yet less and less *traditionally* Adventist. Or perhaps we could say that they don't see some of the traditonal standards of Adventism as central to their practice of religious lifestyle as some others do. We can look at this decision in two ways. This is both good and bad news, depending on your perspective. We will feel comfortable with this news or feel threatened about our failure to pass on approved behaviors to our children, according to how we feel about some of these "traditional standards.

So what should we do?

Nurturing grace, the entrance to mature faith, is pivotal for Adventist youth to experience. These suggestions seem obvious, but what must we do to ensure this transmission to our young people? Here are some observations and suggestions from our research.

() *Provide a grace-oriented presence* in which youth can grow and identify with the Kingdom of God.

() *Build on their growing understanding* of how God saves humanity by clear teaching, compassionate mentoring, and active experiences that reflect the love and grace of God in all of the relationships we have with our youth.

Since personal devotional life (piety) is so important to the sustenance of mature faith, we must:

() *Encourage private devotions* for each young person. And if reading has dropped off in the home or school as much as it seems in the past years, what could we do that would remedy this situation? Should a significant reading program, quiz time, and media-related biblical materials be developed for home, church, and school? Interactive Bible study utilizing computer games, Bible chat rooms, distance learning specifically designed for Adventist youth could be effective. We need to engage our best minds in this endeavor.

() Since students have such a high regard for religion and the church, we could capitalize on this fact and *stress personal relationship with God thorough individual involvement with God's word and the writings of the church* in a new and significant way, using the works of Ellen G. White to begin discussion rather than what is, according to focus groups with youth so often done—ending it!

So what?

We'll have more to say about standards later and a great deal of clarification as to what we might do in one of our last chapters in this book, but from this brief introduction, remember that most of the discussions you will have with young people will center on the popular cultural standards rather than on the substance abuse standards or peculiarly Adventist way-of-life ones. It is encouraging that by far most of the standards are supported by the youth of the church.

In addition, this information challenges us to think about what we might do to encouraging life-affirming choices and eliminate life-denying ones. Teaching how to make good, biblically sound, and clear decisions is the task ahead. And from the point of view of the youth of the church, perhaps time spent becoming expert in this skill would be appreciated.

What is our challenge? Providing good answers and reasons to hold high and clear standards and teaching young people of all ages how to begin to make clear choices that support growth in their spiritual lives.

REFERENCES

1. Ezekiel 16:8 (New International Version).
2. George H. Gallup, "Is a New Awakening at Hand?" *Emerging Trends* (Princeton Religious Research Center) 18, No. 9 (1996), 1.
3. George Barna, *Third Millennium Teens* (Pasadena, CA: Barna Research Corporation, 1999), 18.
4. Ellen G. White, *Christ Object Lessons* (Hagerstown, MD: Review and Herald Publishing, 1900), 65-66.
5. Roger Dudley with V. Bailey Gillespie, *Valuegenesis: Faith in the Balance*, 58.
6. Jeremiah 31:33 (New International Version).
7. Roger Dudley with V. Bailey Gillespie, *Valuegenesis: Faith in the Balance*, 59-60.
8. Roger Dudley with V. Bailey Gillespie, *Valuegenesis: Faith in the Balance*, 65.
9. Raymond F. Paloutzian, *Invitation to the Psychology of Religion* (2nd Ed.). (Boston, MA: Allyn and Bacon, 1996), 7.
10. Summarized from George Barna, *The Millennial Generation* (Pasadena, CA: Barna Research Corporation, 2001).
11. Thomas L. Friedman, *Longitudes and Attitudes: Exploring the World After September 11* (New York, NY: Farrar Strausand Giroux, 2002), 124.
12. Roger Dudley with V. Bailey Gillespie, *Valuegenesis: Faith in the Balance*, 92-93.
13. Roger Dudley with V. Bailey Gillespie, *Valuegenesis: Faith in the Balance*, 94.
14. George Barna, *Real Teens* (Ventura, CA: Regal Books, 2001), 26.
15. John Weir, "Hot Sound," *Rolling Stone* (August 1997), 54.
16. George Barna, *Real Teens*, 30.
17. George Barna, *Real Teens*, 24.

*O*nce while chaperoning a party for one of the local high schools, I (Jim) watched one of our core leadership kids literally being carried out of the party because he had passed out from drinking too much. I was hurt; he was embarrassed. Of course, on Sunday he didn't come to our group. I decided I had to go to him and let him know I loved him and still wanted him in our group. He had to learn that even though he made a mistake, he was still accepted by our group and leaders. Even through this negative experience, he would understand the grace of God in a stronger, more meaningful way. Recently this young man told me that if we had not loved him with unconditional love, he probably would never have come back to church. Don't miss the opportunity to demonstrate God's grace to your students.

— *Jim Burns*

CHAPTER 4

()

A FAITH THAT ENDURES
Valuegenesis and the journey of faith

4

A FAITH THAT ENDURES
Valuegenesis and the journey of faith

A great frustration for many Christian educators is trying to motivate people to serve God. Some Christians seem to believe that God exists to serve them, rather than seeing themselves as grateful servants of the most high God. The primary motivator for serving God is a thankful heart. — *Perry G. Downs*

Let's talk about grace. There is no better place to begin this discussion than in the Bible. So before we can understand how our youth feel about God and His marvelous gift of grace, let's look at some biblical counterparts. Perry Downs in his seminal volume, *Teaching for Spiritual Growth*, says that biblical referents for grace are found first in an understanding of the fear of God.[1] He goes on to illustrate this insight by looking at the mystical encounter of Isaiah with the enthroned God of Isaiah 6 in the year that King Uzziah died. When Isaiah had a vision of a holy God he answered by aiming God's concerns upon himself and crying, *"Woe to me!" I cried. "I am ruined!"*[2]

This declaration, according to commentators on this text, was a typical formula used by the prophets to pronounce judgment on God's enemies. Isaiah shouts it to himself! He was ruined, he was the man of unclean lips and his own eyes had seen the "King, the Lord Almighty." Perry Downs says that "when people are allowed to see something of the glory of God, the response is invariably a profound sense of sadness and helplessness because of their sinfulness."[3]

It is clear that when we truly see Jesus, our lives change. This is the power of grace. Somehow Jesus' life and death provide an incredible power for change. If you look at anyone's life cycle, you can find stories of gentle or dramatic change throughout. History is replete with stories of lives different when Jesus has entered them, and the concomitant results of this entrance is often profound—new-found obedience and conformity to God's will.

It is often claimed that "law" is the other side of "grace." This is far from the truth, however, because the opposite of law should be the concept of lawlessness. Law and grace are two completely different topics, related only in the juncture of the impact each has on one's choices. If saved by grace means anything, it means a recognition of the profound action of God's love towards us that continually is available. And a proper understanding of the function of law implies a sense of conformity to a new set of values and directives understood as a clear message of God's ever-present will on this earth. Simply put, if you want to live a happy life, beneficial to others, and exemplary of the impact of grace, you would follow God's explicit instructions in Scripture. If you want to claim salvation, you must accept Christ's gift of life. First you choose Christ, then you choose to live for and with Him. The prior choice determines the impact of the second one.

Understanding grace begins this recognition. One is not saved by one's works, ever. We can do nothing to get God to move towards us, to facilitate His actions towards us, but we can make choices to follow God and we can choose to live a good, clean, and loving life that is motivated by our new-found relationship with the Almighty.

GRACE GIVES US SO MUCH

G race is the beginning. Understanding it motivates us to new purpose in life; thinking about it can challenge us to act in new ways; and knowing about it can move us to accept God's will in our lives. We talk about being a grace-oriented people. In *Valuegenesis¹* we saw its importance, but in our newer research, *Valuegenesis²*, we wanted to clarify the 1990 statistic that argued a clear two thirds of the youth in our survey were confused about how they were saved and even perhaps failed to understand God's rich, loving grace altogether. We saw them more works-oriented than we had hoped. Just what are we saying now?

All too often Generation Y (Mosaic or Millennial), as we have called it, are products of their GenX relatives. A "postmodern" approach to religious life permeates all of our culture, and its spill-over into the GenY crowd

RELIGIOUS THEMES FOR GENX

"I've found. . .major themes that represent strands of a lived theology in Generation X. This practical theology is both *actual and potential*, both self-consciously lived and awaiting further exploration. . . .The first theme is deep suspicion of religious institutions. Xers challenge religious institution in general. . .they frequently pit Jesus against the Church.[4]

is inevitable. And pitting Jesus against the church is one theme that continues in this generation today. In reality, it is a false dichotomy. After all, the church, rightly understood, is to be an expression of the mission and message of the Messiah Himself. For youth, there is something about the Adventist church that creates some tension in relation to one's personal experience of Jesus.

The bumper sticker, "After Religion, Try Jesus," while it rings a visceral bell among youth, is really quite fallacious theology. Religion here is equated as institutional and often repressive. Sadly, many of our young people seem to perceive salvation in terms of the behaviors, good and bad, that the church promotes. This concentration on actions is all too often translated into a type of works righteousness.

Remember, Adventists have a very clear teaching about God's grace which provides everything a person would ever need regarding his or her salvation. "Obedience and responsibility, we teach, are the result of faith and not its source."[5] But we do spend an inordinate amount of time concerned about the behaviors of our youth. And parents say, rightly so, look at the devastation to life and happiness a series of poor choices can cause. Youth can experience permanent damage and even death if not taught to place value in life-affirming behaviors and choose never to participate in life-denying ones.

Our society is focused on acceptance. When Jesus walked the earth, religious leaders were concerned about rules and judgment. But Jesus challenged that kind of thinking with a message of love and compassion. He said, *"The second [most important commandment] is this: 'Love your neighbor as yourself.'"*[6] Grace is expressed in the way we treat others and our neighbors and not only those who share our faith and beliefs. Unfortunately, while we think correctly about grace, we don't put it into practice where it counts.

We Christians sometimes have a difficult time sharing love in a graceful way to people we consider deeply sinful—people who drink, do drugs, sleep around, or have chosen a different lifestyle than we promote. Some would think these "sinners" are not worthy of love or compassion. To judge others, to make them feel as though they are not worthy of God's love, goes against the real message of the gospel. Jesus died for all of us. God's grace is a gift to all of us, and not one of us deserves it. Sin is sin and God's grace is needed to cover all of ours.

Adventists often confuse deserving salvation with accepting salvation. This was the challenge Jesus faced when confronting the works-oriented Pharisees in the Gospels. Jesus said, *"Woe to you, teachers of the law and Pharisees, you hypocrites! You are like whitewashed tombs, which look beautiful on the out-side but on the inside are full of dead men's bones and everything unclean."*[7] This categorization of works-oriented approaches to gain acceptance by God was condemned by Jesus and the Apostle Paul. *"You foolish Galatians! Who has bewitched you? Before your very*

TEN YEARS AGO (1990)

◌ 88% agreed , "I know that to be saved I have to live by God's rules." Only 9% disagreed.

◌ 47% agreed that, "the more I follow Adventist standards and practices, the more likely it is that I will be saved. 30% disagreed.

◌ 61% agreed that "the way to be accepted by God is to try sincerely to live a good life." 22% disagreed.

◌ 44% agreed that "the main emphasis of the Gospel is on God's rules for right living." 23% disagreed.

eyes Jesus Christ was clearly portrayed as crucified."[8] Accepting Jesus' gift of grace is often very difficult to communicate to youth, and even harder to accept for those that grow up in a works-oriented environment of home, church, or school. And our graceful responses to others reflects just how we understand God's actions of love for our lives.

It is easy to see how confused we were and how it has changed over the past years. In the church's earlier research, even a significant portion of adults were confused as to the process of salvation by grace through faith. And when looking at the youth, clearly two thirds of those studied ten years ago exhibited this confusion. Tragically, after ten years of targeting God's rich and abounding grace in sermons, reprints of Ellen G. White's writings, new Bible curriculum in Adventist schools, and myriad *Review* articles and publications, along with hundreds of public presentations, and even a Sabbath School curriculum with Grace, Worship, Community, and Service at the core, we haven't gotten it all straight yet, as Roger Dudley said ten years ago.[9] How do we know?

SAVED BY GRACE ALONE

A number of items in our survey explored our understanding of the theological concept of God's actions in personal salvation. For the information on grace and law orientation, a five-point response format was used that ranged from "definitely disagree" to "definitely agree." In order to help us interpret the results of this information, we combined ten years ago the two "disagree" and the two "agree" categories. We did the same this time to have an orderly comparison between the studies. When the total is not at 100%, it reflects the percentage of those that chose the category, "I'm not sure" as their best answer. We discovered that there were in actuality two concepts—grace and love. The love responses are contrasted with a clearly works-oriented question below. When you look closely at this "love" index, 95% (85%) endorse this love response to God's attitude towards them. This 10% improvement over the ensuing years is encouraging.

()   I know that God loves me no matter what I do. >1% disagree; 97% agree. (1% disagree; 95% agree)*

()   I am loved by God even when I sin. 96% agree; 1% disagree. (94% agree; 2% disagree)

()   There is nothing I can do to earn salvation. 48% agree; 34% disagree. (29% agree; 58% disagree)

Youth are clear on their understanding of God's love for them. They see God's love as almost entirely unconditional and believe that nothing they can do will change this certainty. But when they are challenged to accept God's grace completely for their salvation, some could not make that declaration. But

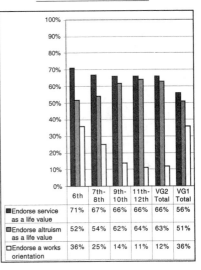

SERVICE AND ALTRUISM

	6th	7th-8th	9th-10th	11th-12th	VG2 Total	VG1 Total
■ Endorse service as a life value	71%	67%	66%	66%	66%	56%
▨ Endorse altruism as a life value	52%	54%	62%	64%	63%	51%
□ Endorse a works orientation	36%	25%	14%	11%	12%	36%

*Remember, the answers in parentheses reflect ten years ago.
**The sign ">" is to be understood as "less than."

we must also note the improvement in this love-oriented question over the past years. The survey says there is an increase in their understanding by some 10% on this question. This reflected a trend in all of the new grace questions. And in addition, as you track the "love" scale across the grades from 6 to 12, the basic understanding of God's unconditional love is a factor that does not decrease as youth mature.

In *Valuegenesis²* we have separated the "grace" items from the "love" items to provide a clearer and more reliable scale score. And in these series of questions students had the opportunity to answer over a continuum of agreement and disagreement. For example, for a typical question like, "There is nothing I can do to earn salvation," the response patterns included from "definitely disagree," "tend to disagree," "not sure," "tend to agree," "definitely agree." This way, the respondents could make a graduated commitment to their answers. The questions about God's rich grace follow with their response percentages responding to the top two answers in the response categories ("tend to agree," or "definitely agree").

	Valuegenesis² Total
() There is nothing I can do to earn salvation.	48%
() Following Adventist practices will cause me to be saved.	23%
() The way to be accepted by God is to try sincerely to live a good life.	45%
() The main emphasis of the gospel is on God's rules for right living.	36%
() Salvation is the way God rewards us for obeying Him.	48%
() We show we are worthy of being saved by doing good to others.	39%
() The gift of salvation is free, yet I must keep the law to be worthy.	51%
() My salvation depends on whether I keep the law perfectly.	11%
() We must be baptized church members before we really are saved.	11%

- () Salvation is God's free gift that we don't deserve and cannot earn. 61%
- () We can do nothing to deserve God's gift of salvation. 48%
- () My good works are a response to God's gift of grace. 63%

In checking with our statistician, Michael Donahue, regarding our Love Scale, you will remember in an earlier chapter the following statement explaining this scale:

Our Love Scale, the mean of two items that can range from 1 to 5, averaged 4.83 (trivially higher than the Valuegenesis[1] value of 4.75), indicating a solid grasp of Gospel principles regarding God's love for these students. A typical item is: "I know that God loves me no matter what I do." Here, about 95% agreed at all grade levels. It should be noted that the original score was so high (4.75; already 95% of the highest it could possibly be, with every single student choosing "strongly agree) that little increase was even possible (a situation known in statistics as a "ceiling effect.)[10]

REGARDING LAW ORIENTATION

In looking at the works orientation of the youth, you will also remember we shared a significant reduction in a works orientation to salvation. This indicates that our youth, in addition to affirming a grace orientation are increasing in their rejection of a works orientation.

In our first research, the news was not as good as it is now. Youth struggled with legalism in a remarkable way. Perhaps they have decided that acceptance of God's grace is just another "work" to perform in order to obtain some sense of surety in their spiritual lives. Youth seemed to be slowly sorting out just the proper place for works in a Christian experience. There is a subtle difference that a maturing faith discerns regarding the relationship between God's rich grace (God's activity) and our regular and significant activities (works). They often forget that sin is a daily struggle for all of us because we are by nature sinful people. If I said I'd never sin again, I'd be lying (1 John 1:8). Now, that doesn't mean I should just give up trying to live a more godly life. It means I must strive daily to follow God, humbly repent when I fail, and accept that it is God's grace, and only God's grace, that saves me.

Here is a summary of the new grace percentage scores as compared with *Valuegenesis[1]* research on some specific items designed to see if students understood grace or were more inclined to be works-oriented. The percentages given are for the total North American Division. The questions asked, *"Salvation is the way God rewards us for obeying Him."* In looking closely at these responses it is significant that 35% definitely agree in grades 6 through 8, while only 21% of high school students definitely agree. This trend of sorting out the nature of God's gift of grace is consistent throughout the questions that deal with the concept of God's grace.

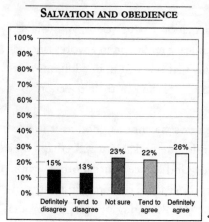

SALVATION AND OBEDIENCE

Another question in this scale was, *"Salvation is God's way of saying 'Thank you' for our good behavior."* The percentages to the left share the total of the study group. Again, when you break these percentages out by grade, only 11% of high school students definitely agree with the statement while 22% of the junior high students feel that way too.

We asked students a more subtle question about law and grace. *"My salvation depends on whether I keep the law perfectly."* Now, we do believe that law keeping is crucial and obviously a result of one's relationship with God, but the question directly equates salvation with that of perfectly keeping the law. The question was based on the Apostle Paul's discussion of this topic with the church in Galatia. The Apostle said, *"Am I now trying to win the approval of men, or of God? Or am I trying to please men? If I were still trying to please men, I would not be a servant of Christ."*[11] And he clarifies the proper function of law

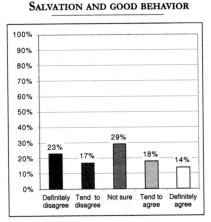

SALVATION AND GOOD BEHAVIOR

SALVATION AND LAW KEEPING

after clearly separating law keeping with the act of God in salvation somewhat later in his epistle by saying, "*Clearly no one is justified before God by the law, because 'the righteous will live by faith.'*"[12]

We continued to try to clarify the student's responses regarding grace and their understanding of the relationship they have to law-keeping. For example, we tried to get as clear a question as possible about the process of salvation. We stated, "*We can do noth-*

"We can do nothing to deserve God's gift of Salvation"							
	Total	6th	7th	8th	9th	10th	11th	12th
Definitely disagree	21%	34%	30%	27%	18%	14%	13%	12%
Tend to disagree	12%	15%	14%	11%	12%	11%	9%	9%
Not sure	20%	22%	24%	2%	20%	9%	15%	14%
Tend to agree	12%	11%	11%	12%	13%	13%	15%	11%
Definitely agree	36%	18%	2%	24%	38%	43%	48%	54%

"My good works are a response to God's gift of grace."							
	Total	6th	7th	8th	9th	10th	11th	12th
Definitely disagree	4%	2%	3%	5%	4%	4%	4%	5%
Tend to disagree	5%	4%	6%	5%	5%	5%	5%	4%
Not sure	28%	32%	33%	35%	30%	26%	21%	19%
Tend to agree	31%	32%	31%	31%	33%	30%	32%	28%
Definitely agree	32%	30%	27%	24%	27%	34%	38%	44%

ing to deserve God's gift of salvation." That seems clear enough. And when we look at the total progression through the grades on the topic of works as a response to God's grace, we can see a growing understanding of this Christian theological concept.

Well, there you have it. The youth in our survey have made a change over the past years in the direction of grace and away from a law orientation towards their salvation. And while there is still confusion about salvation, as students grow older they are more clearly understanding the role of God in the process of their salvation. And what is so wonderful about God's grace is that it works just that way—grows in our lives as we form relationships with Him.

WHAT CAN WE DO?

It seems clear that we must continue to stress the boundless grace of God to the youth of the church. And, in addition, we have to live, modeling that grace in all of our relationships with them. That means the church has to come to grips with any critical, judgmental attitudes they may have towards the youth in our church.

The truth that God loves us and that He came to do things in this world we were totally incapable of doing for ourselves is the secret in the Gospel. As young people experience graceful people, a grace-filled church, and a grace-oriented life themselves, they will come to understand the truth that the Bible announces about our Heavenly Father—that He is full of grace and mercy; He gives me freedom to live as I choose—even when I'm wrong; He is tenderhearted and forgiving; and His heart and arms are always open to me and ready to accept me back just like the prodigal Son in the New Testament story.

And these statements about God are true even if we don't feel like they are. We should often be reminded of the statement in *Steps to Christ* by Ellen G. White as she reflects on this very topic.

In like manner you are a sinner. You cannot atone for your past sins; you cannot change your heart and make yourself holy. But God promises to do all this for you through Christ. You believe that promise. You confess your sins and give yourself to God. You will to serve Him. Just as surely as you do this, God will fulfill His word to you. If you believe the promise—believe that you are forgiven and cleansed—God supplies the fact; you are made whole, just as Christ gave the paralytic power to walk when the man believed that he was healed. It is so if you believe it.

Do not wait to feel that you are made whole, but say, "I believe it; it is so, not because I feel it, but because God has promised."[13]

Many of the youth in the church fear the prospect of facing an angry God, knowing that He is holy and they are sinful. They can't grasp the fact that they are already justified, according to the New Testament. The sins have already been taken care of by Jesus![14] Jesus has already paid the penalty for our sins and we are justified (declared not guilty when we actually are) through his death on the cross. This fear may be evident by the responses youth made to a particular question in our survey. The exact same percentage, 67% in both surveys, even though they were separated by a decade, provided a unique insight into Adventist youth's attitudes toward the Second Coming. While they fully believe in the doctrine of his soon return, they "tended to agree" and "definitely agreed" with the statement that, "I am worried about not being ready for Christ's return." And what is unique about this percentage is that over the years from grades 6 through 12, there was little change: 60% in the 6th grade and 65% in the 12th.

WHAT ABOUT WORKS RIGHTEOUSNESS?

And in spite of the great news about grace and its growth throughout the maturing years of those in our survey group, young people still find it difficult to clarify the proper role of works in their lives. This is not an uncommon problem. In the items in the Law Orientation Scale, the more one agrees, the more one is oriented toward law. In *Valuegenesis[1]* in every case, youth *agreed* more than they *disagreed*.

○ *I know that to be saved I have to live by God's rules.* (9% disagree; 83% agree), 16% disagree; 74% agree in *Valuegenesis[2]*.

○ *The more I follow Adventist standards and practices, the more likely it is that I will be saved.* (30% disagree; 47% agree), 55% disagree; 23% agree in *Valuegenesis[2]* (The question in our newer survey was rewritten to say, "Following Adventist practices will cause me to be saved." This rewrite may have helped students to understand the question more fully and thus explains the more positive scores).

○ *The way to be accepted by God is to try sincerely to live a good life.* (22% disagree; 62% agree), 25% disagree; 23% agree in *Valuegenesis[2]*.

○ *The main emphasis of the gospel is on God's rules for right living.* (23% disagree; 44% agree), 29% disagree; 36% agree in *Valuegenesis[2]*.

Notice that in the scales above, there is 9%, 24%, 39%, and 8% less agreement indicating law orientation now than before. The movement is significantly in the right direction.

As was pointed out in our earlier research, "Unfortunately, not much difference exists on the Law Orientation Scale between those in our schools and those in public schools. The public school students were only .11 higher," according to Roger Dudley.[15] And on the rest of these same questions, students from public education were not much different.

When you look at these questions over time, however, there is some encouraging news. For example, when asked if they "tended to" or "definitely" agreed with this statement, "The emphasis on behavior is so strong in the Adventist church that the message of Christianity gets lost," the change over the grade spread is most interesting. Students feel that this is definitely true. And the older they get, the more they see this as a real possibility. What is the problem?

It may be that young people, understandably, have a developmental tendency to connect any suggestions to live a holy life with their salvation so that feeling saved becomes the result of and the reward for behaving correctly. Thus, as they get older, and more aware of the theological paradox demonstrated by this question, they become more able to express their frustration with this tragic result.

HOW DO WORKS FIT IN?

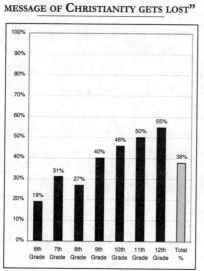

"EMPHASIS ON RULES SO STRONG THE MESSAGE OF CHRISTIANITY GETS LOST"

To say that many Adventists are works oriented is not an understatement according to our research. But we are not alone. Parallel research supports this finding. Perhaps because we care about sanctification (belonging to God), we carelessly equate God's work in our lives with the work we must do as we connect with the power of God for right living. It seems almost impossible to get rid of this notion in the minds of the young. There is a very logical and research-implicit reason for this. As one studies how morality grows in the lives of young, we notice that there is a time during early teen years when young people want things to be black or white, good or bad. They have a difficult time, until they mature, to see the "gray" areas in choice making. Those that research this area of development see this law-oriented phase as something that with time and maturity many can grow out of and balance this concern for concrete morality with a personal law, "written in the heart" as the Old Testament proposes to the faithful.

What actually happens is that when the young grow up, they begin to use their own power to choose and make personal decisions based on values and biblical principles for life. These more reasoned answers govern the life and make commitment and devotion possible. We should expect these younger ones to be more law-oriented, as part of their development. However, we don't want the church to be misunderstood either. The church must reflect a grace orientation in its activities, in its reactions to the young, in its compassion to the world outside of the church, and theologically in order to properly understand the graciousness of God in their own lives.

I personally am not happy with the growth of this attitude over the years of Adventism. The fact that over half of the youth feel that the message of God is lost because of our emphasis on behavior may simply say that the methods we use to encourage good choices and proper behaviors are being coerced by our way of presenting the gospel to the young. We need to study this and decide what picture of God an overemphasis on behavior creates in the lives and impressions of the youth of the church.

How to make a difference

One question I often hear in my religion classes at the university is, "I just can't seem to be good enough!" Remember, the good news of grace is that Jesus was good enough. In fact, it is His life that takes the place of ours in this plan of salvation. It is His life and relationship with His father that takes our place and makes up the difference in our lives and makes possible the good news.

Romans 5:1 says, *"Therefore, since we have been justified through faith, we have peace with God through our Lord Jesus Christ."* We too seldom experience the peace of the battle being over in our lives. Youth professional Neil Anderson tells this story of how he learned of God's love in his life.

> *The school in the small farming town where I was raised released students from school early every Tuesday afternoon for religious day instruction. Some of us went to the church of our choice for an hour of Bible study; those who chose not to go to church went to study hall. One Tuesday afternoon, a friend and I decided we would skip school and church this time, so we went and played in the gravel pit.*
>
> *The next day the principal called me in and confronted me with the fact that I had skipped school. He concluded his remarks by saying he had arranged for me to stay home from school on Thursday and Friday of that week. I was shocked. No way! I was suspended from school for two days for skipping religious day instruction!*
>
> *As I rode the school bus home that afternoon, I was terrified. I walked*

slowly up the long lane that led to our house, fearing my parents' wrath. I thought about faking an illness for two days or getting dressed for school as usual but hiding in the woods each day. . . . No, I couldn't do that to my parents. Lying wasn't the answer.

There was great unrest in my heart as I trudged up that lane. Because I was suspended from school, there was no way I could hide from my parents what I had done. When I finally told them, they were surprised, but then my mother started to smile. Without my knowing, she had called the principal earlier that week and asked permission for me to be released from school for two days to help with the fall harvest. I had already been justified for not going to school those two days![16]

For many young Christians the prospect of facing an angry God in fear, knowing that He alone is the one that is holy and they are sinful, is almost more than they can stand. They can't grasp the truth that they are already justified. Their sins have already been taken care of by Jesus. Jesus has already paid the penalty for our sins, establishing peace with God the Father. So what is it that homes, schools, and churches can do to help this become clear?

◯ *Parents can spend time guaranteeing the kind of grace that Christ's actions represent.* Research confirms that mentoring young people helps them establish clear values and direction in their lives. Parents who spend more time with their children than anyone else have the chief responsibility to be what they want their children to be. So spend time helping them see the grace that Jesus provides through their actions: acceptance and discipline. And when it comes to building a grace-orientation, the family climate, one that is both loving and disciplined, open and accepting is the most crucial variant according to our research. After all, the home must regularly model what it means to understand grace if we expect children to understand it through experience.

() *Schools need to look at those points of contact with students where they can get a subtle picture of the true nature of Kingdom people and their actions.* Check out the discipline process in your school. Look closely at the relationships that are being built between students and teacher, aids and students, administration and the student body. All these relationships must model the goodness, graciousness, and love of God.

() *Churches have a particular responsibility to model the nature of Christ.* Acceptance of worship styles, church music styles, programing that is relevant to youth and young adults, all provide metaphors of God's actions in the world. If the church is too critical, obviously self-centered, and fails to show compassion to others and respect diversity and difference, how can the young ever feel that God is that way? The church is God's agency on earth to picture God's attributes. What a tragedy if it fails to be a good model of God in their community.

The church "is the only reminder left on earth that Christ was here."[17] This comment was made by a teen. Another, Vanessa, said "The church is a family. It's somewhere we can fall down on our knees and repent for our sins."[18] These pictures of the church share what is supposed to be, but so often is not. And when Wendy Zoba asks, "Does God have a face?" she means God's portrait and personality are seen in the people of God—in the church on earth. What a challenge to be representatives of the grace that saves us.

To model that kind of acceptance and love. To be those kinds of people on earth living at the end of time. We have a continuing challenge to communicate just that kind of love and share just that kind of a God.

REFERENCES

1. Perry G. Downs, *Teaching for Spiritual Growth* (Grand Rapids, MI: Zondervan Publishing House, 1994), 46-49.
2. Isaiah 6:5. (New International Version).
3. Perry G. Downs, *Teaching for Spiritual Growth,* 47.
4. Tom Beaudoin, *Virtual Faith: the Irreverent Spiritual Quest of Generation X* (San Francisco, CA: Jossey Bass, 1998), 41.
5. Roger Dudley with V. Bailey Gillespie, *Valuegenesis: Faith in the Balance* (Riverside, CA: Loma Linda University Press, 1992), 97-98.
6. Mark 12:31 (NIV)
7. Matthew 23:27 (NIV).
8. Galatians 3:1 (NIV).
9. Roger Dudley with V. Bailey Gillespie, *Valuegenesis: Faith in The Balance,* 98.
10. Our statistician, Michael J. Donahue, is an Associate Professor at Azusa Pacific University in California. He wrote the chapter entitled, "From the Statistician's Desk" in this book. He works regularly at the Graduate School of Psychology and worked with *Valuegenesis'* research team at Search Institute in Minneapolis, Minnesota. His contribution is immense to the success of this project. As coauthor of this volume, his work represents a major part of the actual analysis of the data sets for *Valuegenesis².*
11. Galatians 1:10 (NIV).
12. Galatians 3:11 (NIV).
13. Ellen G. White, *Steps to Christ* (Mountain View, CA: Pacific Press, 1908), 55.
14. Neil T. Anderson and Dave Park, *Extreme Faith* (Eugene, OR: Harvest House Publishers, 1996), 64.
15. Roger Dudley with V. Bailey Gillespie, *Valuegenesis: Faith in the Balance,* 103.
16. Neil T. Anderson and Dave Park, *Extreme Faith,* 63-64.
17. Wendy Murray Zoba, *Generation 2K: What Parents and Others Need to Know About the Millennials* (Downers Grove, IL: InterVarsity Press, 1999), 78.
18. Wendy Murray Zoba, *Generation 2K,* 78.

T *he first time I went out to "share my faith" door-to-door at college, I got a strange feeling. How could I presume to take all the biggest questions of life—the questions that these students had committed four years of their lives and tens of thousands of their parents' dollars to answer—waltz into their dorm rooms, and answer them in 15 minutes? The reason I was given is that some of the greatest Christian minds of our century had gotten together and honed the Christian gospel into these four propositions.*

But why didn't God just give us a systematic theology book instead of a book of stories, poems, and letters? Why did God gift us with 10,000 years of Jewish and Christian history—and many of the greatest minds ever born trying to examine it all—if he just wants us to simplify his steadfast love for us into a list of propositions?

A helpful definition of propositional truth: containing only logical constants and having a fixed truth-value.

— *Tony Jones,* Postmodern Youth Ministry

CHAPTER 5

FASHION ME A PEOPLE
Loyalty and the content of faith

5

FASHION ME A PEOPLE
Loyalty and the content of faith

For the last few centuries, evangelism was considered mainly a cognitive process (i.e., Christianity is a set of propositions an individual must intellectually agree with and accept as true.) But more recently, the understanding of conversion has been shifting toward the transformation for the whole person. In fact, in the postmodern context, it could be said that we ought to first evangelize experientially and teach the content of the faith later! After all, Jesus says to his disciples, 'Follow me!'—Not 'do you accept me as your personal Lord and Savior?' — *Tony Jones*

Using research on hundreds of adolescents in the early '60s, Ronald Goldman, religious educator and researcher, argued that "we give them too much, too soon."[1] His argument focused on the fact that the "content" of religious life is often the only thing that church groups promote, thus growing young Christians that simply are too young to understand the whole truth about God and a church that presumes they know it all, and therefore, believing the right stuff will guarantee a place in God's kingdom.

And on the other hand, there is what one might call an emotional approach to finding God. This is when the emotional content of the environment or a personal deeply felt recognition of the distance one is from God's kingdom comes home in the youth's life because of some external manipulation. There can be emotional upheaval equal to nothing teens have ever experienced before, and because of it, they equate this "feeling" of religious piety that was generated by these external forces with that of acceptance and presence of God.

I CRY, THEREFORE I'M SAVED

Perhaps it is the end of a long and emotional week away from school, up at a mountain retreat, moonshining, boating, new friendships, or powerful messages of God by prominent youth specialists. Everyone's sad about leaving tomorrow, and everyone is both physically and emotionally exhausted. After all, they've been away from their real world for over two days and now they must go back. But they have to attend one last chapel service of the weekend and the camp staff had gone all out with pageantry—cross lit by the waterside, red felt banners, new songs, and quiet meditation.

The speaker gets up and really lays on a great talk about the cross and Jesus' death. The band plays ever so softly, "Friends are Friends Forever" in the background. Hysterically crying campers come forward during the altar call, one after the other to give their now fully recognized sinful selves over to the new Lord of their lives.

Em Griffin, author of *The Mind Changers: The Art of Christian Persuasion,* shares forcefully about this style of evangelism for teens. He calls it "emotional rape."

> *The average preadolescent is not equipped to withstand the positive incentive of counselor approval or the negative force of group condemna-*

tion. The phrase "age of consent" in our legal code points to the fact that children may be unable to say no to the forceful persuader. Jesus made it clear that leading a child astray is a particularly heinous act. I think this applies to the methods used as well as the intended results.[2]

I was the recipient of just such an evangelistic call during my own teen years. I heard stories about how some teens heard the message of forgiveness but didn't respond and then left the building, only to be hit by a car and therefore lost their eternal chance for eternity. Of course, I responded and walked the long aisle as the Methodists used to say in early American history. And sadly, I watched as many of those same teens gave up their new-found faith only because it, "didn't feel that way anymore" when they returned down the mountainside.

The most interesting thing is that neither the emotional nor the highly cognitive approach are the best models for working with postmodern teens as they find God. This kind of emotionally manipulative approach is an insult to the gospel, in my opinion, and equally so to those who receive it.

I THINK, THEREFORE I'M SAVED

While it is important for Adventist youth to understand and accept the truth as we teach it, we must always remember that if the church of tomorrow does not accept that truth, it is possible that Adventists may find themselves trembling "on the brink of extinction, for if we cease to believe, we will soon cease to behave."[3] We believe that there is a close relationship to belief and behavior. Adventists will not ever forget how important believing is; in fact, we often stress believing way ahead of behaving, and certainly the concept of belonging. One can only read Richard Rice's book, *Believing, Behaving, Belonging: Finding New Love for the Church,* to recognize how deficient we are in understanding the role of community and acceptance in our theology of the church.[4]

Still, knowing what it is that the church teaches is central to understanding a balanced religious experience. Avery Dulles has suggested that there are at least five distinct ways that individuals and those who join together in congregations view their church. None is more central than any of the others, but he simply is giving a formal organizational structure to what we already intuitively know.

For our purposes here, it is interesting to see what others think is a balanced view of the church. After all, people go to church for many different reasons, and there they seek different types of resources and insights from their church. The models Dulles suggests are the following:

() The *church as institution* emphasizing organization, management, and efficiency. Young people with concerns for logic, knowledge, and history are drawn to this model.

() The *church as mystical communion* or community which highlights fellowship, prayer, and interpersonal relationships.

() The *church as worship* or sacrament which concentrates on liturgy, worship, symbol, and the beauty that is attached to the place and process of worship. Central to this concept is understanding God's grace and our response in faith.

() The fourth model depicts the *church as herald.* The focus here is on the communication of the Word of God in the form of proclamation, teaching, Bible study, and passing on the tradition through evangelism.

() Finally, the church is seen as *servant* and emphasizes the role of the congregation as an agent for human betterment and as a responder to human needs. Central concerns here focus on justice, peace, brotherhood and sisterhood among all people, and respect for diversity.[5]

The church's task is in providing members with the skills needed to meet these needs evidenced by each model. When you look at the youth and their religious priorities, building an ideology (a system of beliefs) becomes a concern for at least two of the five models depicted above.

So *knowing* what one believes is central to the religious experience of any growing adolescent, and framing an ideology is a crucial faith stage process.[6] And even after saying this, the research team is ultimately aware that a growing and maturing faith life and commitment to a life of service and modeling after Christ is not formed solely by mental ascent to these propositional forms of belief. Fully knowing something forms the ideology and framework of faith, but being faithful or, better put, being a disciple means recognizing the Lordship of Jesus in one's life. These commitments are made firm in living the Christian way, being nurtured in a loving and faithful environment, and growing close to an understanding of what the love of God is all about.

"Seventh-day Adventists have always put a high premium on the belief components of religion." With this

THINK ABOUT THIS

We have done a disservice to Christ's gospel by making it into tracts and statements of faith. While these methods of evangelism have made many converts, have they made many disciples? The gospel is something to be accepted with our minds, but it is so much more!

The young are won to radical discipleship, not by intellectual assent but by the example of a friend, by a loving and accepting community, and, ultimately by the steadfast love of God.[7]

statement, Roger Dudley began the segment on youth's commitment to beliefs of the church.[8]

SO, WHAT DO THEY BELIEVE?

With these reservations and theological suppositions in mind, we developed a part of the research questionnaire which measured the cognitive part of religious belief in areas of what we might call the historical teachings of Adventism. We wanted to see how committed to these belief statements these young people would be. Originally we called it the Orthodoxy Scale. And in fact, our new research broadened this information with a more complete scale that included all of the basic doctrinal beliefs of the Adventist church, including the original ten we explored before. All twenty-seven basic beliefs of Adventism were explored, including those that are not mentioned in our belief statement such as prayer and personal commitment. First let's look in detail at the same questions we queried about ten years ago in our first research, *Valuegenesis¹*, and see how the students in Adventist schools grades 6 through 12 scored.

The youth were given ten fundamental doctrinal statements. Six responses to each were possible as follows: "I have never heard of this," "I definitely do not believe this," "I am uncertain but lean toward believing," or "I definitely believe this." For each statement the percentage that "definitely believed" is listed in the box that follows. And again, the percentages in *Valuegenesis¹* are listed enclosed in parentheses. The ten doctrines are listed in descending order of commitment, the same descending order as in our first research.

ORTHODOXY I SCALE - ADVENTIST BELIEFS		
() The true Sabbath is the seventh day—Saturday.	91%	(91%)*
() The Ten Commandments still apply to us today.	91%	(91%)
() Jesus will come back to earth again and take the righteous to heaven.	89%	(91%)
() When people die, they remain in the grave until the resurrection.	88%	(89%)
() The body is a temple of God, and we are responsible in every area of life for its care.	79%	(83%)
() God created the world in six 24-hour days.	71%	(67%)
() The wicked will not burn forever but will be totally destroyed.	61%	(65%)
() The Seventh-day Adventist church is God's true last-day church with a message to prepare the world for the second coming of Christ.	46%	(61%)
() Ellen G. White fulfilled Bible predictions that God would speak through the gift of prophecy in the last days.	43%	(53%)
() The investigative or pre-Advent judgment in heaven began in 1844.	27%	(45%)

The four major doctrines—the Sabbath, the perpetuity of the ten commandments, the Second Coming of Christ, and the doctrine of the state of the dead—were "definitely believed" by the young people of the church at about 90%, just as ten years ago by the young people of the church. And what is particularly interesting is that there is little difference between the 6th grade students and high school seniors. For example, using the Sabbath as our illustration, the students in 6th grade "definitely believed" this doctrine at 92%. Those in the 12th grade were at 90%. And as another

*The answers in parentheses reflect *Valuegenesis¹* research.

illustration of this fact, the doctrine of the state of the dead was at an 87% level in 6th grade and at 90% among high school seniors. And remember, this percentage reflects those that "definitely believe." On the two illustrated doctrines above, less than 1% had "never heard" these doctrines, and less than 10% were "neutral" or "disbelieved" it entirely. These doctrines are key to understanding Adventism, and our church has provided sound theological support for these basic beliefs. While there was a slight drop over time in the support for the theological underpinnings of the health message, 79% of our youth hardly puts this belief in jeopardy.

Comparing research again, the five other doctrines received slightly less support, and in some areas the difference over time was particularly significant.

Only one doctrine showed in the original scale to have made some improvement. The belief in a literal creation week increased 4% over the period under study. This may have been due to the fact that considerable money was expended by the Office of Education of the church in this area, and the students who took this survey were in the middle of this new curriculum when they were questioned. If you remember in our first study, when we looked at Adventist students in public schools, they were only slightly more in favor (2% more) of a belief in evolution.

However, the other four doctrines *decreased* in percentage over the study time: the destruction of the wicked, the church as remnant, Ellen G. White's prophetic gift, and the pre-Advent judgment in 1844.

This is a cause for some concern. While these students did not say they "disbelieved" these doctrines, the percentages decreased from 4% on the discussion of the destruction of the wicked, 15% regarding the identification of the remnant church, 10% decrease regarding "definitely" believing in Ellen G. White as fulfillment of the Bible predictions that God would speak through the gift of prophecy at the end time, and a total of 18% decrease regarding the investigative or pre-Advent judgment.

These last three doctrines demand careful discussion in our schools, churches, and homes if they are going to hold relevant meaning for this generation. The teaching of the true church showed that only 7% had "never heard" of this belief, additional 7% leaned towards disbelief, 17% were "uncertain" about it, and 26% "lean toward believing" it with 49% "definitely" believing.

A similar pattern is evident in the doctrine regarding Ellen G. White and her prophetic gift. A total of 11% "never" heard to it, "definitely do not believe it", or "lean towards not believing" in this particular doctrine. 17% are "uncertain" about it, and 25% "lean towards believing." At the same time 47% "definitely believe" it. There seems to be confusion as to the relevant meaning for this age group in the church for support of the doctrine regarding Ellen G. White.

WHY IS IT SO IMPORTANT?

Understanding Ellen G. White's role in Adventist history and the part she played in affirming the beliefs of the church seems crucial if Adventism is to maintain its unique identity among the many other churches proclaiming the gospel message. One might understand the reluctance of students to claim exclusivity as a church, especially in this postmodern age. In our research with college and university Adventist students, this doctrine holds the award for being the least believed among five major colleges or universities in our denomination. It scored low in the research in the South Pacific Division as well. Young Adventists seem to show a tendency to move away from such exclusive claims.

In light of modern thinking, this is probably explainable, yet it does give us pause for concern. If doctrines that make Adventism particularly unique continue to diminish at the rate they are evidenced by this research, these Adventist beliefs will cease to be meaningful to the youth of the church.

Ten years ago we said, "The church needs to focus on new ways to present a defensible and positive view of Ellen White to the rising generation." From our evidence, we have not fulfilled this challenge nor have we even begun to address it. We can only reconfirm this conviction about making these particularly unique Adventist doctrines meaningful in this modern time and leave it to teachers, parents, and pastors who can instill renewed interest in these landmark doctrines.

While this uncertainty among our responders may simply reflect lack of understanding in such doctrines as the sanctuary message, it is more likely a lack of information and relevant presentations by their adult pastors, teachers, and parents, who are ultimately responsible for their spiritual training. But it seems that at all ages this belief is forgotten, if not misunderstood. In *Valuegen-*

esis[1], (36%) of those in the 6th grade "definitely" believed, and the figure rose to (56%) in the 12th grade; now 6th graders "definitely believe" at only 22% and as seniors in high school only rose to 45%. The numbers are simply going the wrong way if these are to remain central to Adventist understanding.

A REASON TO BELIEVE

In our earlier research there was some criticism that we only asked ten items regarding Adventist orthodoxy. With a second chance to look at what Adventist young people believe, we jumped at this opportunity. After all, Adventists understand way more than these simple ten discussed above. So we created an additional set of questions. We labeled them the Orthodoxy II Scale. Since these questions were entirely new, we were curious as how students would respond to these additional statements of belief. We wondered if the same pattern of strong belief from even the early grades could be supported. The response scale for these additional doctrinal questions was exactly as before with "definitely believe" the highest possible response. The questions were phrased to elicit a response to the additional core beliefs of the church. The doctrines were grouped according to theological topics.

The first grouping is the doctrine of the trinity. In the history of Adventism, this doctrinal grouping came relatively late and was included as one of the doctrines of the church in a more recent revision of church beliefs. While the trinity is a complex doctrine, even confusing to the early Christian church, it still explains a significant truth about God's purpose. Being three-in-one, united in purpose, and yet including three distinct personalities is an abstract construction. As children grow, they should grasp this abstract concept in their belief system. And while it is difficult, movement to abstraction is a developmental task that helps this doctrine become more real in understanding. Yet, Adventist youth have a clear commitment to this truth about God, even in the 6th grade. The questions included in this doctrinal group include the nature of Christ and the doctrine of the Holy Spirit and the role this person of the Godhead plays in our life. The charts in this series reflect responses in the top category, "definitely believe."

TRINITY, GOD, JESUS, HOLY SPIRIT

	6th	7th-8th	9th-10th	11th-12th	Total %
God	90%	91%	91%	92%	91%
Jesus' divinity	74%	77%	81%	84%	80%
Jesus' humanity	54%	66%	75%	80%	71%
Holy Spirit	61%	60%	63%	67%	63%
Trinity	80%	86%	87%	88%	86%

The following theological understandings in this grouping are:

() *God*—God, our Heavenly Father, is the Source, Sustainer, and Ruler of the universe.

() *Jesus' divinity*—Jesus is truly and eternally God.

() *Jesus' humanity*—Jesus became truly and fully human.

() *Holy Spirit*—God, the Holy Spirit, teaches us how much we need Jesus in our lives, draws us to Jesus, and makes us as He is.

( ) *Trinity*—There is one God: Father, Son, and Spirit, a unity of three eternal persons.

The next grouping reflects the unique picture of the history of the world in *the Adventist view of the great controversy between Christ and Satan* and related doctrines.

( ) *Adam and Eve*—the first man and woman, created as free beings in the image of God, chose to rebel against God. We have inherited their fallen nature along with all its consequences.

( ) *Great Controversy*—There is a great controversy taking place between God and Satan. It began in heaven with the rebellion of Lucifer and will continue until the end of time.

Again we can see a learning curve as students grow older. By the time they reach their senior year in high school, they definitely believe these great-controversy-related doctrines at a greater percentage. One that is especially low is that of the millennium, and it begins at 40% "definitely" believing, with a full one-third of the young people in 6th grade leaning toward not believing, are uncertain, or simply do not believe. By their

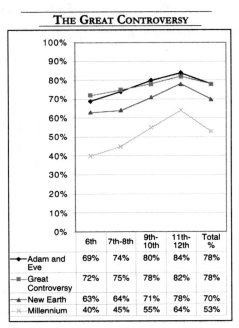

THE GREAT CONTROVERSY

	6th	7th-8th	9th-10th	11th-12th	Total %
Adam and Eve	69%	74%	80%	84%	78%
Great Controversy	72%	75%	78%	82%	78%
New Earth	63%	64%	71%	78%	70%
Millennium	40%	45%	55%	64%	53%

senior year, that percentage is only 17%, with 16% leaning towards belief. There is no question that more time should be spent clarifying this doctrine as youth grow through the grades. Those that have no exposure to Adventist education must rely solely on the church or their parents to clarify this belief. Perhaps a simple Bible study on Revelation 20 would be helpful. In my teaching in the university, I often find students who come from Adventist homes and attend church regularly still have not had, or don't remember having, a Bible study on this topic. Pastors might look at their preaching and teaching schedule and see if they provide ample time to clarify these particular beliefs as youth grow toward the upper grades in high school. It may simply be lack of time. Just as none of my high school history courses ever got past World War II, and none of my Gospel courses ever got to the post-resurrection narratives, maybe Bible courses can't get to the end of Revelation.

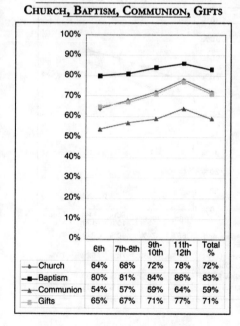

CHURCH, BAPTISM, COMMUNION, GIFTS

	6th	7th-8th	9th-10th	11th-12th	Total %
Church	64%	68%	72%	78%	72%
Baptism	80%	81%	84%	86%	83%
Communion	54%	57%	59%	64%	59%
Gifts	65%	67%	71%	77%	71%

Another theological grouping is that of the church and related doctrines to ministry, evangelism, and nurture. For example, beliefs that relate to the unity in the church—as God's family—are reflected in this category. These include: baptism, communion, and belief in spiritual gifts and are included together here. They are doctrines of:

- () *Church*—The church is God's family on earth, a community of faith in which many members, all equal in Christ, join for worship, instruction and service.
- () *Baptism*—Baptism is a public testimony that we have accepted Jesus and want to be involved in His church.
- () *Communion*—Taking part in the Communion service expresses thanks to Jesus for saving us.
- () *Gifts*—God has given spiritual gifts to each of us that we can use in ministry.

Anyone who has worked with teens knows that one of the most challenging Christian practices is the celebration of communion and the ordinance of service—foot washing. This practice exposes youth to others and involves personal participation. It is no wonder it is the lowest of these in the church group. But the learning curve is evident once more as youth grow through their school grades.

The final doctrinal grouping includes those doctrines relating to God's ownership. Doctrines in this category are Christian marriage unity and stewardship in the broadest sense. The doctrines that relate to making appropriate choices in one's lifestyle are included in the chapter about life affirming choices, so it is not included on the Orthodoxy II Scale. The two doctrines here are:

- () *Marriage*—Marriage is a loving union that should be entered into only by people who share a common faith.
- () *Stewardship*—We acknowledge God's ownership of the earth and all its resources by returning tithes and giving offerings.

These particular doctrines of the Adventist church reflect doctrines that impact one's lifestyle. This may explain why they are some of the lowest in the Orthodoxy II Scale. After all, giving of

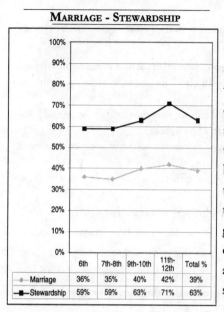

	6th	7th-8th	9th-10th	11th-12th	Total %
Marriage	36%	35%	40%	42%	39%
Stewardship	59%	59%	63%	71%	63%

one's life—including money, time, energy, gifts, etc. require deep commitment to a vision of what God wants in one's life. In addition, the issue of marrying someone of the same faith, for some, borders on meddling rather than clarification of biblical truth. Teens, however, all grow in their understanding of these church positions and share a deeper understanding as they get older.

One of the things we were interested in was the relationship of a strong orthodoxy percentage and a number of other variables in our research.

RELATIONSHIPS AND CORRELATIONS

We discovered that high orthodoxy scale scores are more closely linked to intrinsic religious (I/E) scores than is the Faith Maturity Scale (FMS). Those who report that their religious education programs are of high quality and those who found the group of influences in the "Spiritual-Influences Scale" to be strong, are more likely to rate high on denominational loyalty and to a lesser extent, Adventist orthodoxy. A similar pattern is found for those who personally endorse the "Adventist lifestyle" standards, and who engage in personal devotional practices.

Since this was the first *Valuegenesis* instrument which included Allport's Intrinsic Religious Orientation measure (although somewhat modified to address an Adventist population), we noted that the intrinsic scale correlates more highly than the faith maturity scale with denominational loyalty, at .64 vs. .47; Orthodoxy I and Orthodoxy II, approximately .40 vs. approximately .30; personal standards concerning drugs, .33 vs. 26, popular cultural standards .37 vs. .21; and Adventist lifestyle standards, .49 vs. .40; and slightly higher with the Grace Scale, .34 vs. .30.

But one obvious reality is the fact that Adventist young people learn their doctrines early, and maintain their loyalty and commitment to them throughout their high school years. And a strong ideology and theology should help in providing a clear perspective on the vision the church has about the nature and work of God in the world.

WHAT IS A CORRELATION?

We exist in a field of relatedness, and our theories and ideas about things are usually based on assumed correlations. "Birds of a feather flock together." "Time heals all wounds." "Power corrupts and absolute power corrupts absolutely." No wonder, then, that scientists have tried to make the concept of correlation more precise, to measure and quantify correlations.

When we perceive two things that co-vary, what do we see? There are two possibilities. One is that the change in a thing is concomitant with the change in another, as the change in a child's age co-varies with his or her height. The older, the taller. When higher magnitudes on one thing occur along with higher magnitudes on another and the lower magnitudes on both also co-occur, then things vary together positively and we say this situation is a positive correlation.

The second possibility is that two things vary inversely or oppositely. For example, the more insulation we have, the lower our heating bills; and vice versa. We would say these things are negatively correlated.

What is the most interesting is how soon the youth seem to learn their doctrines. In fact, we would have to study students at a much earlier age and with more qualitative research techniques in order to find why they fail and when they form a clear idea about their church's beliefs. Teachers, pastors and parents must be doing a good job in providing information about their beliefs, for only a few doctrines seem to have problems regarding acceptance among the youth of the church. And if you remember the earlier research, when you compare Adventist students in Adventist schools with those in public education, they were significantly more likely to hold the orthodox view on the Orthodoxy I Scale than those in public schools (64% to 61%).

ADOLESCENT BELIEF BUILDING

Most research on faith development spends time talking about building a belief system. And we have seen that our youth have a firm grasp of the basic beliefs of Adventism, but remember, to live in faith is to act in faith. Responses based only on traditional reasons may produce actions, but since they are not products of a deep faith commitment that is held personally, they often become habitual rather than personal faith responses.

We are aware that there are some givens for establishing a rich and growing faith life. "First, faith must be personal if it is to be truly viable. We cannot give our faith to someone else. But we can structure what we want from others in their faith life and we can structure the situations that nurture faith."[10] Emphasis must be put on the proper teaching of relevant beliefs, if they are to be renewed by youth as they build their own theology of God.

And young adolescents' religion often integrate new symbols with each new age. For faith to be real, the symbols that generate meaning and give excitement to one's religious life often must be renewed and adapted to other meaningful symbols that are being gleaned and used. This means that some youths' religious lives will incorporate new symbols and new approaches, with some new forms that seem to replace the old forms and symbols of the previous generation. We may not like it, but it probably will happen anyway.[11]

Younger youth demand real reasons for establishing their own stories about God. They want to know their own reasons for establishing their behavioral norms, and they need to be committed to their own reasons for belief. These building blocks of personal identity are stressed in James Cobble's insightful book, *Faith and Crisis in the Stages of Life*. He argues that there are really only two fundamental issues that occur in teens' transition into mature faith and adulthood. The first of these is to establish a basis for faith apart from what one's parents or other authority figures believe. The second, and equally important, is to "begin to clarify what one believes to be God's will for his or her life." Understanding this, God's will, is to understand God's purpose and vision for life itself. If doctrines don't point to this clarity and vision of God, they are simply dry beliefs, often as dry as the Hills of Gilboa, as scripture says. Beliefs that have no meaning and impact on understanding God or the way to impact the world itself, are of little use other than being a simple academic exercise.

Salvation is a complex process that involves the individual and the community's distilling of the beliefs in a way that makes them clear and propositional. Of course, the result is supposed to be disciples that bear fruit. However, we don't have a lot of examples of the salvation if the individual in Scripture, perhaps Philip and the Ethiopian in Acts 8 and Jesus and the woman at the well in John 4, are considered typical. And since we believe that salvation is based on the individual's own decision, and not the community's, we just have to make these doctrines they profess to know a product of our community, and their understanding of Scripture personal and real to each youth. Just because they score high on orthodoxy doesn't mean we don't have work to do. Perhaps Dan Kimball said it best:

> I believe that salvation is based on the individual's decision, not the community's. Revelation 20:15 states, "If anyone's name was not found written in the book of life . . ." not "if a community's name." But while we're each accountable to God individually, our faith must be lived out and shared in the context of community. After all, what was the woman at the well's first act after meeting Jesus? She ran off, leaving her pitcher behind, and told to those in her community about Him.[12]

So what is the challenge in light of the information?

To provide a reasoned faith that is both personal and deep, the church has an important agenda for the coming years—to continue to provide clear, relevant reasons for the hope that is within us as well as to encourage creative approaches that reflect insight and biblical consistency for those doctrines that reflect a unique Adventist identity.

REFERENCES

1. For information about the appropriate age to introduce religious content into a child's life, one of the best resources for research in this area is Ronald Goldman's *Readiness for Religion* (New York, NY: The Seabury Press, 1968).

2. Tony Jones, *Postmodern Youth Ministry* (Grand Rapids, MI: Zondervans, 2001) 131-132.

3. Roger Dudley with V. Bailey Gillespie, *Valuegenesis: Faith in the Balance* (Loma Linda, CA: Loma Linda University Press, 1992), 82.

4. See Richard Rice, *Believing, Behaving, Belonging* (Loma Linda, CA: Spectrum Books, 2003). Complete bibliographical information can be found at: (http://www.spectrummagazine.org/store/ricebook.html).

5. See Avery Dulles, *Models of the Church* (Garden City, NY: Image Books, 1978) or several articles in Loretta Girzaitis, *The Church as Reflecting Community: Models of Adult Religious Learning* (West Mystic, CO: Twenty-third Publication, 1977) uses Dulles' models as a base for suggesting approaches to adult religious education and church planning decisions.

6. For a detailed discussion of the process of faith development see V. Bailey Gillespie, *The Experience of Faith* (Birmingham, AL: Religious Education Press, 1992).

7. Tony Jones, *Postmodern Youth Ministry,* 130.

8. Roger Dudley with V. Bailey Gillespie, *Valuegenesis: Faith in the Balance, 81.*

9. Roger Dudley with V. Bailey Gillespie, *Valuegenesis: Faith in the Balance,* 85.

10. V. Bailey Gillespie, *The Experience of Faith* (Birmingham, AL: The Religious Education Press, 1992), 136.

11. V. Bailey Gillespie, *The Experience of Faith,* 136.

12. Dan Kimball in Tony Jones, *Postmodern Youth Ministry,* 119.

We find the image of God as a potter fashioning a people in both the Hebrew Bible and the New Testament. The prophet Isaiah reminds us that we do not make ourselves and points out the foolishness in thinking that we do. "Shall the potter be regarded as the clay; that the things made should say of its maker, 'He did not make me'; or the thing formed say of him who formed it, 'He has no understanding'?" (Isaiah 29:16). Jeremiah also focuses on this image in an even more familiar text: "Behold, like the clay in the potter's hand, so are you in my hand, O house of Israel" (Jeremiah 18:6). In Romans, Paul uses the image too, sobering us with a reference to "vessels of wrath" at the same time that he graces us with the imagery of a God making known the riches of divine glory for the "vessels of mercy" we might hope to become (Romans 9:20-24).

— *Maria Harris*

CHAPTER 6

NOW I LAY ME DOWN TO SLEEP

Personal piety and the quest for spiritual life

6

NOW I LAY ME DOWN TO SLEEP
Personal piety and the quest for spiritual life

The adolescent faith crisis, which can arise in either the high school years or under-graduate college years, can take many forms. For some adolescents, the crisis results in a complete break with traditional value systems and a retreat within the self to dis-cover new meaning. Other adolescents dramatize their reactions to the faith crisis by assuming values and behaviors that explicitly reject the religious traditions from their childhood. For other adolescents, the crisis might lead to the questioning of a limited scale of behaviors or certain religious practices....Still other adolescents might adapt their own religious upbringing without recourse to any sense of rebellion or rejection.
— *Charles Shelton*

While we never really can predict what behaviors and questions will emerge during the developing years of adolescence, what we do know is young people go through a time of questing and questioning both their understanding of themselves and their relationship and understanding of God. Religious youth often find this quest in a religious format, one that tries to sort out the various options they have thought up and selections given by their parents and teachers during their growing years. But whatever the outcome, the process is a spiritual one, and the outcome is crucial for their future faith maturity and life decisions.

One of the first prayers we often teach our children is one everyone can recite. "Now I lay me down to sleep, I pray the Lord my soul to keep. If I should die before I wake, I pray the Lord my soul to take." Regardless of the unbiblical theological implications of that prayer, it points us to a very important and often seen universal religious behavior. Prayer is one of the first, and probably the most regular religious practices impacting the growing spiritual life of the young. It is part of a number of religious disciplines we call evidences of piety. And the regularity of these practices often has a great deal to do with an evaluation of faith maturity and evidence of loyalty to the church.

The spiritual lives of teens are the subject of this chapter. Pastor and author Eugene Peterson says that spirituality is "the attention we give to our souls, to the invisible interior of our lives that is the core of our identity, these image-of-God souls that comprise our uniqueness and glory."[3] So it is imperative we spend a bit more time looking at this aspect of the growing adolescent's spiritual life.

Talking about spirituality is often difficult, however, because its definition is often hard to nail down. "Spirituality" can be a difficult term to understand. In Peterson's book, *Leap over a Wall: Earthly Spirituality for Everyday Christians,* he suggests a quote from Winnie the Pooh as he and his friends are on a trek to find the North Pole. This story illustrates the challenges in the quest for spiritual life today. Along the way little Roo falls into a stream and needs rescuing—everyone pitches in. Pooh picks up a pole and fishes him out. The emergency over, the animals talk it over while Pooh stands there with the pole in his hands. Christopher Robin then says, "Pooh...where did you find that pole?"

Pooh looked at the pole in his hands.

"I just found it," he said. "I thought it ought to be useful. I just picked it up."

"Pooh," said Christopher Robin solemnly, "the Expedition is over. You have found the North Pole!"

"Oh!" said Pooh.

The animals go on with their desultory, haphazard conversation for a while until Christopher Robin finally gets them back to attending to the North Pole that Pooh had discovered.

They stuck the pole in the ground, and Christopher Robin tied a message onto it. It read:

"North Pole. Discovered by Pooh. Pooh Found It."

Then they all went home again....[1]

We often sort out spirituality this very same way—spirituality is a vaguely defined term (the "North Pole"). Every once in a while, one of them picks up something and someone says, "That's it!" Sure enough, it does look like "it." And someone, usually a "spiritual authority" (Christopher Robin), hangs a sign on it: "Spirituality." And then everyone goes home again, until the next expedition is proposed.[2]

Remember, spirituality is the attention we give to our souls, to the *invisible interior* of our lives. Christian spirituality, true spirituality, *takes attention from us and focuses it on another, on Jesus.* One key goal of Adventist Christian education is to help youth become spiritual, to have their lives more focused on Jesus than on themselves. The task to bring youth to this understanding is formidable since the spiritual goal of our institutions is all too often fuzzy at best, and outright dogmatic at worst. But what we do know is that this generation, the one we are beginning to teach and will teach for the next five to seven years, is interested in spiritual life in a new and intense way.

REASONS FOR A FAITH CRISIS

In Charles Shelton's important work on adolescent spirituality he lists a number of reasons that in the emerging developing years of youth, a faith crisis often appears.[3] He lists reasons and identifies some as particularly crucial. We noticed some of the same evidence in our own research. These include:

() *Peer pressure.* It is difficult to overestimate the power of peers in the choices youth make about their future. They can find support and close personal relationships with one or more friends. And these friends have an impact on their choices, faith, and behaviors.

In our research, we see this potential power for spiritual growth evidenced by the relationships youth have with their friends. We

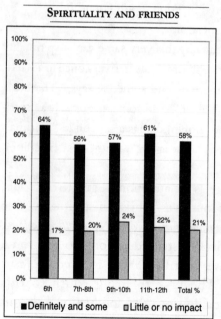

SPIRITUALITY AND FRIENDS

■ Definitely and some   ▫ Little or no impact

asked our survey group, "How strongly do you consider spirituality, morality, or religiousness when choosing a friend?" We wanted to have them choose the one answer which represented most closely their attitude regarding this topic. There were a number of possible responses. "I definitely think it has an impact on me." "It has some impact on my choice of friends." "I'm not sure it has an impact on my choice of friends." "It has little impact," and "It has no impact at all." With these choices, notice how important religious friends really are. Only 7% of the students actually said it had no impact and only 14% said it was of little importance. But around 60% said it was definitely significant.

() *Institutional alienation.* Youth often feel put-off by the institutional forms of worship and practice of religion. And even though a relationship with Jesus Christ may be important to them, the larger, impersonal settings that characterize traditional religious practice usually distract teens and militate against his or her developmental need for a close, personal walk with God. What's the end result? It is an obvious lack of meaning in their religious walk.

When we asked our youth "under what conditions would you consider leaving your local Seventh-day Adventist church to worship in another congregation of another faith?" Some 5% responded they would

---

THINK ABOUT THIS

Faith communities appear to provide strong social networks for youth. They also offer a moral code and behavioral prescriptions that can affect the risk taking and thriving indicators for youth. Religions provide philosophical systems of understanding meaning and purpose in life that may positively influence identity development . . .by grounding principles and behavioral norms in ideological bases and exemplifying them in actual historical events, religion gives a transcendent world-view that gives meaning and purpose to life.[4]

do so if the sermons were boring, 9% would leave if there were no youth activities in their local church. More significantly, some 20% wanted relevance. For them, if the services were not meaningful, they would leave. An additional 25% of the total group said if the church was cold and unfriendly they would seek fellowship elsewhere. The issues are all about climate and relationships and relevancy. This is a clue to what needs to be done if we are to hold our youth in their spiritual walk with God.

() *Separation from parents.* As youth grow, they move naturally away from their parents' beliefs until they formulate their own and adopt the behaviors consistent with those beliefs. Parents, perhaps forgetting what it was like to be a teen themselves, often ally themselves with traditional institutional attitudes and values and in an attempt to separate from their parents' views, youth try to formulate their own idea of God's will for themselves, often personal and "clearly distinct from parental beliefs."[5] Our research explored the youth's ideas about their

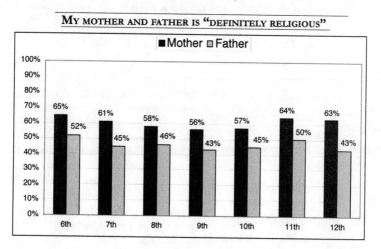

MY MOTHER AND FATHER IS "DEFINITELY RELIGIOUS"

parent's religious life. As you look at the chart below, you notice that there is a time when a parent's religiousness comes into a bit more doubt. It is during the times of 8th through 10th grades, the time when personalization of faith is crucial.

() *Rebellion.* In other publications we have used the Eriksonian expression "negative identity" as another term for rebellion. Rebellion during the teen years is simply an acting out of negative behaviors. These may be as mild as questioning traditional beliefs, or as radical as getting involved in at-risk behaviors or dangerous drug use. And Adventist youth are not exempt from this response as they grow up.

We are amazed at the percentage of young people that use alcohol, for example. We have a strong health message, well-believed by the majority of our youth, but in a reaction to something, we see 35% of 11th to 12th grade students drink alcohol (beer, wine, or liquor) while "alone or with a friend during the past year." Some of this behavior can be attributed directly to rebellion and an "I want to do it myself" attitude, which often is usual in growing teens as they try to determine just what it is they stand for and want to believe. Others are probably related to peer pressure, as we will see in the discussion on at-risk behaviors later in this book.

() *Search for meaning.* We know, for example, that another developmental and spiritual task during these growing years is that of searching out the meaning of life by building his or her own personal value system. Research tells us that the older high school years and probably the undergraduate college or university years are a particularly relevant time during which they try out their new intellectual powers and seek to understand and ask meaningful questions about the purpose of life.

The answers youth have received from their church and

family may not be sufficient now as they grow up. Formulating their own belief system is part of this search for meaning. The childhood naivete is gone now, and their uncritical acceptance of church beliefs is long gone, but the future is still not very clear. Those crucial identity questions of "Who am I?" "Where am I going?" "How is the best way to get there?" "And why am I making this trip at all?" need resolution and reasonable answers. This is a significant factor in an adolescent's crisis of faith quest.

I believe this is why there is a certain cynicism about Adventism that shows up in our research. We'll see it in a later section of this book, but for now it is enough to suggest that this reorientation may explain the reorganization of popular cultural standards in the church as teens try to come to grips with their own century and culture.

The traditional church often sees this as a search that is facing backward because the traditional behaviors of the church don't seem to be practiced or believed any longer, the traditional styles of worship don't provide the same meaning as before, and the style of spiritual music just doesn't sound right—like it used to—anymore!

All this is a part of the youth's search for meaning and identity and can be viewed as a challenge for the church to be and remain relevant during these crucial years. If there were ever an argument for separate worship services for youth and young adults, this may be it. And while this flies in the face of a biblical theology of church, it is directly related to the spiritual relevancy of church and beliefs for growing teens and young adults.

() *Disillusionment.* Before most commitments can be made to the church or to a personal God, the youth must find ways to cope with disillusionment. This is often done by reassessment of their prior commitments. When youth see that many adults don't live particularly "good Christian" lives, this can be unsettling. When asked, "Some adults insist on certain rules or standards for younger Adventists that they do not observe themselves," the answers were revealing. There were a number of choices from "no opinion" to "always true." And they had lots of choices in-between; 46% believed it "often," "almost always," or "always" true.

() *Personal difficulty.* During the personal life history of an adolescent, problems in the home, feelings of insecurity, adjustment problems all mitigate against a call to a deepening faith life. And when you couple these with the growing uncertainties of just being a teen, there is often a distancing from the church and God. Ministry directly to young people is important during such times. And this ministry must target these crises and problems rather than simply attempt to get them involved in the church or to correct their aberrant behaviors. They must feel acceptance and know they are needed by the church at large. This climate issue is crucial if they are ever to build a close walk with God. When we asked youth if their church is "dull or exciting," 23% said it was "slightly" exciting. Another 20% indicated it was "quite" so, and only 17% answered "extremely exciting." All

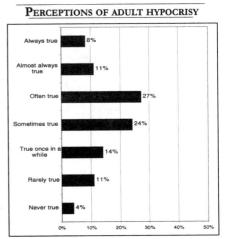

PERCEPTIONS OF ADULT HYPOCRISY

Always true	8%
Almost always true	11%
Often true	27%
Sometimes true	24%
True once in a while	14%
Rarely true	11%
Never true	4%

in all, 60% indicated church was exciting.

() *Environment.* The last reason for the crisis in faith among youth is that of environment. We can't dismiss both the cultural or the environmental factors that influence the adolescent. No one grows up in a vacuum or apart from culture. One may wish that Christians were always against the prevailing culture, but like it or not, we are always in our culture, and on a daily basis it is impinging on our lives.

For example, MTV in 2003 had the largest worldwide programming. The commercialism of TV ads and magazine headlines taunts youth to buy, consume, and become just like the people that are considered by the world as successful. 50% of the youth in our survey said, "Religion doesn't affect my daily life." This percentage is among a group of young people who see themselves as both spiritual and religious and loyal to the church and its teachings. After all, 77% of the youth in our survey said they were "somewhat" religious and only 14% claimed "very" religious as their preference. The culture has its impact. Just look at the popular cultural influences on our youth in the chapter on life-affirming choices and you'll see the impact of today's contemporary culture. A close, spiritual life is crucial. Piety is an essential for teens who want to know God.

FAITH AS A PERSONAL ACTIVITY

One of my favorite religious educators is Thomas Groome. His text is used in most of my graduate youth ministry classes. He has clarified faith in a unique way—as a threefold activity. Faith is best seen as believing, trusting, and doing. Much like Richard Rice's *Believing, Behaving, Belonging,* Groome see faith first as believing because it is a commitment to belief and the tenants of Scripture through the transforming power of God's grace and love. The relationship with God is a trusting encounter. "The call to God's Kingdom is an invitation to a relationship of unbounded trust in the faithfulness of God and in the power of God's saving grace."[6] Trust finds its fulfillment, for Groome, in the activity and practice of prayer. This trusting relationship with God is seen by the Christian through personal activity, works, which he calls "doing." "Doing" means living one's faith in the world.

His contribution to our understanding of piety is just this: While faith is a believing-and-trusting encounter that leads to our response, action also nurtures and sustains belief and trust. "True faith, then, is immersed in, rather than isolated from, the everyday activity of life experiences."[7]

Let's take a closer look at those activities that are often called "spiritual." And while we gave a brief introduction to this in the earlier chapters, we want to look with some clarity to the involvement across the grade span of these crucial behaviors that are often considered indicators of spiritual life and vitality.

Often these actions have been called "disciplines," or "spiritual activities," but whatever they are called, they are the myriad ways that we as humans attempt to acknowledge our relationship with God and build a life of faith. They are the acts of worship that we elect to perform. They are the way that humans respond to God's actions on our behalf. With that theological background, let's look at some of the things that form the everyday life of the youth of the church, things that are results of their life of faith and activities that help build and sustain their belief and trust in God.

A LIFE OF PRAYER

Of the spiritual activities we studied, prayer formed a large portion of the questions which revealed the practical spiritual life of the youth in our research, and there were a number of questions about this crucial and central relationship behavior.

One of the questions we repeated was that of exploring the frequency of personal, private prayer. It is encouraging to see that Adventist young people still believe in and practice prayer. "How often do you pray or meditate, other than at church or before meals?" was the exact question. More than 73% (53%) prayed at least once a day or more, and over 90% (67%) claimed that they prayed on at least a weekly basis. Only 2% (5%) of the youth never prayed personally at all. You can notice by the graph these same figures which reflect a substantial increase in the percentage of youth involved in personal prayer. This is an indication of the place that a personal relationship with God plays in their prayer life. With such encouraging news, it is important to continue to provide opportunities to join other church members in prayer activities.

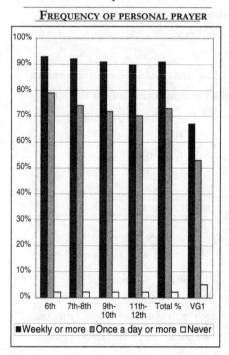

FREQUENCY OF PERSONAL PRAYER

■ Weekly or more ▨ Once a day or more ▢ Never

There were, on the new survey questions, other aspects of this discussion that were not explored ten years ago. When personal devotions is included in a list of 27 influences that have developed your religious faith, personal devotions ranked in a grouping of the top five. Of course, the top influences were, "the family I grew up in, " "attending Adventist schools," their "mother's" and "father's faith," and "personal devotions" was tied with "short-term mission projects," "the youth pastor," and "Week of Prayer at school."

Couple this response with the fact that 57% said they were "very interested" in gaining a deeper relationship with God and another 24% indicated they were "interested" in doing so again shares the spiritual focus by this generation of youth.

Other questions about personal prayer were as follows, and the response format spanned five steps from "I strongly disagree" to "I strongly agree." Here are their responses to "Tend to agree," and "Definitely agree" to the questions about prayer. The following list provides a look at those that tended to and definitely agreed with these statements.

() It is important to me to spend time in private thought
   and prayer.   74%
() I have often had a strong sense of God's presence.   62%
() I pray mainly to gain relief and protection.   53%
() Prayer is for peace and happiness.   63%
() I pray mainly because I have been taught to pray.   23%
() Prayers I say when I'm alone are as important to me as
   those I say in church.   66%

Over time when we look at the question, "I pray mainly because I have been taught to pray," we see that as the student gets older he is less likely to see prayer as simply a function of habit.

The percentages go from a high in 6th grade of 27% to a low in the 12th grade of 18% of those that "tend" and definitely believe" this statement.

Couple these behaviors with those already explored in our chapter on the other side of the story regarding reading the Bible, Ellen G. White's writings, and their involvement in Christian media and you can see that their spiritual life reflects the modern cultural, promedia, antireading model, like most of the youth in national studies of religious behavior.[8]

CHURCH ATTENDANCE

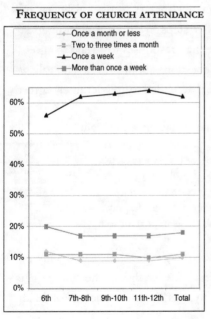

FREQUENCY OF CHURCH ATTENDANCE

Church attendance patterns are another indicator of spiritual vitality in one's personal religious experience. Why? First of all when youth participate in religious activities it helps them learn ideas and values that are not as easily understood if they are passive learners. Also, when a young person engages in decision making, the church sends out a signal that they are important in this process. There is a sense of respect for them which may help them develop a positive sense of self and self-respect along with dignity and self-worth.

It is for just these kinds of reasons that this type of socialization helps them learn the values, beliefs, and traditions of our faith, and ultimately become fully participating members of that religion.[9] Research in other denominations has demonstrated a number of elements that influence youth participation in religious activities:

() Church attendance is strongly related to the religious behavior of a youth's parents. In fact, the principal determinant for church attendance is parental attendance and parental religious values.

() Youth's attitudes towards church depend on past religious education, types of leaders, and beliefs.

() Children and youth need opportunities to be involved as active participants and leaders in the life of the congregation.

() Youth need ways to participate that are meaningful to them and help them relate their religious education and practice to everyday life. For example, children can serve as leaders in worship, greeters at church and Sabbath School, and offer prayers. Also, they can be involved in mission projects in the church and community.[10]

The Bible provides a good model of the importance of involvement in church. *"Let us not give up meeting together as some are in the habit of doing, but let us encourage one another—and all the more as you see the Day approaching."*[11] When we asked the young people about how often they would prefer to go to church, they were consistent with their responses. 63% suggested about once a week and 16% agreed with more than once a week. These percentages stayed close to the same throughout their schooling, and there were no significant differences in their responses.

Since friends' behaviors are so influential to young people as well, we wondered what they would say if we asked about their "friends." We wanted them to indicate if the statement we provided was "completely true, "somewhat true, "somewhat untrue," or "completely untrue." When provided with the statement, "My friends attend church almost every week," 44% said it was "somewhat true" and 43% indicated it was "completely true." And one interesting insight into this type of questioning was when we probed them about their friends to see if they belonged to church teen groups. Below are there responses. First we see their percentages as they said it was "somewhat" and completely untrue" and second their answers to "somewhat" and "completely true.":

"My friends belong to church-sponsored groups for teenagers."

	6th grade	7th-8th grade	9th-10th grade	11th-12th grade
Untrue	49%	42%	45%	47%
True	51%	58%	55%	53%

Almost one-half of the young people did not view their friends involved in a church-oriented youth group. How will these young people learn values and the Adventist faith in practice? Schools provide an academic and cultural experience, but only about 35%-45% of the young people attend Adventist education, so the majority, sadly enough, don't get the benefit of a caring, nurturing teen-oriented ministry. And since church involvement is crucial to a rich, growing faith life, these statistics reflect the reality in our church where local congregations fail to provide the necessary ministry needed to build a deep spiritual life and one that is deeply loyal to the Adventist way of life and message.

REFERENCES

1. A. A. Milne, *The Complete Tales of Winnie The Pooh* (New York, NY: Frederick Wane and Co., 1999), Chapter 8. See Eugene Peterson's "What's Wrong with Spirituality? The Gospel of Mark's Prescription for Spiritual Sanity," quoted in *Christianity Today,* July 13, 1998, Vol. 42, No. 8, 51. This quotation is found in detail in Eugene H. Peterson's *Leap Over a Wall: Earthly Spirituality for Everyday Christian* (San Francisco, CA: Harpers, 1997).

2. Eugene Peterson, *Subversive Spirituality* (Grand Rapids, MI: Eerdmans, 1997), 6.

3. Charles M. Shelton, *Adolescent Spirituality* (New York, NY: Crossroad, 1989), 143-146.

4. Charles M. Shelton, *Adolescent Spirituality, 144.*

5. Linda Mans Wagener, James L. Furrow, Pamela Ebstyne King, Nancy Leffert, Peter Benson "Religious Involvement and Developmental Resources in Youth," *Review of Religious Research* (Volume 44:3, 2003), 282.

6. Thomas Groome, *Christian Religious Education Sharing Our Story and Vision* (New York Harper & Row, 1980), 60.

7. Charles M. Shelton, *Adolescent Spirituality, 149.*

8. R. Kimbrough-Melton (June 2000). "Children's Participation in Faith-Based Organizations." A paper presented at a symposium sponsored by Childwatch International and UNESCO on the topic of children's participation in community settings, Oslo, Norway, 8.

9. Answers to these questions are part of the scale that measures intrinsic religiousness. The remaining three are traditionally associated with extrinsic religiousness. But in its present wording (from the "universal" version of the I and E scales), it is actually associated with *both* scales.

10. Kimborough-Melton, "Children's Participation in Faith-Based Organizations," 9.

11. Hebrews 10:25 (NIV).

What makes a church appealing? The importance of church life in the spiritual development of people cannot be overestimated, nor should it be minimized. But we also know that teenagers are still in a formative stage spiritually. They attend churches for a variety of reasons, and those experiences will shape their desires and expectations regarding church life as they age. What matters to them as they explore church life?

— *Adapted from George Barna*

We live in a fast-paced culture. If the Church stands still and waits for youth to come to it, then the Church will have a long, quiet, empty and frustrating wait. Meeting students on their territory is vital because it breaks down the often imposing walls of the Church. . . .By going into the student's world, you will show them that you are interested in them as people, not just as church participants. One of the most important aspects of ministry is to let them know you care. Your presence and commitment to be in their world communicates care and concern.

— *Jim Burns*

CHAPTER 7

()

SPIRIT MADE FLESH
How to build a Kingdom

7

SPIRIT MADE FLESH
How to build a Kingdom

The trouble with writing about postmoderns is that they don't like to be categorized, explained, observed, limited, reduced, dumbed down, isolated, or put under a microscope. Postmoderns resent our obsession with definition. This generation is longing for relationship, mystery, experience, passion, wonder, creativity, and spontaneity. In other words, they want to go past where the "sidewalk ends." They long for the place just beyond words, the shore of mystery. In other words, they're looking for Jesus. What else do we need to know?
— *Mike Yaconelli*

Just what is the church for our young people? Ten years ago, Roger Dudley asked, "Is there any room for the church in my life?"[1] Research outside of the Adventist church has suggested a number of answers to this question. There have been a few significant correlations between self-esteem and church participation, scales of religiosity and church attendance, as well as building understandings of belonging and interdependence, in which each member is an integral part of the whole.[2] The church could be the one place where young people know they will always be welcomed, never rejected. And life has meaning and purpose for those who belong, because they owe their existence to a Creator. Sadly, this glowing picture of the church only exists in our desire, not often in our reality. After all, we are all in the business of building Kingdom churches—ones that carefully and realistically reflect the nature of the Kingdom of God on this earth. What an opportunity!

If you look at your life, you will notice that there is always time to do the things you like to do. I always read *Newsweek*. If I am traveling and have some extra time, I'll even buy another copy of the magazine I will get at home anyway, just to keep up-to-date on the world's condition and news of the hour. Of course, this behavior is on a micro level—my life. On a macro level in the world, all people usually do just what they want. Perhaps it is so because they don't have any good models of proper love or lack a vision of hope in their lives. Maybe they haven't spent enough time with people that can make a difference in their lives. Or on the other hand, maybe they are so focused on themselves nothing else truly matters.

After all, we all do over and over again those things that bring us good feelings and shun those activities that create problems and frustration. That is why for a young person, following Jesus is so crucial. They are learning about life and what is important. This concept is based on a law of the mind that Ellen White explored in 1901.

> *God desires men and women to think soberly and candidly. They are to ascend to a higher and still higher grade, commanding a wider and still wider horizon. Looking unto Jesus, they are to be changed into His image. They are to spend their time in searching for the deep, everlasting truths of heaven.... And as they learn of Him, their motives and sympathies become firm and unchanging; Christ is our example. By beholding Him we are to*

be changed into His image, from glory to glory, from character to character. This is our work. God help us rightly represent the Saviour to the world.[3]

How does the church fit in?

What are the ways in which the local congregation impacts the growth of faith and feelings of belonging so necessary to youth at certain ages in their growth? Does exposure to religious experiences, regularly shared, modeled after the best of God's ways, provide useful insight into how youth develop their rich growing faith life?

In interviews on the qualitative side of our research, we asked students to share their feelings about church. Some of these students were particularly candid. *"I wish I had something positive to say about the church,"* one young women shared. She continued:

I believe that a narrow approach to the church presented by my parents and school may have forever damaged my view of religion and its place in my life. Whenever I am home, my folks ask if I am going to church. During meals, my mother reads the scripture to me. Each week, now that I am at a local university and no longer living at home, I get a call from my mother asking if I have at-

---

YOUTH AND THE CHURCH

The responsibility of the church to the youth is to support them with:
- Your service and personal involvement
- Your prayers
- Your giving
- A receptive attitude and refraining from "looking down" on youth.

Responsibilities of youth to the church are:
- Believe in Christ
- Learn the Word of God
- Grow in your spiritual development
- Be an example to others in speech, conduct, love, faith, and purity.

now that I am at a local university and no longer living at home, I get a call from my mother asking if I have attended the local church yet. I just want some freedom. I want to understand religion for myself. I am a member of a sorority now at my university. It provides philanthropic services for the community, a sisterhood and loyalty to every one involved, and rituals that have meaning and importance to our group. It gives me all I need from people who really care about me. Why do I need the church?

And during the process of this research, I have received a number of letters and e-mails from concerned parents both encouraging and discouraging about the models of the Kingdom of God local congregations present to their young people. One local church leader shares his concern for his daughters by saying:

My two teenage daughters never felt accepted by the church. They were criticized by some older adults because of their dress and hair style, they were excluded from being up-front because they were not in the group that attended Adventist schools, and they were often forgotten when the church had activities for the youth because they didn't know very many of the leaders in the youth program of the church. I have talked with them a number of times, but they are shy teens and feel that they can't contribute anything to the church. They regularly attend, but that doesn't seem enough. What's wrong with a church that won't make youth a priority in its vision of ministry?

Here are two young ones that attend, believe in the church's mission, and still feel like outsiders. And tragically, we all too often use terms to isolate and separate—unbelievers, outsiders, one of them, etc. Unless churches change this trend they will only reap devastating outcomes. As Roger Dudley says, "Remember, people will not continue in something that no longer proves satisfying. Attitudes toward the local congregation are of vital importance in determining what happens to the religious experience of a person a few years down the road."[4]

So let us begin our exploration into the issues local churches face as they attempt to grow committed Christian young people.

IT'S ALL ABOUT CLIMATE

We asked the youth of the church to spend a moment thinking about the church that they attend and judge the truth of the following statements. A five-point response format ranged from "not at all true" to "very true." Here are the combined percentages of those who answered either "quite true" or "very true." And the research ten years ago is again included using parentheses.

	Valuegenesis[1]	*Valuegenesis[2]*
() It feels warm.	(44%)	51% - +7%
() It accepts people who are different.	(60%)	63% - +3%
() It is friendly.	(61%)	68% - +7%
() Strangers feel welcome.	(49%)	56% - +7%
() It provides fellowship.	(NA)	70%
() I learn a lot.	(34%)	43% - +9%
() It expects people to learn and think.	(40%)	42% - +2%
() It challenges my thinking.	(31%)	37% - +6%
() It encourages me to ask questions.	(28%)	35% - +7%
() Most members want to be challenged to think about religious issues/ideas.	(35%)	35%
() It stretches me in worship.	(NA)	37%

In the list above we combined the first four statements into a scale which we labeled "Warm Church Climate." It measures the extent to which the youth perceive their congregations as warm, friendly, and accepting to people who are different than they are or even see themselves as strangers. A unique way to explore this data is to look at the changes as students mature through the grades from 6th to 12th. Here we see something quite interesting. As students grow up and move from the junior high school grades to those of high school, there is a "blip" on the radar of our statistics. Students seem to have a difficult time moving between these levels of maturity. As students go into the 9th grade, and of course, they are now beginning to move into the next stage of faith development, that of personalizing faith for themselves, their perception of the church becomes more critical. Just when they need to understand their identity in light of the emerging view of the Kingdom of God as seen in the local church members' lives and in the mission and message of the church, they begin to see the problems that their local church has.

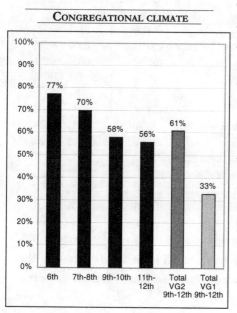

CONGREGATIONAL CLIMATE

Now, even though the Warmth Index is greater now than it was ten years ago, it drops almost 21 percentage points through time. The good news is that our churches are more warm and friendly, full of fellowship and acceptance than they were before, but one can't be happy with only 56% of 11th and 12th grade students perceiving the church this way.

Another interesting insight relating to the warmth climate in churches has to do with what it would take for youth to leave their church. When asked the reasons why they might leave they responded as follows:

()	If the sermons were boring.	5%
()	If the church was cold and unfriendly.	25%
()	If there were no activities for youth.	9%
()	If the services were not meaningful.	20%
()	Misc. others all totalling.	40%

Notice that the climate-related issues had the highest percentages. And when asked if their congregations stretched them in worship, only 37% responded that it was "quite" or "very true." Perhaps this is a warning to local congregations that unless their services are relevant and challenging and unless they continue to become places where youth feel welcome and accepted, young people will continue to drift away as they get older.

CONGREGATIONAL THINKING CLIMATE

In our earlier list of items we noticed the Warmth Scale. The last six items reflect our Thinking Index. It is broader than those in our earlier research; however, the results follow the same pattern. Of the four items that are the same, there was only a 6% average increase in the thinking climate of our churches. Looking at a couple of the items provides insight into the challenge. One question asks, "My church encourages me to ask questions." Looking at the ratings of 4 or higher on a 5-point multiple item index, excluding those who do not attend church at all, over time the percentages drop from 51% in 6th grade to 26% in the 12th.

When we asked, "It challenges my thinking.," those that answered "quite" or "very" true were at 55% (56%) in the early grades and dropping to 27% (23%) in the 12th grade. Unfortunately, as crucial an activity this is for identity formation and especially so for a budding personal, theological ideology, such a climate seems to be scarce in Adventism. Only about a third of the youth in the 12th grade of high school saw their congregations as places that respect and foster thinking and believed that they "learn a lot." And the older the student, the less positive they are regarding a critical thinking climate in local congregations.

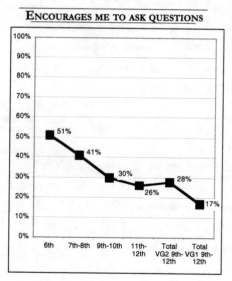

ENCOURAGES ME TO ASK QUESTIONS

This understanding of a thinking church climate is crucial too. The Thinking Climate Scale was correlated among a number of items with some interesting insights possible. A rich climate that is open to new ideas, able to accept divergent opinions, and challenges members to think in a creative way about traditional beliefs and practices is correlated .63 with the student's perception of the quality of the religious education that he or she receives, a high correlation in our research. In addition, it is directly related to denominational loyalty. It is also related in a significant way to personal religious piety. So helping youth develop a clear ability to do critical thinking, and to develop the skills needed to evaluate beliefs and make practical applications without criticism or negative responses from church members and teachers provides a rich milieux for building a sense of belonging to the Adventist church.

Learning to think is all a part of growing up and separating from the beliefs of parents and other people of authority. Showing youth how to think, how to explore issues, to evaluate information, choose a position, and then defend it with logic and passion are all important for a vibrant faith. If one does not know what one believes, or how to defend it, one often never bothers to act with conviction.

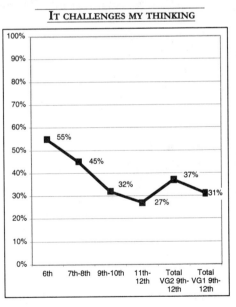

IT CHALLENGES MY THINKING

Youth today are looking for some place where they can feel at home. Theorists often say youth need to explore their own identity. This identity quest comes to play in understanding the faith situations of adolescents. James Cobble in his book,

Faith and Crisis in the Stages of Life, argues that there are really only two fundamental issues that occur in this transition into adulthood. The first of these, he says, is to establish a basis for faith apart from what one's parents or other authority figures believe. The second is to "begin to clarify what one believes to be God's will for his or her life." As the young person grows, he or she begins to define the parameters around their faith experience. Critical thinking plays a crucial role now as they work with their beliefs, values, and feelings of identity to establish a faith that is their own. Because of this, growing a thinking climate in the church is essential.

Since faith is both a construct (cognitively crafted) and an experience of valuing and committing (experientially felt), these first steps in understanding the religious world become important. Giving early adolescents the big picture as often as possible helps these persons to focus on the major concerns of religion rather than on the mistakes of their peers and other church members. Providing adolescents with a frame of reference is an important first step for faith development.[5]

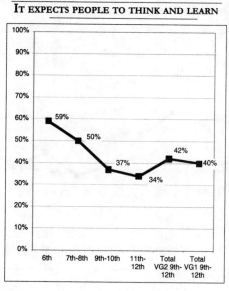

IT EXPECTS PEOPLE TO THINK AND LEARN

One cannot forget how important development of critical thinking skills are to building a faith matrix on which to rely on when making applications in life.

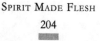

There is often confusion about the nature of what is meant by critical thinking. One simple definition is, "deciding rationally what to do or what not to believe."[6] Or to say it in a more formal way:

Critical thinking is the use of those cognitive skills or strategies that increase the probability of a desirable outcome. It is used to describe thinking that is purposeful, reasoned, and goal-directed—the kind of thinking involved in solving problems, formulating inferences, calculating likelihoods, and making decisions when the thinker is using skills that are thoughtful and effective for the particular context and type of thinking task. Critical thinking also involves evaluating the thinking process—the reasoning that went into the conclusion we've arrived at the kinds of factors considered in making a decision. Critical thinking is sometimes called directed thinking because it focuses on a desired outcome.[7]

And regardless of the current debate in just how to obtain those "desired results," any skills that enhance one's ability to make decisions for themselves is helpful. Ellen G. White encourages us to become involved in this type of process in saying,

Every human being. . .is endowed with a power akin to that of the Creator—individuality, power to think and to do. The men [or women] in whom this power is developed are the men who bear responsibilities, who are leaders in enterprise, and who influence character. . .men strong to think and to act, men who are masters and not slaves of circumstances, men who possess breadth of mind, clearness of thought, and the courage of their convictions.[8]

You can see how important these skills are for mature faith. And every congregation needs to note that there should be improvement in this area. And even though after ten years there is a 6% increase in the total averages in these thinking scores when asked if their congregation, "challenges my thinking," their responses are a bit discouraging regarding the potential power of learning to think critically and to personally decide what young people believe and practice.

The Thinking Church Climate Scale is strongly correlated with the Warm Church Climate Scale as well as the Quality of Religious Education Scale, as mentioned earlier. But in addition, the Thinking Scale is correlated with denominational loyalty at .50 and service at .31. It was correlated between .20 (.20) and .24 (.29) with satisfaction with Adventist standards and endorsement of standards. It was correlated significantly as well with faith maturity, .34, and intrinsic faith at .45.

Unfortunately, as important as this is to our denomination's future, as students get older it seems to decrease. Any denomination whose thinking component is missing is doomed to some degree of failure.

So how do you make a change here? We brought a focus group of young people together to answer just this question, and in their responses you can see the types of concerns that surface. One student said, "I want my church to respect my ideas." Now, this is an important declaration of *independence* by a young teen, even though one might argue that their "ideas" have not yet been fully formed. Another said, "I feel that if I give my own opinion and it's wrong because it is a bit different than a traditional belief or it is less central to my view of God's work in the world, the criticism keeps me from expressing it." Here the theme is one of *unconditional acceptance*. Still, in our discussions with teens in the church another concern emerged. "I don't think that older people respect my beliefs." Again, the issue of *respect* and *acceptance* is seen in this response. All in all, most of the expressions of concern by these young people reflected in our research is that as they got older, they saw less and less openness to new ideas and expressions of personal faith. And oftentimes, these criticisms were not aimed at the content of youth's faith, but rather at the style of worship and expression of their experience with God.

WHAT DO YOU THINK OF YOUR CHURCH?

In our research ten years ago we asked questions about their Adventist churches. We wanted to see if they "tended to agree" or "definitely agreed" with statements that suggested their churches needed to become more modern in their thinking (61%), or if they were exciting and interesting (36%), and if they were turning young people off to Adventism (38%). This time we created a continuum that would explore these same feelings. Dr. Won Yoon, a sociologist at La Sierra University, adapted a series of scales that compared churches with Adventist schools. The results give us a more general picture of their attitude towards their church and school. In the chapter on schools we will explore that understanding, but for now let's look at what they thought of their local churches.

We asked, "Please indicate the image of the Seventh-day Adventist Church you have come to know over the years." The students' responses could be selected from negative to positive and encompassed the following scale: "extremely not" "quite not," slightly not," "neither/nor," "slightly so," quite so," and "extremely so."[9] As you can see, the responses were, on the whole, positive. However, none of the percentages were above 50%, which seems

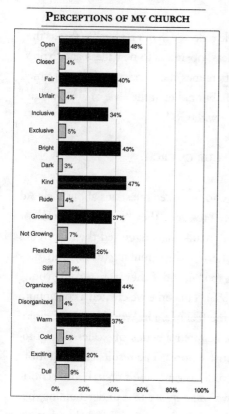

PERCEPTIONS OF MY CHURCH

Perception	Percent
Open	48%
Closed	4%
Fair	40%
Unfair	4%
Inclusive	34%
Exclusive	5%
Bright	43%
Dark	3%
Kind	47%
Rude	4%
Growing	37%
Not Growing	7%
Flexible	26%
Stiff	9%
Organized	44%
Disorganized	4%
Warm	37%
Cold	5%
Exciting	20%
Dull	9%

low to the research team. One would think that a more positive outlook towards the local congregation would be seen.

PROGRAM CHALLENGES

We wanted to see if there was other information about the local church that would be helpful to leaders, pastors, worship leaders, and youth pastors, so we reused a series of questions that gets very specific about the local congregation. After all, Adventist students often view religion through the eyes of the local church. We asked students to think abut their experiences with religious education at their church. We wanted to include more than school education, but things liked Sabbath School, Bible studies, youth groups, camping projects, Adventist Youth meetings, and any other programs that they had experienced in their local church. For each of the statements we provided, we wanted them to tell us how true it was for them. And if they were never involved, they were to mark "does not apply." They could choose a five-point response format which ranged from "not at all true" to "very true." In the list that follows, the percentages represent the combined responses of those who answered "true" or "very true." The research statistics for the 1990 study are again in the parentheses. Some of the questions we asked ten years ago were not included in our new scale. We have listed the percentages according to the new scale in descending order of importance.

() *My teachers or adult leaders are warm and friendly.*	63%	(56%)
() *My teachers or adult leaders care about me.*	62%	(57%)
() *I go to things at church because I want to.*	57%	(50%)
() *I can be myself when at church.*	51%	(45%)
() *My teachers or adult leaders know me well.*	48%	(40%)
() *I look forward to going to things at my church.*	44%	(36%)
() *Programs at my church are interesting.*	40%	(31%)
() *Programs at my church make me think.*	33%	(27%)

Notice that the percentages fall in exactly the same order now that they did before. An in each case, the increase is nearly the same, averaging seven percentage points. Programming got the highest single rise. Teachers and leaders in the church are more warm, friendly, and care more about their youth, and the youth themselves feel that they go to church because of personal motivation and feel comfortable there. Programming, however, continues to be the challenge in youth and preteen ministry.

Now, we don't know what these percentages "should be." We are very happy for the picture of the local church as having improved in all of these areas, but this points out the need for continued concern on personal ministry to the young in our care to ensure that we continue to go in the positive direction in areas of adult caring and personal acceptance. So mark these down as two areas we must continue to stress, and use these insights to plan quality programs for churches and schools.

IF WE COULD DREAM?

One of the programming ideas that was suggested by some of the youth in one focus group we conducted was their need to feel a part of the planning of youth ministry in the local church. They wanted to feel they had made some contribution to their nurture. This reflects a typical preteen and teenage need to feel needed and accepted. They wanted to have a chance to say what they wanted.

We all know, as program planners and adult leaders, that not everything teens *want* is what they *need*. But with this as a rule, it is crucial that they feel a part of the programming of their own ministry. That means creative, inclusive methods must be employed in order to ensure they are actually involved in their own ministry.

We wanted to find out the same thing that any local adult and teen leader does. If they could dream, what would they want to have happen at their church? Their answers share up-to-date concerns, relevant issues, and deeply personal needs.

Listed are some of the things a church could offer that would meet their explicit needs. We wanted to know how interested they would be to learn something about their own church. The percentages of those who indicated they would be "interested" or "very interested" are shown in the box on the next page.

It's good news to see that so many young people would like to study their Bibles as a means to get close to God. It is also exciting to know that 5 out of 10 chose Adventism as a keen interest, while only 28% saw the church as a place where they were interested in talking about sexuality or drugs and alcohol (a percent-

()	Gaining a deeper relationship with God	81%	(77%)
()	The Bible	67%	(67%)
()	How to talk with my parents	52%	(44%)
()	How to talk to a friend about faith	51%	(NA)*
()	Adventism	50%	(55%)
()	Other cultures and ethnic groups	47%	(43%)
()	Sexuality	28%	(22%)
()	Drugs and Alcohol	14%	(28%)

age that had the most significant drop over time). Perhaps it may be that by now drugs are less "cool" and the youth think they have been educated to death about this topic. The rise in the "sex" area may indicate that they like what they are doing. But knowing that very few, percentagewise, of Adventist teens are involved in those at-risk behaviors, it is probably a positive turn.

We have already seen the need for relevancy by the church in order to personalize faith in a significant way in the growth of teens. We have a challenge ahead in this area.

BAPTISM AND COMMITMENT

In the *Valuegenesis*[2] survey a number of questions focus directly on personal commitment and connection through identification with Christ through baptism. But before we discuss this important issue, let's do some biblical study on this topic.

One of the earliest passages of New Testament scripture challenges believers to become connected with Christ through com-

*There are no comparative percentages for *Valuegenesis*[1]

plete identification with his life, death, and resurrection. Baptism becomes the means of remembering that aids all Christians in making clear decisions not to sin according to Romans 6.

In Paul's long list of reasons why we should not sin, even though we have been saved by the marvelous grace of Christ, freely and completely, we are still challenged to make daily life-changing decisions and to put them into action in our lives in order to keep that relationship vibrant and connected. This illustrates the Christian response to grace called obedience. Baptism is the first step in this identification. We are baptized because Christ was, and because through this act we demonstrate to the world the power of new life in Christ. Just like his resurrection, we rise from the watery grave to new life, so-to-speak, in new-found power for Spirit-filled living. This mystical union, called participation in our dying with Christ, helps us believe that we can live with Him.[10]

Youth in our study show a uniquely North American characteristic regarding the age of baptism. As you can see, most of our baptisms occur in the early grades, somewhere between 5th and 7th grade. In Europe, all available research indicates that the age for baptism is usually more towards the late teens. But in the United States our trend is to baptize youth at an earlier age. The mean baptismal age is around 11.9 years of age. No one would argue against baptism for youth who understand this unique union with Christ. Some research shows that youth at a relatively early age are able to understand some symbolic meanings for their actions. However, most would as well argue that as young people move from a concrete thinking posture to a more religious thinking mode (ab-

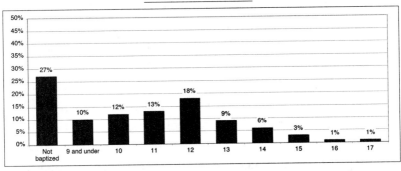

stract), they are better able to internalize the meaning of such issues as the nature of baptism and righteousness.

When we asked the students to explore their commitment to Jesus Christ, we were able to see a unique Adventist position regarding when commitment occurs. The percentages in the graph below share a consistent look at how Adventist youth see their relationship developing in their lives. 44% see it as something that has come to them over time, 32% said that it was formed in their youth, while only 10% saw themselves as not committed or unsure if they were committed to Jesus.

It is obvious to us that their commitment to Christ is im-

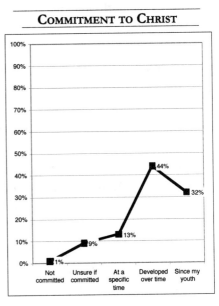

COMMITMENT TO CHRIST

portant to these respondents. Youth of Generation Y have a positive outlook on their relationship with God. And those students in Adventist schools that filled out our survey forms made a clear statement as to their basic allegiance to God. We couldn't be happier with these results.

WHAT COULD CHANGE THE CHURCH?

Many things change slowly, and there are always exceptions. And changing an institution is always risky. It can change too fast and leave those with deep commitments to their history behind, or it can change too slowly and those with no history will feel it is not meaningful or relevant. This conundrum faces all institutions, and especially the church, because the actions, traditions, doctrines, and rituals these institutions participate in have been established not only through long years of challenges and trial, but they have been founded in readings of the Sacred Scriptures that weld many beliefs and behaviors into a moral discussion rather than one which encourages adaptation and personalization along with, contextualization, pluralism, and change. So we asked the youth "To feel comfortable bringing a friend to church, what needs to happen?" They could choose as many answers they felt appropriate. Note that doctrines scaled low on this list, another proof that Adventist youth know their doctrines and don't need to continually be reminded of them. In addition, the items that scored the highest were those personal climate issues—friendliness, acceptance, social events, relevance to their age group. These crucial issues continue to rise to the top of their concerns about the church.

And each is extremely important in building a sense of relevance in the church. This may explain why youth and young adults often want their own church services, after all, if the adults don't accept them, what are the alternatives. However, members that know the importance of these issues for commitment to the church make the necessary changes in their worship and congregational experience in order to include youth in everything in the church.

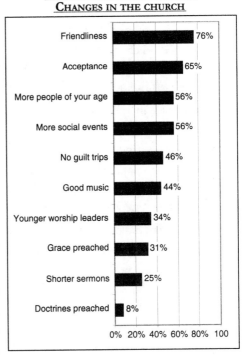

WHAT ABOUT THE FUTURE?

And that brings us to a question posed ten years ago, to the big question—perhaps the most important question of the study—the question that lies at the bottom line: "When you are 40 years old, do you think you will be active in the Adventist Church?"[12]

〈〉 No chance   1%   (2%)
〈〉 Small chance   6%   (7%)

() Fair chance	18%	(19%)
() Good chance	43%	(45%)
() Excellent chance	32%	(27%)

A full three-fourths 75%, (72%) believe that the chances of their staying in the Adventist church are good to excellent. Of course, this is only a predictive opinion. These youth haven't yet lived their lives in the church and have not grown to appreciate or criticize their relationship with the church. But from their point of view now—looking down their short history to their future—they see themselves as Adventists.

In Roger Dudley observed in his ground-breaking research in his longitudinal study of Adventist youth, approximately that 48% of the Adventist young people left the church after ten years. We hope this statistic won't be realized by this group of Adventist youth, and to prevent it we have a great deal of work to do to ensure their loving their church. From this end of the tunnel, most of the youth see themselves as Adventists in the future. The church has made a positive impression on most of the youth and only 9% of the group, (an important percent nonetheless, are sure at this point that they will become distant from their faith community by the time they are 40 years of age.

REFERENCES

1. Roger L. Dudley with V. Bailey Gillespie, *Valuegenesis: Faith in the Balance* (Loma Linda, CA: Loma Linda University Press, 1992), 166.

2. Karen Jones reporting in *EurekAlert!* (http://www.eurekalert.org/pub_release/2001-08/sarn-raa082101.php) on a paper on "Self-esteem of Early Adolescents: A National Survey of 8th Graders," presented August 24, 2001, at the annual meeting of the American Psychological Association in San Francisco, by Yong Dai, Rebecca F. Nolan, and Qing Zeng, 1.

3. Ellen G. White, Volume 1, *Selected Messages*, (Silver Springs, MD: *Review and Herald*, August 13, 1901), 172.

4. *Valuegenesis: Faith in the Balance,* 168.

5. James Cobble, *Faith and Crisis in the Stages of Life* (Peabody MA: Hendrikson, 1985), 47.

6. V. Bailey Gillespie, *The Experience of Faith* (Birmingham, AL: Religious Education Press, 1992), 143.

7. Stephen P. Norris, "Synthesis of Research on Critical Thinking," *Educational Leadership,* Vol. 42 (May 8, 1985), 40-45. For a complete description of critical thinking read Diane Halpern's, *Thought and Knowledge: An Introduction to Critical Thinking* (New York, NY: Pearson, Allyn & Bacon, 4th ed., 2001).

8. Ellen G. White, *Education* (Hagerstown, MD: Review and Herald Publishing, 1903), 17-18.

9. For those familiar with attitude measurement, we used a traditional semantic differential format.

10. Romans 6:8 (NIV).

L ove is a hard thing to explain. "How do I love thee? Let me count the ways," wrote Elizabeth Barrett Browning. "And you shall love the Lord your God with all your heart, with all your soul, and with all your might." What does that really mean, asked the sages of the Talmud. What am I supposed to do to fulfill this Commandment? As rabbis so often do, they answer with a story:

Rabbi Simeon ben Shetach lived in poverty most of his life. His students brought a donkey from an Ishmaelite to present to their master as a gift. When the rabbi brought his donkey home, he found a little bag tied around the animal's neck with a costly diamond inside. He called his students and asked, "Did you buy a donkey with a diamond and pay for both?" The students told their rabbi they knew nothing about the precious stone. Rabbi Simeon immediately returned the diamond to the Ishmaelite. The Arab was so overwhelmed by the rabbi's honesty that he exclaimed, "Praised be Simeon ben Shetach and praised be his God."

That, the rabbis declared, is the very best way to fulfill "You shall love the Lord your God." Act in such a way that God's name becomes beloved by the world because of you.

—— *Rabbi Benjamin Blech*

CHAPTER 8

○

DANCING, MOVIES, AND OTHER SINS
Challenges and choices

8

DANCING, MOVIES, AND OTHER SINS
Challenges and choices

We are drowning in floods of consumer goods and are drenched in showers of media images. We live in a smorgasbord culture in which everything is interesting and nothing really matters. We have lost a vision of the good life, and our hopes for the future are emptied of moral content.

— *Miroslav Volf*

If there was just one gift we could give to the youth of the church, what would you wish it to be? I have asked teens this question during weeks of devotion and at the conclusion of university religion classes only to be surprised at the low expectations that are expressed. "I'd just like to finish school," one young adult opined. "I wish my parents would get along," another said. Still these expectations hit young people where they live. And that is one of the most rewarding characteristics of youth, the fact that they know they live in a real world and their expectations lie there and not in the future.

Of course, this attitude causes some concern for religious people who often use as motivation to be different the fact that someday things will be better and all will be the way God wanted it to be. But these theological dreams are usually not felt in the reality and press of time that demands immediate responses and decisions. Tragically, youth often feel they must decide right now in order to both understand their world and to prepare for one that they feel may never come.

So the choices that students make today truly do impact their future. And it is thus important to talk about how to make good choices and to observe just what choices our youth have already made in regards to their behavior and in relation to their understanding of what God and the community of believers they worship with expect. Just think of that tension. They need to make good decisions that will lead them forward, and they live among a community of people, attend schools with their own expectations, deal with parents that have their perspectives lived in practice on a daily basis, and they are challenged to make good choices and to become good Adventists.

A particularly significant insight about adolescent spirituality and behavior is shared by Charles Shelton in his seminal volume, *Adolescent Spirituality,* where he says,

> *The adolescent's acquisition of formal thought, combined with the new experiences of the secondary school years, i.e., diverse attitudes, greater possibilities, and wider perspectives, provide the opportunity of advancing moral reasoning. Yet in this advancement other experiences also enter the adolescent's life. The adolescent's increasing interactions and experiences of other people, events, and situations bring about a growing sense of relativity. The adolescent discovers that right and wrong vary according to the cultural expectations and norms of society. This growing awareness of relativism is enhanced by the adolescent's own personal life experiences that reflect diversity and ambiguity.*[1]

When you look at such a statement, you realize that the adolescent, while in the middle of this relativity, does not have the same commitment to central and core values and principled reasoning as older youth. Because of this, in the tensions and contradictions of his or her transitions in life and the yet-to-be-realized commitments, the adolescent often shows actions that do not take into account the greater demands and ideals that will come as maturity is realized. Instead, they often seem to be locked in an individualism that only gets satisfied by reliance on their peers. This is a dangerous aspect of adolescing because peers often do not have a broader and more circumspect perspective to share either.

Larry Kohlberg identifies a significant characteristic of being young by quoting their often repeated saying, "Do your own thing, and let others do theirs."[2] This being the case, it may explain just why some of the standards usually associated with Adventism simply are not central or meaningful for many young people today.

Comments from focus groups at the Hancock Center for Youth and Family Ministry at La Sierra University revealed a number of comments that validate this theoretical position. For example, one 18-year-old girl announced, "I don't believe the church has its priorities straight. Instead of focusing on the Gospel and the goodness of God, all I ever hear about is what I should or should not do. Now, I know we don't believe in righteousness by works, but you would never know it from the constant reminders to be good I hear from church members and adults."

Another 15-year-old boy adds, "There are just so many rules to being a good Adventist. I've heard of God's grace, but with all the talk of no movies, no dancing, no dating, no drinking, and all, I seldom have time to think about what my church might really care about. All I hear about are movies, dancing, and other sins."

Roger Dudley entitled his chapter on Adventist behaviors based on the original research, "The Stickiest Point," and he comments,

> *Make no mistake. How we handle church standards is the crucial issue in the determination of whether or not we will retain the rising generation of the church. Acceptance of Adventist standards was the secondmost important variable in the entire study in predicting whether or not the students intended to remain as Adventists by age 40 and the most important in predicting denominational loyalty.[3]*

Today, according to our research we can say much the same thing and in addition, we found that a thinking climate is strongly correlated with the Warm Church Climate scale at .72. But it is an even more important predictor of values and commitment. And the most powerful unique predictors in the present data set were intrinsic religiousness, the quality of religious instruction, and orthodoxy. These three variables predicted over half of the variance in the Denominational Loyalty Scale and become predictors of commitment to the church at a later point in a student's life.

EMPHASIS ON STANDARDS

Emphasis on Adventist rules and standards is so strong that the message of Christianity gets lost.

()	Never true	12%
()	Rarely true	16%
()	True once in a while	13%
()	Sometimes true	20%
()	Often true	19%
()	Almost always true	12%
()	Always true	7%

Often, almost, and always true totals, 41% (11th-12th grade totals, 53%)

With this in mind, let's look at the behaviors that Adventist young people are involved in and their attitude about those standards they have been challenged to accept and follow.

ENDORSEMENT OF STANDARDS

We wondered how youth would agree or disagree with specific Adventist lifestyle standards—we like to call them life-affirming choices as opposed to life-denying ones. Below we list the standards in the rank order of acceptance according to the 1990 *Valuegenesis[1]* surveys so you can see the changes over time with the percentages that "tend" to "definitely" agree and who "tend" to "definitely" disagree with them. The extent to which the two numbers fail to total 100% represents the group that replied, "I'm not sure."

Standard	Agree		Disagree	
Not use illegal drugs	90%	(92%)	7%	(5%)
Not use tobacco	90%	(91%)	7%	(6%)
Observe the Sabbath	90%	(89%)	4%	(5%)
Not drink beer or liquor	84%	(88%)	10%	(8%)
Exercise daily	82%	(85%)	8%	(8%)
Not eat "unclean" meats	72%	(73%)	15%	(16%)
Sex only in marriage	77%	(68%)	13%	(18%)
Wear modest clothes	60%	(65%)	21%	(19%)
Not wear jewelry	22%	(39%)	60%	(42%)
Not use caffeinated drinks	19%	(31%)	63%	(51%)
Not listen to hard rock music	27%	(26%)	53%	(55%)
Not dance	11%	(23%)	75%	(57%)

Not attend movie theaters	7%	(19%)	81%	(64%)
Wearing a wedding ring	6%	(14%)	81%	(64%)
Not engage in competitive sports	5%	(10%)	84%	(78%)
Not play violent video games	36%	(NA)	43%	(NA)

When you look closely at these typical Adventist standards, you observe a number of interesting insights into the behaviors of young people in the church.

There seem to be three types of standards evidenced by acceptance and support in the list of sixteen. The first group can be labeled, Substance Abuse Standards. They evidence strong support by the youth of the church. Those related to health came out the strongest with percentages of 84% to 90%, a slight dip from *Valuegenesis¹*.

The next group are called by our research team Adventist Way of Life Standards. This group shares a majority of support as well. Such issues as Sabbath observance, sexual standards, modesty, exercise, and healthful living are included here. Percentages from 60% to a high of 82% are evidenced, with an average for this group of 76.5%, over three-fourths of the study group support

---

ACTING BY DUTY OR AND IDEAL

The history of ethical theory reveals two major approaches to understanding the basis on which one makes a moral decision. One stresses the notion of duty and has its roots in the right decision to our sense of obligation. When we act according to duty. . . then we are doing what is right. This is the *dontological* view. . .in which rules and law play an important role.

The second approach, called the *teleological* view. . .stresses the ideals or goals of our decision making. This view roots the morally good action in the end or goal by which one acts. The language here is not that of law or rule, but of a guiding ideal or value.[4]

Adventist Way of Life Standards. The biggest change is in the areas of sexual activity outside of marriage. Perhaps this reflects a culture concerned now about AIDS and the push for teen sexual purity, because the data agreeing that there should be no sex outside of marriage is up 9% over the past years. The decrease in those *disagreeing* is also notable. Nonetheless, the percentages of agreement of these types of standards have changed a little over time overall.

The third category of standards shows the most change. We call them Popular Cultural Standards, and they show significant disagreement ranging from 43% to a high of disagreement of 83% with increases in almost every category. "Not dancing," "Not attending movies in theaters," "Not participating in competitive sports," and "Not wearing of wedding rings" all took the greatest hit over the past years. And when you look at these standards over time, the support from 6th to the 12th grades stays within one percentage point the same. These are standards that are not supported in our earlier research about young people's behaviors. In the new research we added a new one regarding the playing of violent video games. We were surprised that only a little over a third of the group agreed, while 43% disagreed with it altogether. This is an ominous sign of the times. Perhaps we need to spend some time thinking carefully about how to teach youth to make good choices in the areas of media.

At any rate, the drop in endorsement from the sixteen standards is evidenced by eight of the sixteen—all popular cultural items. It is safe to say that the research indicates that the wearing of a wedding ring is simply not an issue with young people, nor are competitive sports, with an additional 5% drop in support over time. The standards of attendance of movies in theaters has been muddied by the evolution of DVDs, TV, and videos. This standard, too, suffered a significant drop, some 12% in agreement and an additional 17% in disagreement. Not dancing is only slightly ahead of movies in becoming a nonissue for youth. Perhaps they could be considered a lost cause now with less than 1 in 10 supporting them.

The church needs to continue to consider whether its traditional stand against such activities is warranted and how it is going to instruct the young to make good choices. This is perhaps the most significant issue here. How long does the church want these standards to be considered at all? And if they are not accepted now, what does the future hold? If those standards are based on good ideals and significant values, then we cannot abandon them. But perhaps now we will begin to provide clear guidelines as to how to teach values and clarify good choices in media, lifestyle, and involvement in areas that Adventist youth no longer understand as a vibrant part of their Adventism.

At the conclusion of this chapter we want to extend some questions for parents, church workers, adult youth leaders, pastors, and youth professionals that might help in this area. When church standards, are ignored, how long should the church try to enforce them? How do you ensure that the values which are behind the standards are clearly seen when you spend most of the time harping just on the behaviors? On the other hand, where do we draw the line? Are various standards more or less central, and if so, when do we say, with Martin Luther, "Here I stand, I can do no other. God help me."

BEHAVIORS RELATED TO WHAT?

Often people criticize discussions about standards and ethical behavior as being a form of legalism—a type of works righteousness—due to the overemphasis on behavior. Others are deeply concerned about what seems to be the slipping standards that many Adventist youth have regarding traditional popular cultural items in our scale. And as we have seen, these continue to be depreciated by the youth of the church. In fact, a number of books have been published that are quite critical of an open-ended discussion about lifestyle choices and popular cultural standards. While this criticism is usually illogical and misplaced, it is appropriate here to provide understanding of the relationship of clear life-affirming choices with other theological issues Adventism sees as important

We don't want to be misunderstood. Because we report the findings of our research, it does not mean we approve of the choices many youth are making. Those that criticize the study on this basis don't understand the whole of the matter. Let me explain.

Adventist care about the standards of behavior that the Bible presents to us as we live our lives for and in Jesus Christ. We have always relied heavily on the Bible because it bears an authority for the faith and life of the church and its people that nothing else can claim. This being the case, we still hear arguments over the extent of the Bible's role and its authority for living a moral life. As Adventists, we recognize that the Bible reflects in many ways the moral standards and the cultural values of ancient Israel and early Christianity. As modern, thoughtful Christians we are compelled to choose some principles of interpretation to understand how to consistently and appropriately apply the Bible's moral authority to today's living. How do we do that?

First, the Bible provides a set of commandments and teachings that give us our moral code. The Ten Commandments are our basic moral resource and are stated so matter-of-factly that we can use them safely as our moral handbook, our guideline for moral behavior in many situations. From them we derive principles of behavior for our lives. We always go to the commandments first in any moral discussion.

Next, the Bible's moral impact comes from God's involvement in our lives and in our history. This is the reason we must interpret how to apply basic moral principles revealed in Scripture to our everyday lives. The situations we face today are often not the same as the 1st Century church or those of the Old Testament characters, and that is where our personal and institutional reflection come into the picture. We learn to reflect on the moral dimension of life and apply the revealed moral guidelines to those situations and make good, clear, life-affirming choices. This is a sign of maturity of faith and something every parent hopes for in their children.

In addition, the moral guidelines of Scripture are applied by our Christian heritage and tradition. Adventism has some things that Adventists have cared about. For example, we see an overuse of jewelry as a symbolic thing—identification with the world, perhaps. But we have not spent as much time talking to youth about the use of sugar or being overweight, both serious problems for United States teens. We often fail to provide a basis for decision making and eliminate possible clear thinking by making declarations about their actions. As we build community, trying to live in correspondence with the understanding of the Bible as seen in our Adventist history, we try to do responsible interpretation of Scripture to provide a theoretical foundation for our moral life and the lives of our children. And the traditions of our faith community provide some concrete moral directions for faithful living as members of that community. And we care about that.

Finally, the Bible does not always provide a unified, coherent basis for *all* moral decisions. Jesus left many decisions for the church to make under the direction of the Holy spirit, and the wisdom of our forbears. Consider, for example, that the early church was unclear about how much of the Jewish law one had to keep to be a Christian!

It is fair to say that the Bible is not primarily a book about moral choices. It does give us examples of moral decision-making, however. It is a book that serves a people of faith, shares stories of God's presence in life, and contains information that has high moral substance.

We can conclude by saying that without a doubt, our life of faith is a call for moral responsibility. That is why we have to care more about the *reasons* we do or do not do something than the *fact* that others do or don't do what we have considered inappropriate.

While we would love to have certainty in the form of absolutes (perhaps even a biblical directive) and some clear answers to what is right to do, we can seldom reach that certainty on the more challenging life situations and issues we face, because they often involve a number of complex issues and are not as simple as we would like.

The Christian life is ultimately all about being faithful—faithful to Christ's calling and purpose, faithful to God's clarity in Scripture, faithful regarding our own weaknesses, and faithfulness to our commitment to God's will as we have studied it and as we understand it. That is not an easy assignment, but the process of learning to choose and making faithful responses to Christ in life situations is what God hopes for when He says, "I will put my law in their minds and write it on their hearts. I will be their God, and they will be my people."[5]

ENDORSEMENT OF ADVENTIST STANDARDS

What are the influences that assist in the endorsement of Adventist standards? The Endorsement of Standards Scale has a number of important relationships with other attitudes and behaviors. Below are the three categories of Adventist standards and their *significant* correlations. And remember that in painting a portrait of an Adventist young person, the items listed below each group of standards simply describe the significant things that assist in its endorsement and practice.

Adventist Substance Abuse Standards.

- () Endorsement of Seventh-day Adventist lifestyle standards, .50
- () Denominational loyalty, .36
- () Intrinsic religion, .33
- () Quality of religious education, .27
- () Personal religious piety, .27
- () Endorsement of popular cultural standards, .27

( ) Faith maturity, .26

( ) Family climate, .26

( ) Adventist orthodoxy, .26

Seventh-day Adventist Way of Life Standards

( ) Denominational loyalty, .50

( ) Endorsement of substance abuse standards, .50

( ) Intrinsic religion, .49

( ) Endorsement of popular cultural standards, .47

( ) Family climate, .45

( ) Faith maturity, .40

( ) Personal piety, .37

( ) Quality of religious education, .34

( ) Service, .30

Popular Cultural Standards

( ) Family enforcement of popular cultural standards, .63

( ) Endorsement of Seventh-day Adventist way of life standards, .47

( ) Faith maturity, .40

( ) Intrinsic religion, .37

( ) Denominational loyalty, .37

( ) Personal piety, .37

( ) Quality of religious education, .27

What is significant is that in each case, the quality of religious education has impact. In addition, support for other types of standards seems to go hand-in-hand. Popular cultural standards are best reinforced when the family is involved, and an open and loving yet constrained family system seems to assist in this area too.

In our earlier research, Roger Dudley said, "In addition, it is clear that believing church standards to be reasonable and right constitutes a part of a package of beliefs and behaviors which indicate that youth will continue in the Adventist church."[6] The recent study supports his claim. And like his research, in all cases the correlations and relationships were positive with good and desirable attitudes and showed up as negative with those that were undesirable. Again, as you can see, acceptance of Adventist lifestyle standards of all three types is closely related to loyalty to the church.

In looking closely at the types of standards in our church and examining the types which have support, it is obvious that there is no clear picture emerging. There is not uniform acceptance of the standards as a whole, popular cultural standards are the most debated. There is ample room for discussion and open-ended dialogue as youth make decisions to support things which affirm life and refrain from things that deny life as a whole.

We probably need to revise some of the popular cultural standards that seem to have all but disappeared, according to our research. But rather than suggest that we acquiesce because of the research, we should find better ways to discuss ways to

---

AT-RISK INDICATORS

() Ten years ago we said, "It is alarming to find that (60%) of our youth in grade six had at least one at-risk indicator and that this rose to (73%) by grade twelve. Also (14%) of the sixth-graders had at a least three at-risk indicators. This figure increased over the grades to (23%) for high school seniors.

() Now we can say 48% in grade six had at least one at-risk indicator, and this rose to 58% by grade twelve. Also, 5% of the 6th graders had three or more at-risk indicators. This figure increased to 36% by grade 12.

make good choices in areas of media, relationship with the culture, and lifestyle. After all, these areas impact us all. Families have challenges with television and movies having a grip on American culture in ways that negatively impact Adventist youth by their power. Rather than simply condemn the lifestyle choices of our youth, we would love to see the church provide resources to help members make positive decisions about what they let into their lives. We believe that this promotes mature faith, critical thinking, and personal commitment to what is holy, just, and good.

There are a number of good resources that can assist parents in this all-important task. If education about these lifestyle choices is not made in the home, the church and school can never do what the home has failed to accomplish. And while they have a serious impact as evidenced by the regularity of quality religious education in the endorsement of standards of all types, without the home as a central source of reinforcement and discussion, the other two venues are less effective.

The John Hancock Center for Youth and Family Ministry at La Sierra University School of Religion has a number of resources in this area to assist parents in this regard, but more are needed.[7]

A UNIQUE ADVENTIST ATTITUDE IDENTIFIED

Belief and behavior go together. Understanding and decisions are closely related. But one important thing is the attitude that youth have towards the church. All too often this attitude is connected with the way and methods used to enforce Adventist standards. How youth perceive the church is closely related to perceptions they get in areas that touch their lives most closely. And of course, helping students make choices that impact their lifestyle always provides a rich context out of which one's attitudes of the church or authority are formulated.

We have identified this scale as the Adventist Attitude Scale, and it contains eight statements concerning standards and enforcement to which they could respond from a seven-point format ranging from "never true" to "always true." One of the questions in our first survey was not repeated and was replaced with one that was better suited and more relevant to our discussion. (See the last statement in the side-bar). This side-bar provides a close look at each of these statements. They are often worded in a negative way. But using factor analysis we discovered a strong relationship between these issues, and a reliable scale was formed which helps us see how the enforcement of Adventist lifestyle standards impact their attitudes towards the church in general.

ADVENTIST ATTITUDE SCALE

( ) Adventist rules and standards serve a useful purpose. (66%)—1990 only

( ) Non-Adventists laugh when they hear what Adventists are forbidden to do. 39% (50%)

( ) Some adults insist on certain rules of standards for younger Adventists that they do not observe themselves. 46% (47%)

( ) The feeling is conveyed in the Adventist Church that *how* one behaves is more important than *what* one believes. 44% (45%)

( ) Emphasis on Adventist rules and standards is so strong that the message of Christianity gets lost. 38% (41%)

( ) Adventists are loaded down with too many restrictions. 29% (27%)

( ) Student breaking a school standard or rule in Adventist schools are punished too harshly. 27% (26%)

( ) Adventist rules and standards just don't make sense. 18% (17%)

( ) People respect Adventist for their high moral standards. 41%—2000 only

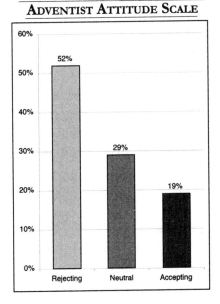

There is actually little change over the ten years between questionnaires, except for the question about their perceptions of what others think of them for their behavior choices. There is significant improvement here from (50%) to 39% over ten years. Slightly over one-third said that we emphasize rules and standards so much that the essential message of Christianity seems to get lost. And again, almost one-half of the respondents suggest that adults don't "walk as they talk." The issue of hypocrisy among the older generations causes some concern. This scale provides us with a particularly useful insight into this attitude and how to lessen its impact on the youth of the church. Let's get more specific.

IT'S ABOUT PERCEPTIONS

When we look at the whole set of data on Adventist youth in Adventist schools, the Faith Maturity Scale is closely correlated with volunteer hours. This is not a surprise because it has items about that topic in it. Another interesting insight is that the

Grace Scale is slightly more strongly related to the Faith Maturity Scale than to the Intrinsic Scale, but it is important and still central to a mature faith. As you look at the Adventist Attitude Scale we see that it is negatively related to "warm" and "thinking" congregational climates. We don't know whether the perception of the climate causes opinion towards the Adventist church or vice versa, but the scale seems to be a valid measure of a perception of hypocrisy among the youth of the church. The mean score is 3.88, almost exactly in the middle (4.0) of the 1 to 7-point scale. When we look at the total number of students that have this "Adventist Attitude," we note that 19% of the total group have a negative outlook, and three out of ten are in the middle of the scale. 57% of the students reject this attitude.

If you look at the class development of this attitude, it is interesting to see that the percent rejecting this attitude decreases from 70% in the 6th grade to 44% in the 12th grade. The percent who are in the "middle" position increases from 17% to 35%. And the proportion at the good end of the scale increases from 13% to 20%.

Some 20% or one-fifth of the youth display this attitude. There is a unique spike at the 9th to 10th grade level in each of the three categories. Since the 6th grade respondents are usually more optimistic on most scales, this jump is significant. What is happening during this time of their faith growth that may increase this attitude?

One explanation is that this simply parallels a well-documented increase in negative attitudes and behaviors when students change schools—from grammar to middle school (these data do not begin early enough to reflect that change) and from middle to high school.

The students who possess this negative attitude are more likely to declare they will not be Adventists when they are forty years of age. The correlation between this attitude is negative with respect to support of Adventist standards, except for health and sports issues: Tobacco, -.22; Alcohol, -.28; Binge drinking, -.22; Rock music, -.30; Dancing, -.29; Sexual activity, -.29; Modesty, -.31.

Conversely, the more youth like their church services, the less of this attitude they demonstrate. The more important attending an Adventist school is to your faith development, the less of this attitude you exhibit. But Weeks of Devotion in schools have the least impact on this negativeness.

In summary, school climate is driving an intrinsic attitude toward religion. If you want your children to build a deep personal relationship with God, one that is both devotional and compassionate, the positive warmth and thinking climate in the school and church are central. Or better said, the initial evidence is that positive climate scores reduce the negative Adventist attitude. The warm and thinking climate assists in making the students more positive towards the Seventh-day Adventist church than anything else. And if students say that they like their schools, they are less likely to see hypocrisy in their church. In other words, do your job well, and nice things do happen. There is a more mature faith, more intrinsic faith, and more positive view of Adventist culture. This can only spill over into less hypocrisy and a closer relationship with the church in regards to loyalty.

We didn't want to only find out about standards and their acceptance and importance. We also felt it was important to look at the enforcement of particular standards contrasted between the home and school. In order to understand this, we presented the students with a list of the seventeen standards we explored before and asked them to tell us how strictly each is or was enforced by (1) your family and (2) the Adventist school you now attend. We gave them a four-point response format which ranged from "Not at all strictly enforced" to "Very strictly enforced." Look at the responses the students provided. We've listed the percentages in parallel columns along with the information from the *Valuegenesis[1]* research project.

FAMILY AND SCHOOL STANDARD ENFORCEMENT	Family	School
() Not smoking tobacco.	91% (88%)	93% (90%)
() Not drinking beer and liquor.	91% ((87%)	94% (91%)
() Not wearing jewelry.	32% (53%)	78% (78%)
() Not listening to rock music.	30% (32%)	53% (55%)
() Not dancing.	25% (46%)	62% (61%)
() Not attending movie theaters.	19% (39%)	30% (47%)
() Not using illegal drugs.	95% (94%)	96% (94%)
() Having sex only in marriage.	87% (84%)	88% (64%)
() Not eating "unclean" meats.	66% (72%)	65% (64%)
() Observing the Sabbath.	83% (83%)	85% (72%)
() Wearing modest clothes.	58% (62%)	85% (76%)

() Not doing competitive sports.	7% (16%)	21% (21%)
() Exercising daily.	32% (30%)	44% (27%)
() Not wearing a wedding ring.	17% (32%)	30% (44%)
() Not using drinks that contain caffeine.	23% (30%)	51% (46%)
() Not playing violent video games.	38%	60%
() Not watching R-rated videos.	44%	74%

What can we conclude regarding the enforcement of Adventist standards? Several issues seem to stand out.

(1) *The commitment to Adventist standards of all types is basically paralleled by family enforcement of those standards.* However, there are some interesting exceptions to this rule. Of the sixteen examined personal standards, ten were more highly enforced than personally accepted by each student (drugs, tobacco, beer or liquor, jewelry, caffeinated drinks, rock music, dancing, movies, wedding rings all lost ground as contrasted with family enforcement percentages).

Of those sampled, four were more agreed to than enforced by the family. (Sabbath, exercise, unclean meats, sex only in marriage, and modesty all had higher percentages personally than in the family). In addition, two were about the same: competitive sports and violent video games. All in all, school enforcement of Adventist lifestyle choices was significantly higher than seen by students as they rated their own homes. And some were dramatically more enforced at school than at home. For example, while only 19% saw any family enforcement for not attending movies in theaters, 30% saw the school more strict than their families. Not dancing was two and one-half times as likely to be enforced at the schools than at home. In fact, all seventeen in our recent research were enforced at the school slightly or significantly more strictly. This leads us to our next conclusion.

(2) *The school enforces standards more strictly than the family does.* And this is especially true when you look at the popular cultural choices such as dancing, movies, competitive sports, and music. Families of students in Adventist schools differ in important areas over what should and should not be enforced. This may explain why it is often hard for schools to hold the line on what have been called "traditional" Adventist standards. After all, there is all too often little support from the home for some of them.

As we saw earlier, the parents are key to building clear choices in those life-enhancing daily decisions. Without support in the homes, the schools are faced with a clear problem. And what seems all too often to be the case is that many parents send their children to Christian education to do what they themselves have been unable to do themselves in the home.

(3) *There is continued erosion of popular cultural areas of Adventist standards.* Perhaps it is time to clarify just what the church's position is on these controversial issues. And while no one wants to let youth do anything and everything, the church has a responsibility to assist the home and school in clarifying methods of encouraging high standards and good choices in regards to adolescent behavior. Perhaps our statement of fundamental beliefs says it best and outlines what is important for Adventist Christians. It is found under the heading of Christian behavior and emphasizes general principles of behavior rather than identifies specific activities that may or

may not be good or bad. And while it is true that many Adventists elect not to see the best movies in theaters, this statement of belief stands as a strong indication that the church is working to instill clear values, based on eternal principles in the lives of its membership. I believe it is a clear, definitive statement that clarifies the church's position in the area of life-affirming behaviors. Here is the baptismal statement of belief in this area:

We are called to be a godly people who think, feel, and act in harmony with the principles of heaven. For the Spirit to recreate in us the character of our Lord, we involve ourselves only in those things which will produce Christlike purity, health, and joy in our lives. This means that our amusement and entertainment should meet the highest standards of Christian taste and beauty. While recognizing cultural differences, our dress is to be simple, modest, and neat, befitting those whose true beauty does not consist of outward adornment but in the imperishable ornament of a gentle and quiet spirit. It also means that because our bodies are the temples of the Holy Spirit, we are to care for them intelligently. Along with adequate exercise and rest, we are to adopt the most healthful diet possible and abstain from the unclean foods identified in the Scriptures. Since alcoholic beverages, tobacco, and the irresponsible use of drugs and narcotics are harmful to our bodies, we are to abstain from them as well. Instead, we are to engage in whatever brings our thoughts and bodies into the discipline of Christ, who desires our wholesomeness, joy, and goodness.[7]

It would be well to rehearse this statement with our young people. It provides both value-laden reasons and direction for life choices. This approach is by far the best if we plan on making significant impact on the formation of the choices young people select and clarify as they grow.

Here are some interesting statistics about Adventist youth that could fit into this discussion about Adventist standards, as well. We asked the students, "How often do you eat any kind of meat (for example, beef, chicken, fish, etc.)?" The response format allowed youth to check "never," "occasionally, but less than once a month," "between once a week and once a month," "one to three days a week," "three to six days a week," or "daily." The graph on the right provides their responses. 20% of Adventist young people never eat any kind of meat. The team members from Loma Linda University were interested in vegetarianism and wanted to clarify this area even more, so they asked "How often do you eat any kind of dairy product (for example, milk, ice cream, cheese, yogurt, etc.)?" Only 1% of the total sample of Adventist students said "never." 81% did so three to six days a week or daily. 65% indicated that they ate dairy products on a daily basis. Now what should we do to encourage high and biblical standards among the youth?

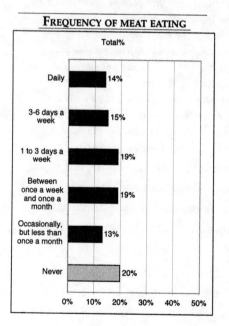

FREQUENCY OF MEAT EATING

Total%

Daily — 14%
3-6 days a week — 15%
1 to 3 days a week — 19%
Between once a week and once a month — 19%
Occasionally, but less than once a month — 13%
Never — 20%

0% 10% 20% 30% 40% 50%

We published a book a number of years ago entitled, *Shall We Dance: Rediscovering Christ-Centered Standards*. Some thought this was a question, but in reality, it was a statement about engaging in discussion about standards. The same holds true today. So, should youth go to the movies, listen to rock music, or dance? The answers to these questions are not easy or quick in coming. I always tell parents that if they want to discuss popular cultural standards in the church, I will need at least two hours of their time. First I want to establish principles of behaviors based on biblical values, and then I want to see the local church culture, ethnic makeup, and traditional concerns of the local congregation. Then, and only then, do I want to establish methods to make clear, value-laden choices that can impact behavior. Our research is a clear indication that we need such a process in order to clarify to parents and youth what is of ultimate concern for their walk with God. As Roger Dudley said ten years ago about the importance of church standards, they should be "clearly Christ-centered, biblically based, and culturally relevant."[8]

There is a wonderful illustration of the concerns God has about establishing clear guidelines and the importance of being clear about what is important. It comes from a column in the *Riverside Press Enterprise* just after the 9/11 terrorist's attack on the World Trade Center.

> *Those suicide hijackings were such an evil act that they shattered your faith in human beings and in the wall of civilization that was supposed to*

constrain the worst in human behavior. There is now a big jagged hole in that wall.

What to do? For guidance, I turned to one of my mentors, Rabbi Tzvi Marx, who teaches in the Netherlands. He offered me a biblical analogy. "To some extent," said Tzvi, "we feel after 9/11 like we have experienced the flood of Noah—as if a flood has inundated our civilization and we are the survivors. What do we do the morning after? The story of Noah has a lot to offer."

What was the first thing Noah did when the flood waters receded and he got off the ark?" asked Tzvi." "He planted a vine and made wine and got drunk." Noah's first response to the flood's devastation of humanity, and the challenge he now faced, was to numb himself to the world.

"But what was God's reaction to the flood?" asked Tzvi." "Just the opposite. God's reaction was to offer Noah a more detailed set of rules for mankind to live by—rules which we now call the Noahite laws. His first rule was that life is precious, so man should not murder man." (These Noahite laws were later expanded to include prohibitions against idolatry, adultery, blasphemy and theft.)

It's interesting—you would have thought that after whipping out humanity with a devastating flood, God's first post-flood act wouldn't have been to teach that all life is precious. But it was. Said Tzvi: "It is as though God said, "Now I understand what I'm up against with these humans. I need to set for them some very clear boundaries of behavior, with some very clear values and norms, that they can internalize.'"

And that is where the analogy with today begins. After the deluge of 9/11 we have two choices: we can numb ourselves to the world, and plug our ears, or we can try to repair that jagged hole in the wall of civilization by insisting, more firmly and loudly than ever, on rules and norms—both for ourselves and for others.

"God, after the flood, refused to let Noah and his offspring indulge *themselves in escapism," said Tzvi, "but he also refused to give them license to live without moral boundaries, just because humankind up to that point had failed."[9]*

The enforcement and clarification of standards is a concern for us as well. We want clear, high standards for our young. We are often afraid that making grace central will somehow eliminate our concern for clear directives by God. This is so far from the truth we hardly need comment. We have all types of styles of enforcement evident in schools, churches, and families. *How* it is done has an important impact on the faith development of children, youth, and young adults. *How* we do it is the crucial question. There is no question that it *should* or *must* be done. Our next chapter on parenting may help clarify this, but for now remember that we have a three-fold task if we want standards to be important and useful in guiding our children's behaviors. These are:

(1) *We must identify the central issue in the standard and continue to clarify its significance and centrality for the life of faith.* Unless young people see the real reason to make choices that benefit them and their church, they often see standards observance as a test of authority or loyalty rather than an act of response (worship) to their Creator and Lord. So first, find the values that are in the Bible and begin there.

(2) *Young people should learn how to make good personal choices as a means of internalizing these values into their daily lives.* Unless these choices have been made through critical evaluation, logical deduction, examination of the facts and options, often these choices only reflect a church's authority and needs, or even their parents' hopes rather

than clear decisions on the part of the young.

(3) *We have to assist young people in their discovery of what is important to them with regards to keeping close to God.* These three important tasks will never go away as we continue to make religion relevant to our children and important for daily life.

On the other hand, what is it that makes youth dissatisfied with the standards of the church? Ivan Blazen, faculty member at Loma Linda University provides some important direction.

> How then does a pastor go about the practical work of healing fractured relationships? Not with 'you ought,' but with 'you are;' not with a list of what we are to do but with a delineation of what God has done for us in Christ Jesus as the basis for how we ought to see and treat each other.[10]

All too often we are guilty of this response. We forget that change and behavior happen best in relationship to our understanding of Jesus Christ.

We ran some tests that would help clarify and predict dissatisfaction with the enforcement of standards. According to our matrix, the major factors that prove positive in building attitudes towards Adventist standards are warm church climates; the quality of religious education and instruction; denominational loyalty; personal endorsement of Adventist standards (lifestyle, substance abuse, and popular cultural ones).

The major factors that facilitate a negative attitude towards the enforcement of these same standards are materialism as a life value, extrinsic religiousness, the lack of quality of family worship, absence of caring teachers, negative perceptions of a thinking climate in churches, their perceptions of how much their leaders and teachers care for them, the family enforcement of church standards, and the lack of religiousness of family members.

So what are we to do? Family enforcement of Adventist lifestyle standards is the most productive. As enforcement increases, so does faith maturity and intrinsic religiousness. Even popular cultural standards are strengthened when enforced by the family. *In other words, strong enforcement is less powerful in our schools than in families.* We have responsibilities as parents to provide both good examples and clear messages that support life-giving behaviors and to teach our children how to make clear, decisive and good choices regarding their actions, friends, and lifestyle. We must learn to clarify those values which lie behind the choices we hope our children make. We are to do so in a loving, open, affection-oriented style. And here the home is the key.

Our consideration of enforcement and decision making at the family and institutional levels has stressed a number of things that are important to remember.

( ) *As individual Christians and as a church, we need to be clear about who we are and the nature of our faith.* What is called for here is a balanced Christianity. One that is not obscured by the nonessentials and unimportant, but that understands its place in a world that does not care to hear about the essentials of living for Christ. Early Adventism clearly touted the excitement of accepting a new understanding and stressed the importance of clearly studying their place in perspective with living for Christ. Christ is the example of godliness and godlikeness— an example that nudges us ". . .that we should follow in His steps."[11]

(\) *Because grace abounds and God is just, we need to act boldly and deci-
sively as we learn God's will for our families.* This is a clear call for
action.
(\) *A Christian life involves our response to both law and gospel.* God's
word that both orders and constrains our lives and inspires us
to selfless action on behalf of others becomes the guide for
decision making and a handbook for family decisions regarding morality and life choices.
(\) *Responsible decision making always involves being informed, whether acting as a youth, parent, or community of faith.*
(\) *Responsible decision making requires the capacity to be self-critical, recognizing our tendency both as individuals and as groups to act in ways that are self-
serving.* Families are not exempt from this attitude.[12]

Making life-affirming decisions is both a challenge and a
struggle. From within, we have to deal with our own weaknesses. It
is a struggle from without as we seek to cope with the difficult and
complex circumstances that defy our best intentions.[13] The question of dancing and movies, illicit drug use, exercise, morality, and
modesty are decisions that are best made first in the home. Only
then can the church and school help young people affirm their
decisions and clarify their options for positive living.

REFERENCES

1. Charles M. Shelton, *Adolescent Spirituality* (New York, NY: Crossroads, 1983), 50.

2. Lawrence Kohlberg and Carol Gilligan, "The Adolescent as a Philosopher: The Discovery of Self in a Postconventional World," *Dadalus, Journal of the American Academy of Arts and Sciences,* 199, (Boston, MA: Fall 1971), 1074.

3. Roger L. Dudley with V. Bailey Gillespie, *Valuegenesis: Faith in the Balance* (Loma Linda, CA: Loma Linda University Press, 1992), 147.

4. Paul Jersild, *Making Moral Decisions* (Minneapolis, MN: Fortress Press, 1990), 44.

5. Jeremiah 31:33 (NIV).

6. Roger L. Dudley with V. Bailey Gillespie, *Valuegenesis: Faith in the Balance,* 152.

7. Resources for discussion and education in the areas of lifestyle choices can be found in the following publications available from the John Hancock Center for Youth and Family Ministry or AdventSource through your local Adventist Book Center. For specific resources see: V. Bailey Gillespie, Judith Gillespie, Tim Gillespie, and Cheryl Webster, *A Guidebook for Spiritual Parenting* (Lincoln, NE: AdventSource, 2002); Steve Case, *Shall We Dance: Rediscovering Christ-Centered Standards* (Riverside, CA: Hancock Center Publications, 1999).

8. From the statement of Adventist Fundamental Beliefs: Christian Behavior, Texts that support this position are found in Rom. 12:1, 2; 1 John 2:6; Eph. 5:1-21; Phil. 4:8; 2 Cor. 10:5; 6:14-7:1; 1 Peter 3:1-4; 1 Cor. 6:19,20; 10:31; Lev. 11:1-47; 3 John 2.

9. Roger L. Dudley with V. Bailey Gillespie, *Valuegenesis: Faith in the Balance,* 161.

10. Paul Jersild, *Making Moral Decisions,* 121.

11. Thomas Friedman, "Noah's Flood and the Morning after 9/11," *The Press Enterprise* (Wednesday, September 11, 2002), A-12.

12. Ivan T. Blazen, "Reconciliation, New Creation, and New Lenses: A Study in 2 Corinthians 5:14-6:2" (An unpublished paper presented to the Adventist Society for Religious Studies, November 21, 2003). 2.

13. 1 Peter 2:21 (NIV).

*S*uccess in life is a reflection of the inner life of a person. The practical importance of family life is that it shapes the persons who are part of that unit. A nurturing environment can equip people to function well with life's ups and downs. A hostile setting can warp personality or provide motivation for escape. No matter who we are, where we've been or hope to be, we are a product of our families and our faith.

— *Monte & Norma Sahlin*

A Philadelphia father said, "As our children got older, I think they appreciated that we didn't pretend we knew everything about everything. We told them about occasions when we weren't disciplined, and we'd even ask them to pray for us so we could get back on track. Though we intentionally shared spiritual struggles and victories with our kids, I don't think that hurt our leadership in the home. We just emphasized that our journey had taken us a little farther than theirs, but we were both on the same road."

— *Greg Johnson*

CHAPTER 9

()

THE MOST PERDURING FACTOR
Nurturing spiritual families

9

THE MOST PERDURING FACTOR
Nurturing spiritual families

Childhood is no longer perceived as a time of innocence. Indeed, the steady diet of TV violence, sex and social problems ensures that kids are not innocent anymore. Children are now viewed as competent and sophisticated. This view can lead the parents of teenagers to feel that it is unnecessary for them to provide limits, guidelines and supervision.

—David Elkind

I f you are a collector of insights about families, then you've seen the wealth of information that we now know about the centrality of the Christian home. In fact, the concept of family is so central in Adventist theology we even have a Doctrine of the Family based on Scripture and built on an understanding of the role of parents in the development of mature and faithful children. This doctrine begins with an important statement. *"Marriage was divinely established in Eden and affirmed by Jesus to be a lifelong union between a man and a woman in loving companionship."* Ellen G. White comments on this relationship with another compelling statement. *"Society is composed of families. The well-being of society, the success of the church, the prosperity of the nation, depend upon home influences."*[1]

While preparing for my university class in Faith Development and Nurture, I stumbled across a fascinating piece of data that has forever changed my thinking about helping others find God. It was written by the first editor of one of my books, James Michael Lee, editor of the Religious Education Press where he writes, "Early family life is the most perduring factor in building strong commitment to God."[2] His research-based dictum regarding families has proved to be an important piece of information in the building blocks of faith development in understanding the limits of our ministry to children, youth, and families.

There have been a number of academic studies regarding this subject that provide credible and important insights into the power of the quality of family life in the building of a mature life of faith. In Adventism, one of the most significant is that of Bradley Strahan and his work with the South Pacific Division *Valuegenesis* Research.[3] In it he details those factors that have influence in this process. He states,

> *The evidence from a broad range of family studies has suggested that how parents relate to children is of more significance than whether there are one or two parents in the family. Thus a strong emphasis in the family research literature is directed toward the quality of relationships within the family, of family process variables.*[4]

Strahan suggests that both connectedness to and separation from the family have been seen as vital aspects of family relationships that facilitate adolescent development as well.[5] As we explored the family dynamic in the *Valuegenesis²* research, we decided to use the same scale that was used in the South Pacific research in 1994. It was called the *Parental Bonding Instrument (PBI)*.[6] It targets those that are in high school (grades 9-12). The scale is divided into two types of parenting styles, the "Caring Parent Style" and the

"Overprotective Parenting Style." Students were asked to respond to the attitudes and behaviors illustrated by their parents. Specifically they were asked, "Which best describes the extent your mother and father were like or unlike each of the statements." For example, the Caring Parenting Style is illustrated by statements like, "Spoke to me with a warm and friendly voice," and "Appeared to understand my problems and worries," or "Frequently smiled at me." While on the other hand, the Overprotective Parenting Style was demonstrated by such statements as, "Tried to control everything I did," "Invaded my privacy," or demonstrated such attitudes as, "Felt I could not look after myself unless she/he was around."

Students had a variety of possible responses represented by a four-point format: "Mother/Father is very unlike this," to "Mother/Father is very like this." The item percentages for the responses by students about their parents who are "moderately like this" and "very like this" are below:

Statement	Mother	Father
() Spoke to me with a warm and friendly voice.	91%	24%
() Did not help me as much as I needed.	83%	14%
() Let me do those thing I liked doing.	77%	91%
() Seemed emotionally cold to me.	82%	56%
() Appeared to understand my problems and worries.	81%	31%
() Was affectionate to me.	92%	21%
() Liked me to make my own decisions.	67%	81%
() Did not want me to grow up.	91%	45%
() Tried to control everything I did.	42%	36%
() Invaded my privacy.	83%	91%
() Enjoyed talking things over with me.	72%	38%
() Frequently smiled at me.	79%	12%

Continued	Mother	Father
() Tended to baby me.	86%	19%
() Did not seem to understand my needs.	30%	27%
() Let me decide things for myself.	49%	47%
() Made me feel I wasn't wanted.	54%	22%
() Could make me feel better when I was upset.	63%	34%
() Did not talk with me very much.	23%	73%
() Tried to make me dependent on her/him.	79%	32%
() Felt I could not look after myself.	39%	90%
() Gave me as much freedom as I wanted.	15%	66%
() Let me go out as often as I wanted.	28%	22%
() Was overprotective of me.	19%	52%
() Did not praise me.	48%	42%
() Let me dress in any way I pleased.	24%	61%

What can immediately be seen is that the perceptions of fathers are challenging. The youth responded with startling insight that their fathers were warm and friendly, 24%, and a slim 14% were seen as helping these youth when it was needed which contrasted with 83% when asked about their mothers' responsiveness. In fact, 13% of the total group showed that fathers were less responsive than mothers. In addition, fathers were seen as more permissive and less controlling than mothers in many ways.

Those scoring over the midpoint in the Caring Parenting Style Scale (in this case 18) are considered caring; those below that are labeled as indifferent. The styles of parental bonding then are usually identified as the following four types.

Overprotective + caring = affectionate constraint parenting
Overprotective + indifferent = affectionless control style
Promoting independence + indifferent = neglectful parenting
Promoting independence + caring = optimal parenting

Since the participants in this part of the survey were high school students, we can contrast the lower grades with the higher grades in a number of areas to look at the type of parental style and bonding that is evident. When we look closely at the types of parental styles, we notice an interesting perception of the survey by the youth. Affectionate constraint is the most prevalent style among mothers of the students studied.

As we contrast the fathers as perceived by the young people in high school, we see another trend. Fathers are by far more affectionless in most of their relationships, coupled with a controlling style, 60%. Adding to that, 12% are affectionate -constraint while 13% have absent or weak bonding with their children, and only 7% have what we call optimal bonding. Research has a long record of facilitating father involvement in the rearing of children, and not surprisingly, research supports a link between religious belief and responsible fathering.

Research documents that very religious fathers are more likely to be both highly involved and warmer in their relationships with their children than are fathers that are somewhat or nonreligious. You will remember in our research 47% of fathers were

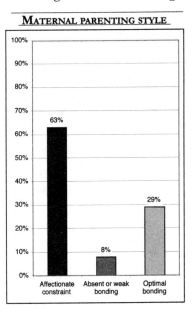

MATERNAL PARENTING STYLE

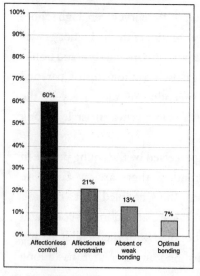

seen as "deeply religious" by their teens while 60% of mothers held that category. We have some work to do with fathers of the children in our church if these perceptions are correct.

In a more recent national study of a number of denominations, the link between good fatherhood and religion was evident in all denominations according to *The Journal of Marriage and the Family*, "Conservative Protestant affiliation" exerted an "independent effect" on some aspects of fatherhood. Conservative fathers were more likely to be involved with their children in personal activities such as private talks than unaffiliated and mainline Protestant men." And they are more likely "to have dinner with their children and to participate in youth-related activities."[7]

Gordon Parker's research on parental bonding labels the combination of high care with low protection as Optimal Parenting. The subjects of his research who place their parents in this category consistently have been shown to be the most psychologically healthy. On the other hand, the combination of high protection and low care (What is called Affectionless Control), has shown to be associated with psychological vulnerability. Strahan in doing a literature search suggests that "parents in the Affectionless Control quadrant have been shown to be up to nine times more likely to experience a neurotic illness."[8] The blending of low protection and low care is called Neglectful Parenting and is also associated with low vulnerability, while the association of high care and high protection is called Affectionate Constraint.

The South Pacific Study carefully analyzed this scale and concludes, *"The quality of the parent-child bond is more important than parents' religious practice for predicting adjustment and support for Adventist religious faith."*[9] And the bond is strengthened by warmth and affection and encouraging independence. Here are the parenting percentages that range through the whole catalogue of parenting approaches. You can see the challenge ahead if this is an accurate perception of parenting by the youth of the church. Listed next are all the possible combinations of parenting styles we explored.

Parenting style	Total % (9th-12th Grades)
() Mother: Constraint; Father: Control	40%
() Both Affectionate Constraint	12%
() Mother: Constraint; Father: Weak	8%
() Mother: Constraint; Father: Optimal	3%
() Mother: Weak; Father: Control	3%
() Mother: Weak; Father: Constraint	3%
() Both absent or weak	1%
() Mother: Weak; Father: Optimal	1%
() Mother: Optimal; Father: Control	19%
() Mother: Optimal; Father: Constraint	7%
() Mother: Optimal; Father: Weak	1%
() Both Optimal Bonding	1%

If you look closely at the parental styles merged together, we see that 40% of the parents had a mother that used a constraining style while the fathers were more controlling.

The most effective type of parenting, the Affectionate Constraint model, was the third highest but just slightly over one in ten parents. We obviously have some significant parenting work to do in regards to encouraging both parents to become actively involved in the lives of their children.

PARENTAL INVOLVEMENT

It is easy to identify the challenges and pitfalls of parenting. Anyone that has tried to build a strong family faces the task of appropriating time properly, being available, and at the same time providing guidance and example to the younger generations. Add to this the difficult and growing demographic in churches of single parenting and you can see the road ahead. It is filled with detours and bypasses that such challenges dictate.

Whiile researching for this book, we looked at the issue of single- parenting. 20% of our survey group came from single-parent families. This number equaled the number of divorced parents among our respondents as well. When pastors who specialize in ministering to single parents were asked how those parents successfully raised faithful children, they responded by saying, "The only single parents I see who are approaching success are those who don't fall into the tremendous trap of self-pity." Another said, "These single moms are forced to go to the work force; they don't have a social life; and the kids demand a lot of time. It's not fair, and most singles recognize that parenting is a difficult, sometimes impossible task."[10]

These situations make parental bonding an especially important task, and the church and other adults in the lives of youth can make an important contribution to faith growth.

When "...parents are exemplars of personal faith...[our lives] become the product of all of our witnessing to His majesty and power. Just think, you and I are coworkers in this plan of salvation. Now, we haven't had anything to do with the gift, but we have everything to do with its discovery."[11] So being involved in those special moments of your children's lives becomes a crucial educational method to model the Kingdom of God and the nature of Christ.

We surveyed a number of ways parents could become involved in the lives of their children and asked the youth to respond. We wanted to understand the types of interaction parents have with their children and to contrast that to other significant adults in their lives—their teachers and pastors. The results suggest an openness to talk about important issues on the part of the youth and parents. Students were asked, "Do you feel your parents accept you unconditionally?" The response format was a typical five-point scale with 1 = "Yes" and 5 = "No." Respondents could select the middle, which was the median or "neutral" response.

It is obvious that the youth in our survey felt the unconditional, "gift love" that exemplifies the type of love that God shares in his acceptance of each of us. So, even though the families seem overprotective, and at times to the extreme, this overprotectiveness is often interpreted as an unconditional love. A loving family with guidelines and constraint seems to be the optimum.

We asked the young people if they felt they could talk to their parents about sensitive things such as sex and drugs, etc., and we asked the same questions about their teachers and pastors. Using

UNCONDITIONAL ACCEPTANCE

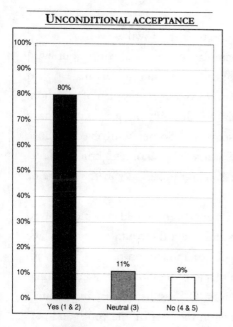

the same response format. However, this time the ends of the continuum were "not willing" to "willing," again with the middle choice being neutral we got encouraging insights into these relationships.

Even as youth felt strongly about the acceptance their parents provide, they were also more willing to bring these issues to them before they shared them with other mentors in their lives. Fully 17% more students were "willing." Again, we see the enduring impact of excellence in parenting in order to develop clear direction, moral action, and relationship with parents in the lives of the youth.

WILLINGNESS TO TALK ABOUT ISSUES

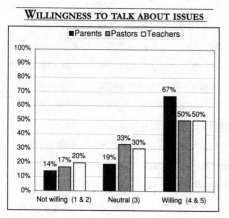

In contrast, we wanted to know about how often they talked to their parents, teachers, and pastors about faith in general. Here we see that 57% "never or rarely" spoke to their pastors about this aspect of their development. In addition, 19% of the youth spoke to their fathers often about it, while their mothers had nearly a third of their children talking to them about eternal issues of faith.

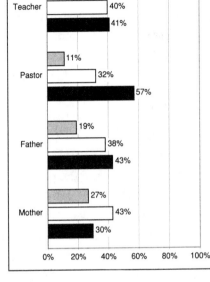

Another important family contribution to building a mature intrinsic faith experience is family worship.

IT'S CALLED THE FAMILY ALTAR

When Noah came out of the ark after those long days rocking on the newly created sea, one of the primary acts of worship he and his family enacted was to build an altar and offer a sacrifice to the God who created, sustained, and kept them during those trying hours amid animals, loneliness, and isolation. Because of this act of faith, family worship came to be known as an altar. Here we offer up our thanks for the same issues that faced Noah and his kin in those hours immediately after striking land.

We discovered early on in our *Valuegenesis* research that meaningful and interesting family worships provide a rich resource for building family faith. And this can begin early and has long-term impact.

While holding family ministry worship workshops in local churches, we found that almost every Adventist has a family worship story. Sad to say, many of them are negative. "A time when our family would always seem to get into an argument," one young adult said. "It was always a family time, interesting and meaningful most of the time, except when Dad would read some obscure text from a book he had just bought that didn't relate to anything I was doing or even thinking about," another student wrote in her journal for her university religion class.

One of the principal ways to model religious values is the family altar. The survey asked: "How often does your family have family worship?" We defined this concept as "prayers or religious devotions you have together as a family, away from church." The frequencies are listed below (with *Valuegenesis¹* figures in parentheses) on the next page. But what is obvious is that fewer students are having family worship now than before. The data shows that those having worship once a day or more is down from (23%) to 7% and over a week or more it is down from 49% to 32%—down one-half to one-third.

"How often does your family have family worship?"

	Total	6th	7th-8th	9th-10th	11th-12th
Never	13% (26%)	10%	13%	14%	12%
Less than 1/mo.	22% (11%)	19%	20%	22%	24%
About 1/mo.	16% (6%)	14%	15%	16%	18%
About 2-3 x/mo	19% (8%)	16%	17%	18%	19%
Once a week	13% (15%)	15%	13%	12%	12%
Several x/week	12% (11%)	13%	13%	11%	11%
Once a day	4% (15%)	6%	5%	3%	3%
More than 1x/day	3% (8%)	6%	4%	3%	2%

Obviously, there are now fewer students *who never* experience family worship. The frequency of family worship is correlated at

.27 with endorsement of popular cultural standards, .25 with denominational loyalty, .24 with intrinsic religion, and .22 with the endorsement of Adventist lifestyle standards. Obviously, families who stress the uniqueness of Adventism and commitment to the denomination have more regular worship.

But the fact that we families do have worship is really not the question, because frequency is not as crucial as the quality of family devotions. Just what is happening during family worship? Is its influence positive or negative? We asked the youth, "Which of the following best describes the way in which your family most often worships together?" Six answers were possible, but they could only choose one correct one for their family.

DESCRIPTION OF FAMILY WORSHIP	
() We don't have family worship.	20%
() We hardly ever worship together.	18%
() Mostly reading together.	19%
() Mostly praying together.	9%
() Mostly sharing our ideas with each other.	7%
() Usually a combination of the above.	28%

It would seem that more creative effort must be exhibited by parents if they want their worships to be more appreciated; however, of those having worships at home, 70% told us that they were interesting, while another 82% said that family worships were meaningful. It seems that if families have mastered the art of creative and relevant family devotions, the youth who participate see its significance. And only 14% claimed that their family worship was a waste of time. (Those percentages reflect almost exactly the data from ten years ago). But what of the 38% who say they don't have regular worship together? Over one-third of the youth feel this way, and you will remember that only 32% of the homes, down from 48%) ten years ago, seem to have worship outside of church once a week or more. We have some work to do in this area.

The approaches to religious life that correlate with the quality of family worship, whether or not the student said that family worship was both interesting and meaningful, were those whose family climate was loving and disciplined, .38; those whose religious life could be described as intrinsic in nature, .37; those with high denominational loyalty, .31; and students with high faith maturity, .28.

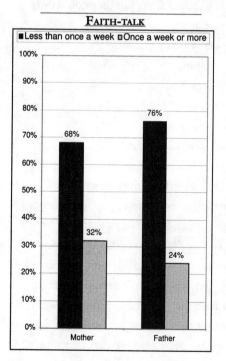

FAITH-TALK

■Less than once a week ▫Once a week or more

THE IMPORTANCE OF FAITH-TALK

We've already stressed the importance and frequency of significant talks between parents and their children about faith, but now we want to explore this important subject in a more careful way. We've labeled positive communication about our own faith as "faith talk." Sharing how God is now and has worked in your life is the basis for the content of this type of communication, and we've already seen its importance. Now for the details.

We wondered how often the young person and their fathers and mothers talked together about faith or religion. After all it, seems that an inordinate amount of time is spent on things like clothes, friends, times to get home, room cleaning, and school grades. Just how much time is really spent talking about eternal things? Less than one in three parents spend time talking to their children once a week or more, while two-thirds to three-fourths have time for this less than once a week.

We wanted to break down this discussion even further to see if we could understand this important activity. We asked, "How often does your father or mother talk with you about his or her faith or religious experiences he or she has had?" These two questions provided a more detailed picture of the faith talk issue.

When asked about this, 29% of youth said their fathers talked to them once a week or more and 37% of the young people claimed their mothers did so. One of the crucial issues in sharing your faith with your children is the level of

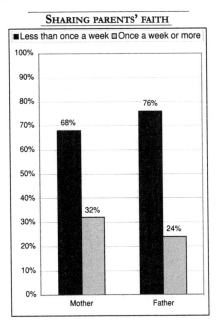

SHARING PARENTS' FAITH

■Less than once a week ◻Once a week or more

Mother: 68%, 32%
Father: 76%, 24%

comfort you have and the relative comfort youth perceive that their parents possess. We asked a series of questions to understand this issue.

The question was, "How comfortable are the following people in talking with others about their faith and what God means to them?" We targeted the youths' understanding of their father, mother, and themselves. We wanted to know if they were "not comfortable," "comfortable," or "very comfortable." Their answers follow:

() *Your father*

Not comfortable	19%
Comfortable	20%
Very comfortable	42%

() *Your mother*

Not comfortable	9%
Comfortable	43%
Very comfortable	48%

() *Your own comfort*

Not comfortable	19%
Comfortable	51%
Very comfortable	30%

Perhaps due to the developmental issues of identity and the feelings of belonging youth are not as comfortable talking about their faith experience; however, if they heard more of this type of discussion from both of their parents, they would grow to understand how easy it is to talk about what God has done and is doing in their lives. Again, parent modeling is crucial here. Time spent is well worth it in establishing close relationships with our children and learning about their personal faith life.

Paying attention

The family is the place where spiritual development is nurtured and facilitated. It has an enduring impact in the future life of faith. And what is required of us is that we learn to pay attention. We've said it before:

> *We embark on a spiritual journey with our family to the extent that we learn to pay attention to each other, and our lives, and let the journey teach us through the power of the Holy Spirit's gentle calling and nudging. All spiritual traditions recognize this truth. And many believe that the only requirement in developing a spiritual life in your home is that you pay attention....Pay attention to God, to each other, and to the vision of what the Kingdom of God might be like as we learn to accept the grace of God seen in the life, death, and resurrection of our Lord, Jesus Christ.*[12]

We'll talk about the conclusions we have drawn about the significance of Christian parenting in the last chapter of this book, but right now remember that there are a number of themes that seem to assist in the building of a strong faith in the lives of our children. They are *a focus on the parents themselves*—their spiritual lives, their sharing and discussions about faithfulness with their young people. It is insight into *parenting itself*—the support, love, openness, protection, and care that make a difference. And finally, but certainly not the least significant, is the *modeling of the Kingdom* done in the home, including holding high standards and enforcing them fairly and lovingly, while holding the line against the infringements of the worst in the world and setting limits for young people, all the time guaranteeing what the love of God is all about through interesting and relevant worship and faith talk or sharing of their own personal relationship with God. These are central to building faithfulness and giving young people a sense of mission and vision of God's purpose for their lives.

REFERENCES

1. Ellen G. White, *The Ministry of Healing* (Mountain View, CA: Pacific Press Publishing Association, 1905), 349.
2. For complete research basis for this claim see James Michael Lee, *The Flow of Religious Instruction* (Birmingham, AL: Religious Education Press, 1971). His book gives the *basic rationale* for the existence and practice of religious education as a form of social science and not a branch of theology. A review in *Religious Education* states: "This is a ground-breaking event for religious education. Lee covers an enormous amount of ground with utmost clarity. He provides the field a more solid grounding than it has had for years."
3. Bradley J. Strahan, *Parents, Adolescents and Religion* (Coranbong, New South Wales: Avondale Academic Press, 1994).
4. Bradley Strahan, *Parents, Adolescents and Religion, 19.*
5. Bradley Strahan, *Parents, Adolescents and Religion, 20.*
6. The scale was developed by Gordon Parker, Hilary Tupling and L. D. B. Brown and measures two distinct scales termed "care" and "overprotection." It measures fundamental parental styles as perceived by the child. The measure is "retrospective," meaning that adults (over the age of 16) complete the measure for how they remember their parents during their first 16 years. There are 25 items in the questionnaire including 12 "care" items and 13 "overprotection" items. See G. Parker, H. Tupling, and L.B. Brown, "A Parental Bonding Instrument," *British Journal of Medical Psychology*, (Volume. 52, 1979), 1-10.
7. W. Bradford Wilcox, "Religion, Convention, and Paternal Involvement," *Journal of Marriage and the Family* (Vol. 64, 2002), 780-792.
8. Bradley J. Strahan, *Parents, Adolescents, and Religion*, 36. Dr. Strahan is quoting studies done by Gordon Parker and L. B. Brown in 1979 shared in the *British Journal of Medical Psychology*, 52, 1-10.
9. Bradley J. Strahan, *Parents, Adolescents, and Religion, 94.*
10. Greg Johnson and Mike Yorkey, *Faithful Parents, Faithful Kids, (Wheaton*, IL: Tyndale House Publishers, 1993), 263.
11. V. Bailey Gillespie, Judith W. Gillespie, Timothy Gillespie, with Cheryl Webster, *Keeping the Faith: A Guidebook for Spiritual Parenting* (Lincoln, NE: AdventSource, 2001), 41.
12. V. Bailey Gillespie, Judith W. Gillespie, et al., *Keeping the Faith, 72.*

The bottom line in youth ministry is not how religious your children are or how well they will master their doctrines. The bottom line is where will your kids be five to ten years from now. Will they be in the church, will they be thinking about Jesus, and will they be excited about being a child of God?

— *V. Bailey & Judith Gillespie*

Here is a mind-set list for the class of 2007 that was created to help us understand and overcome the cultural-reference gap between those students and adults. Here are some on this year's must-know list for youth ministry:

- *"Ctrl + Alt + Del" is as basic as "ABC."*
- *Bert and Ernie are old enough to be their parents.*
- *The snail darter has never been endangered.*
- *They never heard Howard Cosell call a game on ABC.*
- *The Osmonds are just talk-show hosts.*
- *Car detailing has always been available.*
- *Banana Republic has always been a store, not a puppet government in Latin America.*
- *Yuppies are almost as old as hippies.*
- *Killer bees have always been swarming in the United States.*
- *Rock 'n Roll has always been a force for social good.*
- *They can still sing the rap chorus to the Fresh Prince of Bel-Air and the theme song from Duck Tales.*

— *Kellie Bartlett*

CHAPTER 10

YES, YOUTH MINISTRY IS IMPORTANT
Making a difference

10

YES, YOUTH MINISTRY IS IMPORTANT
Making a difference

Why should not labor for the youth in our borders be regarded as missionary work of the highest kind? It requires the most delicate tact, the most watchful consideration. . .The most kindness, courtesy, and the sympathy which flows from a heart filled with love to Jesus, will gain their confidence, and save them from many a snare of the enemy. . .There must be more study given to the problem of how to deal with the youth, more earnest prayer for the wisdom that is needed in dealing with minds. . .We should seek to enter into the feelings of the youth, sympathizing with them in their joys and sorrows, their conflicts and victories. We must meet them where they are if we would keep them. . . Let us remember the claim of God upon us to make the path to heaven bright and attractive.[1]

—*Ellen G. White*

Wisdom declares that *any church is only one generation away from extinction!* If we lose our youth from the church, the results could be devastating. Their spiritual well-being and connection with the church is a barometer that tells us how we are doing as a whole. If our children are not convinced by our message and become committed to the church, we have to ask, "What hope is there of reaching the wider community at all?"

It is a truism in education that if you want to help young people learn, you need to understand the process of how they learn. That is why we study how youth develop faith, with a view of trying to derstand what we can do to facilitate a rich, growing faith life.

We have a clear idea of the kinds of key factors that, when present, promote faith in the growing lives of youth. In examining congregational factors that promote faith growth and maturity in mainline congregations, "Christian education and youth ministry are the most vital factors. Nothing matters more than Christian education." Peter Benson, Director of Search Institute suggests, "Done well, (Christian education and youth ministry) has the potential, more than any other area of congregational life, to promote faith and loyalty." In fact, Christian education has twice the impact that other factors have in congregational life. "The more a congregation embodies the Christian education effectiveness factors," his report claims, "the greater the growth in faith by youth and adults, and the greater the loyalty to congregation and denomination."[2] Many of the factors below are present in both congregational religious education and youth ministry:

() Teachers who have mature faith and who know educational theories and methods.

() A pastor who is committed to education, devotes time to Christian education and knows educational theory and practice.

() An educational process that applies faith to current issues, examines life experiences, creates community, recognizes individuality, and encourages independent thinking and questioning.

() Educational content that blends biblical knowledge and insight with significant engagement in the major life issues each age group faces.

() A high percentage of adults active in a congregation.

() An educational program with a clear mission statement and clear learning objectives.

Seventh-day Adventists have a unique advantage in the area of Christian education. With one of largest private educational enterprises in the United States, our school system provides additional educational opportunity. And while the survey cited above deals with congregational religious education, think what the study might show if both were involved, the church and the school, all dedicated to promoting a clear vision of the love of Jesus and targeted on building faith in the lives of the youth to whom they minister.

The *Valuegenesis²* survey gives us an unprecedented profile of Adventist youth in the early twenty-first century and allows us to be optimistic about the future. As we study what makes a difference in local congregations and in Adventist schools, we can again see what was discovered in studies of other denominations. Things we do, do make an incredible difference.

We've seen how Adventist youth believe in the basic doctrinal positions of their church and by and large are committed to its special mission. And in our chapter about grace orientation, we've seen a significant shift from *Valuegenesis¹* in the overall understanding of grace. This is a heartening result! The major tenets of the faith are still believed by the vast majority of students—in many of those beliefs their "definitely believe" percentages are well over ninety percent.

Professionals in youth ministry and local church youth ministry leaders who are committed to long-term youth leadership are intuitively aware of the impact youth ministry has on attitudes, beliefs and values of the youth. Until now, little research has been undertaken that documents this "gut" feeling. *Valuegenesis²* wanted to see just how much impact ministry to, for, and with youth would make. A number of scales in youth ministry were first explored in the South Pacific Division *Valuegenesis* report while Dr. Barry Gane was the Division youth director and before he began to teach youth ministry at Andrews University. This research has sought to better understand the impact of both local church and conference-based youth ministry.

So what about youth ministry?

Our survey instrument included a series of questions on the importance of various factors on the development of the student's faith. And looking at youth ministry, *per se*, gives us special insight. Using factor analysis, it was revealed that the students saw various clumpings for these questions and gave us a school factor, a home factor, a church factor, and a youth ministry factor which can be useful in understanding the role of each ministry in the life of the young people we studied. We could now use these to see the impact of each on the religous lives of the young people in our study.

We were able to look at the data in terms of these factors and address the question,

---

What is factor analysis?

Factor analysis is used to uncover the underlying structure (dimensions) of a set of variables. It reduces a larger number of variables to a smaller number and sets a priority among them.

A nontechnical analogy: A mother sees various bumps and shapes under a blanket at the bottom of a bed. When one shape moves toward the top of the bed, all the other bumps and shapes move toward the top also, so the mother concludes that what is under the blanket is a single thing, most likely her child. A smaller group, which move independently from the first are most likely the dog. Similarly, factor analysis takes as input a number of measures and tests, analogous to the bumps and shapes. Those that move together are considered a single thing, which it labels a factor.

"Does youth ministry really make a difference?" Using this method, we could see the attitudes to and perceptions of the local church.

The following two charts give an indication of how different age groups perceive the church. They tend to become less positive as they get older. The areas that show the biggest shifts with age are in the area of tolerance and openness to strangers, friendliness and acceptance of difference.

The older students feel it is much more difficult to be themselves, but this is understandable as they seek to differentiate themselves from their parents and often challenge much that the church and their parents believe. These are things that they were either unaware of or ignored when they were younger.

The older students tend to see the church as exclusive and

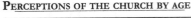

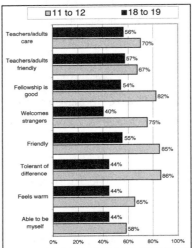

HOW THE CHURCH SHAPES UP

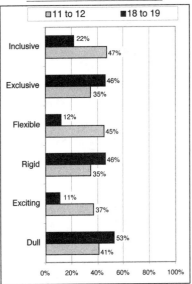

YES, YOUTH MINISTRY IS IMPORTANT

rigid and are bored with the whole approach to worship. Sadly, there are just over 10% who would rate the church as exciting, while the majority view it as dull.

This is probably not news to those who work with or take an interest in the church's youth, but it is still a cause for concern. If we include youth ministry in the formula and ask the same questions dividing the responses into those who have youth ministry and those who don't, we get some surprising results.

Notice in the chart below the major differences between the two groups. These differences are most marked in the areas of their perception of growth, flexibility, and excitement. Even if the same pastor had the same program running in two different churches but in one he had a youth ministry program being offered, he would have youth who were more positive about what the church is offering. Although we still have much to do, there is a 100% increase in the number who see the church as exciting when youth ministry is present. Most churches who have a youth ministry program are

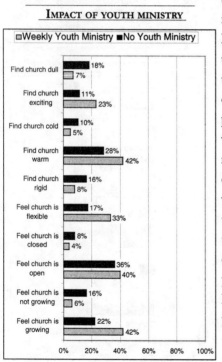

IMPACT OF YOUTH MINISTRY

of necessity more flexible, and this does not go unnoticed. Does youth ministry make a difference? Of course it does. And if the perception of ministry is significant, the attitude about church moves to the positive side.

The question is, If we do more youth ministry do we get better results? Would students who are receiving ministry specially designed for them actually want to have more to do with the church? The next chart gives a resounding YES to both these questions.

The youth who attend churches where no youth ministry is available do not look forward to going to church and do not as a whole go because they want to. These same students find the religious education program of the church uninteresting and only 17% feel it makes them think. These students are already on the fast-track out of the church. They see the church as rigid, cold, dull, and not open to their friends. They feel forced to attend and do not appreciate or enjoy what the church is offering. However, weekly youth ministry brings about major changes.

There is over 100% increase in the number who look forward to going to

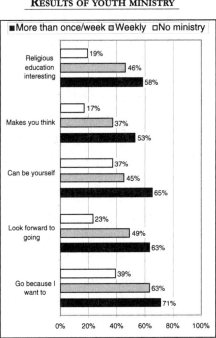

RESULTS OF YOUTH MINISTRY

■More than once/week ▫Weekly ▫No ministry

Religious education interesting
19%
46%
58%

Makes you think
17%
37%
53%

Can be yourself
37%
45%
65%

Look forward to going
23%
49%
63%

Go because I want to
39%
63%
71%

0%   20%   40%   60%   80%   100%

church, and this increases almost another 50% when they receive youth ministry more than once per week. There are major shifts in all the areas with a sizeable move in the area of religious education. Here we see an increase well over 200% for those with youth ministry more then once per week. These figures alone are a compelling argument for doing youth ministry in the local church. But we still have more data to explore.

THE INFLUENCE OF THE PASTOR

When was the last time you heard students praising the pastor and encouraging their friends to come to church? We seldom hear, "Our pastor is the greatest. He is always there for us. Hey, you should really come to our church!" The chances are that those who make this statement have a strong youth ministry program going. We wanted to explore the impact of youth ministry on the students' perception of their local pastor. 45% of students in our research see the pastor as important in the development of the faith. This fact is encouraging. Almost half of the youth recognize the centrality of pastoral ministry when it comes to growing their personal faith.

We cannot overemphasize the power of mentoring in building the Kingdom of God. We've already stressed the importance of this fact, but look what happens when youth ministry is alive and well in the local church. Our research showed that when the church has youth ministry running just one time per week the importance of the pastor in faith development rises to 62% and increases still further to almost three quarters (72%) when their church has youth ministry more often than once a week. Pastors who have experienced this connection with youth are likely to facilitate youth ministry in their churches to raise the perception and actuality of ministry for teens and young adults.

It seems that youth ministry, even when it is perceived as poorly done results in better attitudes toward the pastor's role in their lives than when there is no youth ministry at all!

Another interesting insight is that most of the students see church going once a week as their preference. Only 10% of the youth who felt "no ministry" thought they would like to go more than once a week, but that number increased to 34% when youth ministry was seen as happening "more then once a week."

WHAT ABOUT BEHAVIOR?

The common factor for all these students in this research is their attendance at an Adventist church school. Because of this, we don't have current information about those that do not attend Adventist schools. But we do have recent information as to how these students might compare with those in public education regarding youth ministry's impact.

There were dramatic differences in the results of the *Valuegenesis* studies in the South Pacific Division. The students in this study *(Valuegenesis2) are* less likely to attend parties with nonchurch friends or even have too many friends outside their church. This is not the case where students attend a public school. But having said that, we should note that there are still important differences.

In some of the areas there is as much as 100% positive increase in factors explored when there is an active ministry for youth in the local church and school.

The changes are in the areas where very few of the youth concur with the church's position to begin with (see the areas of dancing and movie going). In all the other areas the increase is between five and eight percentage points.

Even if youth ministry is only offered once per month and not even greatly appreciated, there is usually a difference. In some cases it was as much as or more than 5% (alcohol, tobacco and illegal drug use). In my opinion and based on earlier research, it is clear that adding youth ministry to a strong church school program enhances the results that we are striving for in the transmission of beliefs and values and in helping students make life-affirming choices. And when you look at our recent research, you can see the transforming power of youth ministry in the area of church standards.

There appear to be some areas of standards

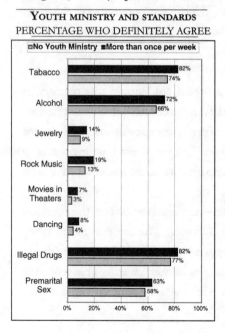

YOUTH MINISTRY AND STANDARDS
PERCENTAGE WHO DEFINITELY AGREE

□No Youth Ministry ■More than once per week

Tabacco 82% / 74%
Alcohol 72% / 66%
Jewelry 14% / 9%
Rock Music 19% / 13%
Movies in Theaters 7% / 3%
Dancing 8% / 4%
Illegal Drugs 82% / 77%
Premarital Sex 63% / 58%

0% 20% 40% 60% 80% 100%

that the students see as more cultural then biblically based, and the score in these areas have deteriorated in the last ten years. These include dancing, attending movie theaters, listening to rock music, wearing jewelry, and taking part in competitive sports. I am reminded of Roger Dudley's statement in our first book on *Valuegenesis.* His words are almost prophetic:

> *The standard on movies seems especially a lost cause. . .the church must consider whether its historic stand is still desirable or even realistic. If it is, then it must mount a massive selling campaign in order to convince the youth to reverse their beliefs here. Given the lack of support from those who will be running the church tomorrow and the anecdotal evidence that most Adventists attend the theater, the present standard seems to be but a joke. When any church "rule" becomes that disregarded, it seems it has a very cloudy future as having much significance in impacting youth's lives.*[3]

The comments he made about theater going could now be readily made concerning dancing, jewelry, rock music, and competitive sports, as you remember the results in our chapter on life-affirming choices earlier in this book. But we must remember, at least if we are serious about these positions, youth ministry appears to give us an additional way of transmitting these crucial choices and actions to the next generation. Couple strong youth ministry with family life and guidance in these choices and you have a powerful approach to assisting young people in their choices in life. And even here, we will have to be intentional about this ministry. If your church has failed to provide this important ministry, spend some time talking to your church board about it and begin to recruit, resource, and train leaders who can build the foundations of a strong and targeted youth ministry in your church.

FUTURE INTENTIONS

We have seen that the frequency with which youth ministry is offered has an effect on so many areas of belief and life among the youth in our schools. Does it affect their intention to be part of the church in the future? We know that many of the young people who sever connection with the church begin the process in their teen years, so this is an important question to try to resolve.

If there is one "should" that is consistent throughout the church, it is the "should" of sharing our faith.[4] Along with this aspect of membership, being a Christian means also "to become a part of a caring community, a community that reflects the love of God."[5] So there are myriad reasons why young people do not elect to remain in the church. For example, some get discouraged because of the attitudes of adults toward their journey to find a personal God; others become disenchanted due to worship that is not perceived as relevant; and still others simply drift away because they don't find friendship. It is seldom because of doctrinal disbelief, however. So determining the reasons for leaving is important. Competent youth ministry in local congregations and in schools often answers some of the issues we have raised.

We asked, "Do you still think you will be active in the church when you are 40 years old?" Surprisingly, 68% of those *without* youth ministry said "yes." When they had exposure to youth ministry only "one time per month," the figure grew to 73%. When ministry was offered "more than one time each week," the figure increased to 81%. When we asked if they were satisfied with their local church, 55% of those *without* youth ministry told us that they were, while the figure for youth ministry, just "once per month," rose to 68% and increased still further to 78% where they had access to a youth ministry program "more then one time per week!"

We said before how loyal Adventist youth in Adventist schools are. It seems that most of the teens felt they would be going to an Adventist church even if they moved cities, and the youth ministry effect here only moved the figures from 84% to 87%. That shows the importance of identifying with an Adventist community, a concept that is well bred in Adventist youth.

How about Pathfinders?

When we look at individual aspects of youth ministry such as Pathfinders and do the same kind of study, we find more interesting and helpful information. Some 72% of those without Pathfinders intend to be in the church at age 40. In looking at the group that says their faith has been "somewhat" affected by Pathfinders, the figure is 81% and 83% if they were very much affected by Pathfinders. It is an important statistic and shows the importance of this aspect of youth ministry in local congregations.

This same trend is repeated when we ask questions about satisfaction with their local church. Those who have not experienced Pathfinders share a figure of 68% satisfied, while those who said Pathfinders "somewhat" affected their faith growth, the percentage stood at 76%. And if you ask the next step in this series, has Pathfindering affected their faith "very much," some 80% were satisfied.

When we asked the same questions of local church youth ministry, the figures show the same trend, 69% who said they were "satisfied" with the church. The percentage moved to 80% for those who saw this ministry affecting their faith development "very much."

Even when we include those students who are negative about everything, nothing we do affects their faith growth, we find that figures are more positive for inclusion of both Pathfinders and youth ministry.

Seventh-four percent of youth with Pathfinders intend to be active at forty years of age in the Adventist church while those with no Pathfinder indicated this at a 71% level. When you look at the youth with youth ministry some 75% see themselves active in the church when they get older with only 73% saying that when there is no active youth ministry in local congregations. And while these percentages are slightly better with active "Pathfindering" and ministry to youth, we can say that every bit helps in building faith in the lives of our youth.

There is a down side of this research too. For example, of the youth who are involved in Pathfinders, only 50% tell us that the program has a positive effect upon their faith growth—the figure is only slightly better for local church youth ministry. This demands urgent attention and cries out that training for the leadership at local churches is a necessity if we want these historic and vital ministries to be successful and meet their purpose in changing the spiritual outlook of the youth of the church. The bottom line, then, is that every church needs ministry for young people. Pathfinders, youth ministry, Sabbath Schools, midweek ministry, all of these are essential.

There is some good news and some bad news in the *Valuegenesis* results. It is clear that if our only goal were to produce young adults who give mental assent to the doctrinal positions of the church, then we are having reasonable success. And there may have been a time when some would argue, "What more do you want?" Adventist young people are bright, well-educated, articulate and on the whole, committed Christians. However, there are a sizeable number who seem to be also anxious to sever connection with their church. Just like their contemporaries in society, they will not give loyalty to an organization just because their parents are part of it. Religion has to become their own, the faith must be personalized, and they must find an ideology that they can feel deeply committed to, along with a community of faithful friends and peers that represent in a clear way the Kingdom of God. The time of youth provides a unique opportunity for ministry. In faith development lingo, it is:

An important situation for faith. The faith situation is formed due to both an emerging self-identity and a sense of autonomy. Adolescents have begun to discover that they are finally their own person. At last, they can decide their fate and future. They really do not have to take "it" anymore. This newfound freedom of choice comes as a welcome relief to the structure of the past and has theological significance to the budding religious expression of young people.[6]

Ellen Charry tells a fitting concluding story in her lecture on youth ministry at Princeton Theological Seminary. As she shares,

When I was a child, my father would tuck me in at night. I loved saying my prayers with him. It was a special time of quiet, just the two of us. I would go through the ritual with all the "God blesses," and then I would straighten my body for what I now realize was my father's special blessing for me. He would slowly run his two large and beautiful open hands over me on top of the covers from head to toe saying, "Grow big and tall and straight and strong." I would point my toes to be as long as possible. I see now that in doing this he was not only praying for me, but also daily giving me of his strength and righteousness. He was telling me that his strong hands would protect me and help me grow. It was what I now understand was his own sacramental rite for me. The outward and visible sign, proclaimed both tactilely and verbally, of an inward and spiritual gift of grace and power.[7]

This is the role of the youth ministry of the local church and school. To provide a concretized gift in every interaction we have, whether it is by taking them on a field trip, going to a sports activity, or teaching them how to paint a room or saw a board. This visualization of compassion provides the grist for the mill of life. It is the way grace is shared—through the practice of competent ministry to children, youth and young adults. If done well, the church will grow; if done carefully, lives will be shaped towards the Kingdom; and if not done at all, many will never find the peace that is in Jesus.

Ellen White assures us that this church will triumph.[8] She provides clear counsel to the church and to parents regarding their role in this ministry. Let's remember that the youth of this church are committed to its message and its special mission in this time in history. They need encouragement, recognition, acceptance and a part in leadership. They have energy, vision, and are prepared to "roll up their sleeves." Confidence in them will be rewarded—it is long overdue!

REFERENCES

1. Ellen G. White, *Gospel Workers* (Washington, D.C.: Review & Herald, 1948), 207-212.
2. For a complete and careful review of this research, see Eugene C. Roehikepartain, "What Makes Faith Mature," *Christian Century* (May 9, 1990), 496-499.
3. Roger L. Dudley with V. Bailey Gillespie, *Valuegenesis: Faith in the Balance* (Riverside, CA: Loma Linda University Press, 1992), 150-151.
4. Barry Gane, *Building Youth Ministry: A Foundational Guide* (Riverside, CA: Hancock Center Publications, 2000), 226.
5. Barry Gane, *Building Youth Ministry,* 128.
6. V. Bailey Gillespie, *The Experience of Faith* (Birmingham, AL: Religious Education Press, 1992), 126.
7. Ellen T. Charry, "Grow Big and Tall and Straight and Strong," from the *Princeton Theological Seminary Youth Ministry Lectures*, 25. Ms. Charry's book *Inquiring After God: Classic and Contemporary Readings* provides other stories of compassion and caring for adolescents in the local church.
8. Ellen G. White, *Selected Messages*, Vol. 2, 380.

If you want to be happy for an hour, take a nap. If you want to be happy for a day, go fishing. If you want to be happy for a month, go on a honeymoon. If you want to be happy for a year, inherit a fortune. If you want to be happy for a lifetime help other people.

— *Paul M. Steinberg*

When I send my children to an Adventist Christian school, I expect that during the course of their study they will meet Jesus as their Lord and Savior. Because the more I understand about religious experience, I recognize that religion is more than content and having a correct ideology, as important as that is in building faith's content. It involves all aspects of my children's lives. I want them to understand God with all of their minds, their bodies, and their emotions.

The religious educational enterprise is an ideal place to teach how to care about others. Service, mission, helping, sharing, caring, loving, understanding, acting, doing, and growing are all vocabulary words that identify a well-balanced Christ-centered environment.

—*V. Bailey Gillespie*

CHAPTER 11

()

SCHOOL DAYS, SCHOOL DAZE
Valuegenesis and Adventist schools

11

SCHOOL DAYS, SCHOOL DAZE
Valuegenesis and Adventist schools

Why have Adventist schools? Earlier Adventists were clear on the topic: to preach the Third Angel's Message to all the world and do the work of the church. Ellen White would sum up that ultimate educational aim as "service." But being able to serve implied training in both the intellectual and moral realm. The early Adventists were in general agreement that character development was crucial and that the common branches of study along with the arts and sciences were important, but they also believed that it was the biblical world view that provided the matrix in which Christian understanding takes place.

After attending his first day of school at Glendale Adventist Academy, my son's assessment was a welcome one. When he came home the first thing he said was, "I like my teacher!" I remember the feelings of joy and satisfaction that my wife and I had because our son's first day in school was a positive experience. Jared liked his school because he liked his teacher.

Unfortunately, not everyone feels the way Jared's parents feel. The evening television news and newspaper headlines often remind us that parents are not happy with their schools. When physical and emotional safety is not secure and academic success is questioned by the latest standardized test, parents and legislatures demand accountability.

Many Adventist parents share the same concern for accountability that the majority of public school parents have in the United States.

Are Adventist schools fulfilling their mission statements for academic achievement, spiritual commitment, social development, emotional and physical wellness? Adventist students in our schools do well when examined. Standardized achievement tests annually testify that our students' scores rank above public school national averages. These achievement scores tell us that our students are being academically challenged. But how do we assess our other goals? Are Adventist students being spiritually nurtured? And how do students assess their spiritual, social, and academic experience in Adventist schools?

These questions lie at the heart of the *Valuegenesis* surveys. As researchers, we wanted to know how our Adventist students perceived their school and their growth both academically and spiritually. Do our students believe that Adventist education is on the right track? Do they believe that they are spiritually nurtured as well as academically challenged?

KUDOS ARE IN ORDER

I believe there are many reasons to pass out kudos and rejoice as we look for the answers to these questions in the *Valuegenesis²* survey. The first question to ask is "Do Adventist students like their school?"

When asked whether they agree or disagree with the statement, "I like my school," 73% responded with an "agree" or "strongly agree." Over three-fourths, 77%, of the students in grades 11 to

12 responded in a positive manner. It is significant that three out of four students feel good about their school. What are the reasons they feel this way? Since feelings usually follow thinking and behavior, on what evidence do the students base these positive feelings about their school?

COMPETENT TEACHERS

First, students in the *Valuegenesis*[2] survey believe that their teachers are competent. When we asked students to agree or disagree with the sentence, "The teaching is good," 81% of respondents agreed or strongly agreed with the assertion. As a long-time observer of Adventist education, I agree with these students. High student achievement scores on standardized assessments is one indicator of teacher quality. Students are learning. Professional teaching credentials and master's degrees also point toward excellence in the Adventist teaching profession. Most Adventist teachers also share a common calling to a teaching ministry that indicates their belief that both God and their school board want them to lead children academically and spiritually. Whatever the reason, it is a compliment to our teachers that their students perceive them as competent—Adventist teachers know their stuff.

INTERESTED AND LISTENING TEACHERS

Secondly, students perceive their teachers to be caring. Eighty percent of the 6th through 12th graders agree with the statement that their "teachers are interested in students." In addition, 75% of the students say that their "teachers listen to what students say." These two positive responses indicate that Adventist educators seek to connect in a personal manner with their students. One current researcher states it this way: "Effective teachers care for the student first as a person, and second as a student."[1]

Today's research confirms what Ellen White stated a century ago. "The true teacher can impart to his pupils few things so valuable as the gift of his own companionship."[2] She states again that teachers should "come sufficiently into social relation" with their students.[3] She also believed that teachers should "manifest an interest in all their [students'] efforts, even in their sports" and "gain their love and win their respect."[4] Ellen White believed that this personal relationship is especially important when spiritual truths are at stake, for she counseled teachers to "win their affection, if you would impress religious truth upon their heart."[5]

RELATIONSHIPS ARE IMPORTANT

In the past, much of the teacher effectiveness research focused on various teaching methods. More research is now focusing on the social and emotional behaviors of teachers that demonstrate the importance of the relationships between them and students. Current educational research on teacher effectiveness shows that student achievement increases when teachers know their students on a personal level. Effective teachers consistently behave in a friendly and personal manner.

Relationships, friendship, companionship, connections— all those words imply that master teachers care deeply about their students as people. Teachers listen, play, and share their passions with students because they first love people and know that the pathway to their minds and hearts is through a trusting, personal relationship.[6]

My experience tells me that I learn more from a teacher I like. To this day, I remember more how I felt towards my teachers than the content they taught. I remember studying harder for teachers that showed a personal interest in me. Now as a teacher, principal and superintendent, I observe it over and over again. Students who are socially awkward or shy, academically slow, or physically challenged are "won" by caring teachers that motivated them to learn and grow.

AFFIRMED STUDENTS

A long with views that their teachers are caring and competent, Adventist students feel affirmed by their teachers. As you can see on the right, seventy-one percent of students "agree" or "agree strongly" with the statement that "when students work hard, teachers praise their efforts." Coupled with this feeling of affirmation is another finding: 39% perceive that "students often feel put down by teachers." Although 39% see "put-downs" by teachers, 61% disagree with the "put-down" characterization. Hence, a large

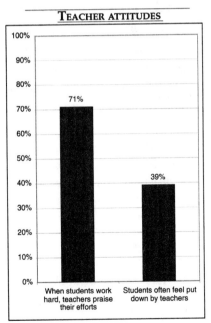

TEACHER ATTITUDES

percentage believes that teachers do not use put-downs. Findings from both these questions confirm that teachers tend to make students feel affirmed as a person and praised for their efforts.

Current educational research again supports that appropriate praise helps teach students one of the most valuable lessons they can learn –"The harder you try, the more successful you are."[7] Our survey results, then, testify that Adventist educators are perceived as caring, affirming teachers.

RELIGIOUS FAITH FACILITATED

Most important to parents and teachers is what Adventist schools do to foster spiritual faith. The findings suggest that students like their school because attending an Adventist school helps them develop their religious faith. When asked "How much has each of the following helped you develop your religious faith?" 74% responded that attending an Adventist school "very much" 36% or "somewhat" 38% helped them. Specific statements of note that positively helped them develop their faith included the following:

() *Personal devotions – 70%—29% very much, 41% somewhat*
() *Week of Prayer at school – 70%—29% very much, 41% somewhat*
() *Student Week of Prayer – 65%—27% very much, 38% somewhat*
() *Bible classes at school – 63%—22% very much, 41% somewhat*
() *Bible/Leadership Camps – 59%—25% very much, 34% somewhat*
() *My friend's faith – 57%—21% very much, 36% somewhat*
() *My teacher's faith – 53%—19% very much, 34% somewhat*

Even though we would like to see higher marks in the "very much" column, the majority of students still perceive that their teachers, friends,

Bible classes and weeks of prayer facilitate their growth in religious faith. And that is good news for Adventist education.

Associated with this perception that Adventist schools assists students in their faith development, our research also asked them about how much interest they have in eight selected topics for their additional study. We've already talked about these, but they are important enough to review. Students selected "interested" or "very interested" in learning more about the following topics:

()	*Gaining a deeper relationship with God*	81%
()	*The Bible*	67%
()	*How to talk to a friend about faith*	51%
()	*Adventism*	50%
()	*Other cultures and ethnic groups*	47%
()	*How to talk to my parents*	42%
()	*Sexuality*	28%
()	*Drugs and alcohol*	14%

Though all these topics are important, I believe it is noteworthy that topics of faith resulted in high student interest for further study. Again, interest in spiritual topics demonstrates a thirst for deeper spiritual understanding, both a sign of this generation and of youth in general as they begin to personalize their faith experience and explore for themselves their need for God.

FAIR STUDENT DISCIPLINE

Another reason why students like their school is that they perceive fairness in student discipline. Sixty-one percent of students surveyed agreed with the statement that "discipline is fair at my school." Since fairness is a value young people strongly cher-

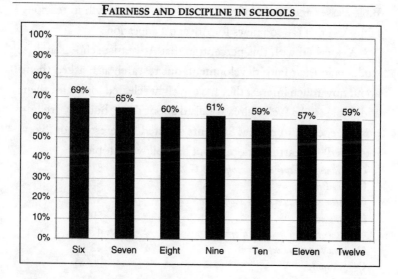

ish, it is significant that a clear majority feel fairness in how discipline is administered in their school. And as you can see by the graph above, as they progress through the grades the percentage seeing fairness in discipline changes very little. This is a good sign that schools are clear in the way they transmit their requirements. And while there will always be a group that disagrees with discipline, it is good to see that they are in the minority.

SCHOOL CLIMATE

Even though we do not know what students had in mind when 58% selected "there is real school spirit" in their school, it is another indicator that Adventist schools are appreciated by the students we serve. Experience and research tell us that a positive school climate, culture, and spirit is essential if learning is to be at its optimum. It does not take a student or visitor long to feel the warmth and acceptance that is evident when a positive school climate exists.

Valuegenesis[2] addresses school climate in a new and creative way. As Bailey Gillespie describes in Chapter 2, this new scale contrasts positive and negative feelings about school climate issues. It asks students to rate the image of the Adventist school they attended.

The results reveal that students view their school as:

() *More exciting [48%] than dull [22%] with 30% viewing their school as neitherexciting or dull.*

() *More warm [53%] than cold [16%] with 31% neutral in their perception.*

() *More organized [53%] than disorganized [18%] with 29% neutral.*

() *More flexible [46%] than rigid/stiff [23%] with 31% neutral.*

() *More growing [49%] than not growing [23%] with 28% neutral.*

() *More kind [52%] than rude [18%] with 30% neutral.*

() *More bright [57%] than dark [12%] with 31% neutral.*

() *More inclusive [46%] than exclusive [17%] with 37% neutral.*

() *More fair [45%] than unfair [25%] with 30% neutral.*

() *More open [55%] than closed [15%] with 30% neutral.*

Even though we wish that fewer students were neutral in their perceptions, we are happy to see that students were two to three times more likely to view their school as exciting, warm, organized, flexible, growing, kind, bright, inclusive, fair, and open. These are perceptions that money cannot buy. We commend the school administrators, teachers and staff for facilitating these feelings about their school. And in addition, we are happy that students see their schools in such a positive light. It is the students' perception that we, on occasion, do an excellent job, and they are perhaps our most exacting critics.

EDUCATIONAL ASPIRATIONS

An additional reason that Adventist students are excited about their school is that *their desire to learn is nurtured by their school experience.* Their educational aspirations are sky-high. In response to the question, "How far will you go in school?" 92% of students said they intend to graduate from a four-year college or higher before they finish their formal education. Sixty-one percent of the 11th and 12th graders want to receive either a master's, doctorate or post-graduate degree. It is evident that both the home and school cultures have nurtured an expectation that college is essential to success. One of the challenges in Adventist education is to advise students not only of four-year colleges, but also professional schools where many may find success and employable skills. We are proud that many Adventists graduate from a four-year college in the United States, but we are similar in percentage to the national average of 26% of the general population that graduate from a college or university.

AT-RISK BEHAVIORS

Another reason that students give for why they appreciate their school is that there is less peer pressure to participate in at-risk behaviors. Chapter 2 summarizes the research that dealt with at-risk behaviors of our students. In reviewing the results there, one finds behaviors such as alcohol use, marijuana, cocaine, fighting, shoplifting, tobacco and eating disorders are not what the majority of our young people participate in. As Gillespie points out, our research findings are much lower in these areas than any public school statistics supported by national research. Though not perfect, Adventist schools provide a climate that is more protective than what public schools provide when it comes to participating in at-risk behaviors. "Just one more very clear reason to support and promote Adventist Christian education," says Gillespie.

It seems to me that if I were going to pick one essential aspect of Adventist Christian education that places us head and shoulders above the world, it would be in the protection it provides children and youth in a world where the distractions of Satan seem to be so pervasive. Any shelter the church can provide is deeply needed and certainly appreciated.

BETTER THAN PUBLIC SCHOOLS

Another indication that students like their school is that 54% of the students perceive their school as "better than public schools." Only 23% of students disagreed with the statement. Though we can demonstrate that academic achievement and educational aspirations are higher and at-risk behaviors are lower in Adventist schools than in public schools, I prefer to describe Adventist schools as different, not better. Our goals are different, our vision for our students has a different focus and, I believe, our students arrive at school better prepared to learn, and our teachers are able to have a broader mission than our public school friends. We are different. We should be. We are proud of that. And that difference should translate into more positives for our students and clearer resolve for Adventist parents for support for our schools.

POSITIVE PERCEPTIONS

In summary, we should celebrate the positive perceptions as seen through the eyes of our students. They like their school. They believe their teachers to be competent and caring. Students feel affirmed by their teachers. They also believe that their peers and teachers are helping them develop their faith in God. A majority of students believe that discipline administered in their school is fair. They wish to continue their formal education, since 92% of them intend to graduate from a four-year college. They also see their school to be safer than public schools when it comes to their peers participating in at-risk behaviors.

STILL CHALLENGES AHEAD

It is a clear consensus that our students give high marks to their schools. But the *Valuegenesis* surveys were administered to not only see our strengths. We asked students to point out areas that also need our attention. It's important to listen to what our students say and allow their perceptions to set our agenda for church, home and school improvement.

Wanting to hear their ideas for improvement, the survey included a set of nine questions entitled "The need for change in Adventist schools." Students were given five ways of responding.

For this summary, I have collapsed "I tend to agree" and "I definitely agree" into the category "agree." "I tend to disagree" and "definitely disagree" are reported in the category "disagree." The following statements with frequency of responses are:

() *Schools need to become more modern in their thinking*
68% agree, 9% disagree and 23% are not sure

() *Schools are exciting and interesting*
39% agree, 35% disagree and 26% are not sure

() *Schools should stay just as they are*
16% agree, 59% disagree and 25% are not sure

() *Schools are turning young people off to Adventism*
32% agree, 27% disagree and 41% are not sure

() *Schools are in need of a great deal of change*
50% agree, 18% disagree and 32% are not sure

() *Schools need to put more emphasis on traditional Adventist values*
28% agree, 31% disagree and 41% are not sure

() *Schools are healthy*
55% agree, 15% disagree and 30% are not sure

() *Schools are dying*
21% agree, 43% disagree and 36% are not sure

() *Schools are helping young people accept and appreciate Adventism.*
44% agree, 20% disagree and 36% are not sure

What do these nine statements and student responses teach us? We learn for sure that change is needed. Since excellence demands continual improvement, students rightly point out that change is essential. Since improvement is essential, change is good if it comes from a desire to become better.

As adults—parents, teachers, administrators, and board members—we need to pay particular attention to the perceptions regarding Adventism. While more students agree (32%) than disagree (27%) with the statement that schools are turning young people off to Adventism, more students (44%) believe that schools are helping young people accept and appreciate Adventism than those students (20%) who disagree. Our concern should not just be on the clear positive or negative percentages, however. Our biggest concern is the high percentage of "not sure" responses. Why do a substantial number 75% either agree or are not sure (75% as well in 1990) that our schools are not a positive influence for Adventism? Should we wonder what their perception would be if we substituted the word "Christian" for "Adventism?"

As a church and school system, we need to ask ourselves some hard questions. We challenge our teachers and administrators to take the lead in discovering reasons for this perception. Most important, we need additional insights from in-depth student conversations as we address this serious concern and student indifference.

A second concern focuses on the responses to questions regarding relationships with teachers. In response to the question, "How willing are you to seek out a relationship with teachers," 55% responded that they were either unwilling or not sure whether to take the initiative in developing a relationship. Another question asked, "Generally speaking, how available are teachers at your school to talk in times of need?" Fifty-one percent said that their teachers were available, while 49% were not sure or perceived their teachers to be unavailable. A final question asked, "How willing are your teachers at your school to talk to you about sensitive issues like sex, drugs, etc." Again, 50% were not sure or perceived that their teachers were not willing to have conversations about sensitive topics.

Previous questions in our research revealed that students perceived their teachers as caring and supportive. The data from these three questions show that teachers must take a more proactive approach with many students in developing a personal friendship. Teachers, administrators and staff are also challenged to intentionally demonstrate their willingness "to be there" and to be more perceptive in realizing when a student needs to discuss sensitive topics. These student responses remind us again that students want a personal friendship with their teachers.

Finally, students want to learn more about grace. Even though our students are more grace oriented that a decade ago, 76% of our eleventh and twelfth graders agree with the statement that "Adventist schools should spend more time teaching about God's grace." We rejoice with our growth in grace, but students want to see these themes explored even more in our classrooms.

AND FINALLY

The school report card is clear. Students have graded their schools with both above average and below average marks. Commendations abound, but recommendations for improvement keep us humble and poised for change. From an educational standpoint, the *Valuegenesis* survey is the largest needs assessment that has been conducted by a private school system. What a tragedy it would be if we do not listen to what our students tell us. But after we listen, what will we do with this treasure of information? My dream is that we should be proud of our successes while making action plans for improvement. "Something better" must continue to drive us to excellence and continued improvement. Our church believes in it. Our parents demand it. And our students deserve it.

REFERENCES

1. James H. Stronge, *Qualities of Effective Teachers* (Alexandria, VA: Association for Supervision and Curriculum Development, 2002), 15.

2. Ellen G. White, *Education* (Mountain View, CA: Pacific Press Publishing Association, 1903), 212.

3. Ellen G. White, *Fundamentals of Christian Education* (Nashville, TN: Southern Publishing Association, 1923), 18.

4. Ellen G. White, *Counsels to Parents, Teachers, and Students* (Mountain View, CA: Pacific Press Publishing Association, 1913), 269.

5. Ellen G. White, *Fundamentals of Christian Education*, 68.

6. William Glasser, *The Quality School Teacher* (New York, NY: Harper Perennial, 1993).

7. Robert J. Marzano, Debra J. Pickering and Jane E. Pollock, *Classroom Instruction That Works* (Alexandria, VA: Association for Supervision and Curriculum Development, 2001), 59.

*O*ne of the most dramatic—yet perhaps least noticed—developments of the last decade has been
the explosion of interest among the United States popu-
lace in spiritual matters. The percentage of Americans
who say they would like to experience spiritual growth in
their lives has shot up to eight in ten from six in ten in
the early 1990s.

*A*mple evidence can be found to show that religion
or religious faith is broad but not deep. And the
public themselves readily attest to this. The fact is, de-
spite the relatively high figures among Americans in terms
of attested belief, many Americans have long questioned
the impact religious faith is having on individual lives
and society as a whole.

— *George Gallup, Jr.*

CHAPTER 12

( )

THE SUM OF THE MATTER
Discovering positive influences

12

THE SUM OF THE MATTER
Discovering positive influences

In our culture, adolescence is a period during which a young person undergoes physical, emotional, intellectual, social, and spiritual growth. While who they are reveals itself slowly, and often in deep, intangible ways, they are actively, moment by moment, establishing who they are not by testing the tethers which bind them to parents, teachers, and peers. It requires great energy to undertake the passage from family to worldly life; and great understanding, attention, and concern on the part of parents who must come to know their children anew.[1]

— *Sydney Lewis*

Over the past years I have been privileged to participate in hundreds of board meetings, school faculty meetings, church convocations, youth ministry meetings, youth pastors' updates, conference pastoral sessions, teacher conventions, local church presentations, international teachers training and graduate teaching, along with classroom lectures. Most have targeted this research we now know and love called *Valuegenesis*. When I first began this project, there were a number of colleagues who assisted the John Hancock Center, but over the years they have taken other jobs, become involved in their own ministries, or simply lost touch or interest in what we have discovered. The task has fallen on the Hancock Center for Youth and Family Ministry at La Sierra University and a cadre of young, enthusiastic, and committed graduate students whose lives are channeled towards professional ministry with children, youth, or young adults. I've been the happy recipient of their scholarly work and questioning minds. And over the past ten years there has been so much that has been written and explored.

One particularly interesting doctoral dissertation had to do with an evaluation of just how well the information in this research back in 1990 was implemented in the local churches, schools, and homes in the North American Division. The myriad presentations, articles and books that emerged then and are now on the drawing boards over the coming years all point to one thing: The children and youth of the church are an important resource for the church. If we lose these young people to our church, we lose much more than the numbers they represent. We lose their enthusiasm and energy that they bring to a movement now a church. We simply can't afford to overlook any information if it informs our understandings, decisions, budgets, and actions in all three venues of concern—the home, the church, and the school.

But the *Valuegenesis* research team is not so naive as to believe that they can do it all themselves or so self-centered as to believe that they alone can do it best. We know that change only happens when everyone—local church leaders, pastors, parents, teachers, administrators, and even youth—become committed to making a real difference. The research describes the qualities inherent in what young people might become; it doesn't make what we would like actually ever happen! So these last two chapters are meant to be a football play, a hand-off, so to speak. We want to pass this information on to you with a challenge to try to become what the best of what we've seen seems to be.

But first I want to share some particularly interesting information about Adventist youth. Our survey probed a number of issues that were in many ways isolated bits of information. The questions were posed because we wanted to determine the factors that influenced mature faith and deep commitment and loyalty to the church. Some of these factors proved significant. Others remain isolated bits of information. Before we draw some basic conclusions, we wanted to share these with you.

EXPERIENCE AS THE TEACHER

Not everything we do is positive. Guess what? Most parents are not perfect either. Not one of them has gone through the many years of child rearing without making some mistake or doing something wrong.

As playwright Oscar Wilde once wrote, "Experience is the name everyone gives to their mistakes."[2] Or as the circularly logical saying goes: "How do you gain experience? By making mistakes. How do you stop making mistakes? By gaining experience."[3]

While talking with young adults while I was writing a book about youth involvement in the church, I discovered that many older youth wished that their parents had taken the time to sit down and talk about their faith or their future or just spent time sharing some of the things that were important to them. This discussion was often phrased as, "I just wish they had taken the time to talk about important things." We don't want to miss the opportunity to talk about the important influences that impact the spiritual growth of children and youth.

Throughout this book we have been sharing the three venues of influence that impact on the spiritual and social growth of young people. We've implied a number of areas of concern and affirmation. It's now time to explore these influences in a more organized way.

FAMILY POSITIVE INFLUENCES

We've identified nineteen positive influences in our research that target family and home life as they relate to an intrinsic faith, faith maturity, denominational loyalty, and commitment to God. These influences can be grouped into four categories: Positive Parenting, Family Climate, Loving Constraint, and Spiritual Parenting. Let's detail each grouping, many of which are scales of a number of survey questions and not single items.

Positive Parenting. This first grouping of positive influences involves characteristics of parents that have a powerful influence in building mature faith of an intrinsic nature. For example, this theme describes mothers and fathers who are comfortable talking with their children and young people about their own faith and, in addition, are willing to spend regular time communicating with them about their lives, activities, and values. Another description is that of the level of commitment and religiosity the parents demonstrate in their homes, choices, and family lifestyle. Below are the percentage of participation in such descriptors as expressed by their children. They are listed in descending percentages and describe aspects of positive spiritual parenting.

()	Mother comfortable with faith-talk	91%
()	Father comfortable with faith-talk	81%
()	Mother is highly religious	60%
()	Father is highly religious	47%
()	Regular mother and child communication	32%
()	Father shares faith-talk (together)	29%
()	Regular father and child communication	24%

Family Climate. Nothing is more important than having a rich, loving, and caring family life. The descriptors here include: when parent-child communication is frequent and positive; when family life is experienced as loving, caring, and supportive; along with parents who frequently help their children with schoolwork. These types of homes help develop youth who are more likely to possess mature faith and loyalty to their church.

()	Loving, caring family (climate)	71%
()	Regular parent-child communication	67%
()	Parents help with homework	22%

Loving Constraint. This category describes when parents have their own strong standards and enforce them in a fair, firm, and loving way. In addition, they punish wrong behaviors and set limits on a number of issues such as time, internet use, video games, and the like. If this occurs, the young people are seen to grow in a mature faith and show loyalty and commitment to the Adventist denomination. And we've already seen that constraint is always best served in a loving, open, and affection-filled family. The effect of these areas of life are positive when experienced in the home; in fact, more so than when stressed in the schools or churches of our denomination. Parents have a real challenge here to discuss these issues in a clear and open way. You will notice, however, that there is much less enforcement for the three types of standards than there might be in the home. If done properly and with consistency, the schools and churches would not have to spend time on these issues and would be more successful when they clarify them.

() Parents set limits 65%
() Parents oppose alcohol use 86%
() Family enforces substance abuse standards ... 36%
() Family enforces popular cultural standards 28%
() Family enforces Adventist way of life 28%

Spiritual Parenting. There is no better power for change than when parents live the religion they believe. This experiential faith models both spiritual traditions and values that are so important in growing up in a world where the secular tempts and draws them away from the stability of religion. We often look back with fond memories to the traditions our parents attempted to build. "We lit candles on Sabbath." "We always prayed before opening our Christmas gifts." "We never missed the Christmas concert." "We always worked in a soup kitchen as a family." Spiritual behaviors in families are the substance of memories and the content of personal commitment. As it is said, "Boot up forty megabytes of great family memories that revolve around your spiritual life. If you do, the output could yield dividends for generations."[4] We surveyed for these concepts and recognized that when parents live their religion and lovingly discipline when wrong occurs, other positive things link. Frequent, interesting, and meaningful family worships, and family helping projects with everyone in the unit working together on something that improves life for others are also of inestimable value in modeling faith. These youth de-

FAMILY INFLUENCES	
Total 0%-25%	5%
Total 26%-50%	37%
Total 51%-75%	42%
Total 76%-100%	16%

velop a strong sense of mission and purpose along with loyalty and maturity and intrinsic faith. Here are the percentages of these descriptors of positive influence in the family.

() Parents punish wrong behavior   72%

() Interesting and meaningful family worships   65%

() Youth involved in family helping projects   60%

() Frequent family worship   48%

To gain an "overall" image, we oversimplified these nineteen positive family influences into "yes/no" categories and then looked to see how many of each of the nineteen influences students reported. 16% of the students reported "a lot" between 76% and 100% of the time. That corresponds to fifteen or more of the total of nineteen.

CHURCH POSITIVE INFLUENCES

Our research identified an additional eight positive influences in the local congregation. They follow three themes: Congregational climate influences, local ministry influences, and congregational support influences.

Congregational Climate. We identified the tone of the local congregation, whether or not it was seen as warm, open, and accepting in nature, and if it provided an open, challenging, and thought-provoking environment in which to grow towards God.

The warmth and thinking climate scales percentages are below:

() Warm congregational climate   53%
() Thinking congregational climate   23%

Local Ministry. Many of the activities of the local church fall into the rubric of ministry: Providing programs for young people that are intergenerational and involve children, youth, and young adults on a regular basis. Churches that are "user friendly" to the young are central in building an intrinsic and mature faith. Along with this is the need for programs to be thought-provoking and challenge the critical thinking skills. These draw youth into discussion about central issues that the church and its members care about and help them clarify their budding ideology and theology. Below are the positive influences in the local church and their percentages of participation.

() Programs are interesting   40%
() Programs are thought-provoking   33%
() Frequent intergenerational programming   30%

Congregational Support. Such influences as the experience of being nurtured by caring peers and adults and being exposed to Sabbath School teachers and leaders who are supportive and compassionate are crucial if maturity of faith and loyalty to the church are to be the result. The scales for these descriptors follow:

CHURCH INFLUENCES	
Total 0%-25%	50%
Total 26%-50%	22%
Total 51%-75%	16%
Total 76%-100%	11%

◯ Teachers and adult leaders supportive and caring   52%

◯ Often experience caring peers   29%

◯ Often experience caring adults   29%

Only 11% of the youth experienced "a lot" between 76 and 100 percent of these influences.

SCHOOL POSITIVE INFLUENCES

Eight positive school influences were identified. They circle around the themes of quality teaching, Adventist values, and school climate influences. Schools that participate in these and make them a central concern have significant impact on the faith maturity, intrinsic faith development, and commitment to the Adventist church. It is interesting to note that half of these issues identified in the *Valuegenesis* research for schools are just the things that make the school system so positive a spiritual influence. They indicate issues in their practice that cannot be duplicated in the public environment yet have been demonstrated to make a difference in the spiritual growth of students.

Quality Teaching. Three scales provide the information about these influences. Teachers that are seen as competent, caring, and supportive provide the best possible nurture to young people. Adventist schools are blessed with quality teachers, certified and educated. One of the evidences of the kind of support teachers provide is the fact that they don't "put down" students. This is an indication of respect. And while 49% of the students have some doubt about this, a clear 61% agree that teachers respect them.

Quality teaching provides the best environment to model the grace of God. What follows are the percentages of the school influences regarding quality teaching.

() Good, competent teachers   83%

() Caring, supportive teachers   68%

() Teachers don't put down students   61%

Adventist Values. In our chapter on standards we examined the role of the home in imparting a clear sense of values to the youth of the church. Here we see the role of the school in enforcing the standards we have identified as Adventist Way of Life Standards, unique to Adventists' core beliefs—Sabbath, modesty, purity, and health-related choices. Schools can be a clear help here as they enforce these values in their schools.

Another influence is the regular contact in faith-talk with teachers that students in Adventist education can experience. This is part of the Adventist mission. And since many baptisms are directly related to schools, the role of teachers in commitment to Jesus cannot be overstressed.

() Enforces Adventist Way of Life Standards   64%

() Students talk to teachers about faith   59%

School Climate Influences. Couple these concerns with the climate influences in schools that care about school spirit and involvement in school decisions where appropriate, and you have a positive Christian influence for your children that only Adventist education can provide. And while popular cultural standards and substance abuse are not as successfully enforced in this venue, the way that discipline is administered is crucial here. Discipline must be seen as fair and reflect God's attitude of grace. This is not a plea for permissive decisions; rather, it is a clear call for careful review of the discipline policies in Adventist schools to ensure that it is always provided in a fair and equal way. Here are the percentages for the positive school influences.

() Discipline is fair   61%
() School spirit is high   58%
() Students have a voice in school policy   39%

A total of 25% of the students experience "a lot" of these influences while only 39% experience less than half. While the schools scored the best as to participation in these influences, there is still a long way to go as we continue to make the home, church, and school models of the King-dom of God and its members representatives of love and grace.

SCHOOL INFLUENCES	
Total 0%-25%	14%
Total 26%-50%	25%
Total 51%-75%	36%
Total 76%-100%	25%

THE FAMILY OF GOD

Each of the venues we have explored make up a part of the whole family system of Adventism. Adventism, as do most religions, offers "guidelines about how family members should treat one another that cut across nuclear and extended family relation-ships and structures. In fact, most religions direct family members to care for each other with dignity and respect, make sacrifices for one another, and forgive one another for wrongdoings."[5] In short, they are to behave as Christians in spite of a world that seldom, if ever, acts that way.

This research is intended to provide insight into all of the systems of relationships that frame the faith life of children, youth, and young adults. It is best intended to provide a portrait of what seems to be working and what we might do to help young people function at their best in their homes, churches, and schools. And a benefit of this research is to provide for the leaders, parents, teachers, adults, pastors, and youth professionals some challenges for change in those same venues. It is not a formula for change, but rather provides touch points that can help form the decisions regarding ministry, administration, and home life.

ETHNIC RESPONSES

It would not be appropriate to ignore the unique makeup of the constituencies in our research. For example, there are a number of other ethnicities represented in the research data sets. One percent of the sample respondents were Asian or Pacific Islanders. Twenty-eight percent represented the African American community, while 22% claimed Latino or Hispanic identification. And while 15% had multiple ethnic backgrounds, by far the largest groups represented were the Hispanic and African American communities. What do these unique communities contribute to our knowledge about how young people develop an intrinsic and mature faith and build denominational loyalty? All in all, the data of the total North American Division is representative of each of the ethnic communities. In fact, it is safe to say that for the most part, Adventist young people here in the United States are a lot alike. Where respondents, in contrast to the North American Division average, which stood at 72%. Almost six to seven out of every ten of our youth represented in the study came from warm, loving homes in all ethnic categories. It is also important to keep in mind possible cultural differences in the expression of parental love which might also influence such statistics.

Faith Maturity. When we look closely at the faith maturity scores of the ethnic communities represented in our census you can see that the scores do not vary from the North American Division statistics. Faith maturity continues around the 45% mark, while the Hispanic group represented the lowest percentage at 40%. All of these percentages are well above the 1990 values.

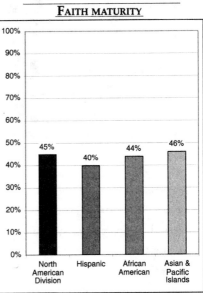

FAITH MATURITY

Family standard enforcement. You will remember we contrasted the enforcement of Adventist standards in the home with that of the school enforcement. When you extract the ethnic communities we have been discussing, we see a distinct difference. Using a two-level approach between "Less strict," and "Strict," in each of the standards types, the percentages are below for "Strict" in each of the groups in this discussion. (See the chart on the next page).

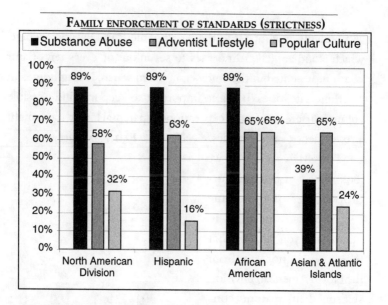

FAMILY ENFORCEMENT OF STANDARDS (STRICTNESS)

■ Substance Abuse ▦ Adventist Lifestyle ▢ Popular Culture

Values. Many of the youth of our study, because of their age, would fit into a time of personalization of faith. This is a time when building a personal faith (personalization of faith) becomes important. It is a time when young people build a sense of freedom through learning to respond to meaningful information and begin to make personal choices.[6] It is during this time that the young person begins to understand the symbols of faith that emerge to help provide daily realities in the realm of ideals, values, and truths that the budding faith life is experiencing. During this crucial time the young person is becoming involved in the community, participating in family and community life, and building realistic models of what the Kingdom of God is like. These values permeate their lives and exploring these values provides us an idea as to what is central in their growing value system. Below are the percentages of our young people who scored four or higher on five-point scales, measuring various values.

Value	NAD	Hispanic	African American	Asian/Pacific Islands
Service	67% (56%)*	70%	68%	70%
Materialism	27% (47%)	36%	43%	31%
Altruism	59% (51%)	55%	56%	63%
Love Scale	96% (85%)	95%	96%	94%
Works Scale	19% (36%)	29%	30%	21%

A typical "works" item would involve disagreeing with the statement "there is nothing I can do to earn salvation." The "love" items are "I am loved by God even when I sin," and "I know God loves me no matter what I do." And a typical "service" value item is "How important for you is the goal of helping people who are poor or hungry?"

When you look specifically at the Altruism measure, it concerns the number of hours in a typical month the student helps those less fortunate, helps friends and neighbors, promotes social equality, and is involved in community affairs.

Standards. We compared the four ethnic groups when we asked, "How often, if ever, did you do each of the following during the last year." The response format ranged from "never," "less than once a month," to "more than once a day" in eight steps. The questions dealt directly with behaviors that might put the young people at risk and would probably place them at the periphery of most of the church. The second lowest frequency (after "never") was "less than once a month." We considered this to be what we have labeled "experimental behaviors" and not regular use. All other categories depict a regular usage—from "About once a month" to "More than

*The *Valuegenesis[1]* study percentages are in parenthesis

once a day." The two lists below provide these two groups of answers listed under "regular" and "experimental" usage.

REGULAR AT-RISK BEHAVIORS

At-risk Practice	NAD	Hispanic	African- American	Asian/ Pacific Islands
Smoke tobacco	7% (6%)	5%	6%	6%
Wear jewelry	52% (36%)	45%	42%	51%
Listen to "hard" rock music	53% (83%)	46%	19%	44%
Attend movies	60% (47%)	59%	51%	60%
Club dancing	6% (NA)	10%	11%	10%
Play violent video games	42% (NA)	34%	47%	49%
Attend party where alcohol is served	14% (NA)	21%	16%	16%
Ever had intercourse (2 or more)	8% (13%)	11%	13%	9%

EXPERIMENTAL AT-RISK BEHAVIORS

	NAD	Hispanic	African- American	Asian/ Pacific Islands
Smoke tobacco	6% (5%)	7%	6%	5%
Wear jewelry	16% (16%)	16%	20%	18%
Listen to "hard" rock music	12% (6%)	11%	8%	17%
Attend movies	27% (26%)	24%	26%	27%
Club dancing	10% (NA)	11%	11%	10%
Play violent video games	22% (NA)	20%	21%	24%
Attend party where alcohol is served	18% (NA)	23%	21%	20%
Ever had intercourse (1x/yr)	4% (4%)	5%	5%	2%

The ethnic sample is, you will remember, a significant part of the census size, so the results are important. A close look at family life, church climate, programming and support and involvement in the local church may be very different according to the cultural traditions and priorities of local churches in these particular groups. Two reports deal with this topic in detail and have been published by the Hancock Center.[7] The number of at-risk behaviors for each group provides another interesting insight

L ooking back is a proleptic activity. In reality, looking back always points us somewhere else. Looking back is problematic, and more than likely it is an exercise in frustration and depression. The early research on Adventist young people brought us to understand that we needed to work on a number of issues and practices in the local church and in families. It encouraged us to recommit to solid, quality Christian education, and it pointed us to the beginnings of change in the church.

Institutions like churches often face important moments of truth. They travel through periods of history that challenge their very survival, redefine their values, make them stronger or do them lasting damage, and, at best, propel them into the future. Some of the time they move in new, uncharted waters. The directions are often unknown, and at other times they march down very clear and predictable paths. And if the church is important to us, if its history and values, mission and power are somehow linked to our own, then we play a kind of role in its crisis too. And it is said that we become an actor on the stage, yet simultaneously a critic in the front row. Because change inevitably invites action, we are the arms and legs of the institution.

And whenever we talk about change, we talk about an illusive creature—as Glenn Frankel shares in his insightful book about Jews and Arabs entitled, *Beyond the Promised Land.* Change, he says, "darts from hole to hole, seldom pausing long enough to allow a clear sighting, its presence and impact often concealed beneath the familiar surface of the old."[8] And because of this we are at times surprised when it surfaces in its own form.

The challenge of change is to make something new that is built on the values of the old, to take a long look at what is at the core of our lives and churches, and to do something better and more Christlike, clearer and more refreshing and vibrant. We can't run from the future, so let's get specific now about change and what we need to do to make a difference.

REFERENCES

1. Sydney Lewis, *A Totally Alien Life-Form—Teenagers* (New York, NY: The New Press, 1996), 17.

2. Quotation is from Oscar Wilde (1854 - 1900), Lady Windermere's Fan, 1892, Act III.

3. Greg Johnson, Mike Yorkey, *Faithful Parents, Faithful Kids* (Wheaton, IL: Tyndale, 1993), 75.

4. Greg Johnson, Mike Yorkey, *Faithful Parents, Faithful Kids,* 8.

5. Annette Mahoney, Kenneth I. Pargament, Aaron Murray-Swank, Nichole Murray-Swank, "Religion and the Sanctification of Family Relationships," *Review of Religious Research* (Vol. 44, No. 3., March 2003), 224.

6. V. Bailey Gillespie, *The Experience of Faith* (Birmingham, AL: Religious Education Press, 1988),125-130.

7. If you are interested in the data from these particular groups, please contact the John Hancock Center for Youth and Family Ministry at La Sierra University. Our e-mail address is: (hcyfm@lasierra.edu). The reports you want to request are: Hispanic Research Report by Dr. Edwin Hernandez, African-American Research Report edited by Dr. Ella Simmons, and the Asian/Pacific Island report by Dr. Won Kil Yoon, all on the research team of the *Valuegenesis²* project.

8. Gary L. Chamberlain, *Fostering Faith: A Minister's Guide to Faith Development* (New York, NY: Paulist Press, 1988), 32.

It was there, massaged by the Mediterranean breeze, that my head started to clear and I finally gave birth to the thought that had been bothering me most: "What kind of world are my two girls going to grow up in?" And it was there that I first completed the sentence: "Regrettably, ladies and gentlemen. . .egrettably, ladies and gentlemen, my girls and yours will not grow up in the same world that we did. History just took a right turn into a blind alley and something very dear has just been taken away from us."

— *Thomas L. Friedman (September 11, 2001)*

CHAPTER 13

()

STARSHIP BEYOND
The way to the future

13

STARSHIP BEYOND
The way to the future

Through these later stages of adolescent development there is a growing realization that the expereinces of life, both painful and joyful, are encounters in which the Lord speaks in a special way to each person. The road yet to be traveled by youths is one which challenges them to identify the special-personal relationship to which God calls. . .It is the role of the youth minister to encourage adolescents, late in their development, to step back from their eager search for careers, for friends, for answers to question of marital and vocatonal future, so as to pause and quiet the search and become faithful listeners. Adolescents may need help in learning how to quiet their busy days, their harried searches, in order to be open to the unique "life call" which is theirs.

— Richard Parsons

When I was much younger, I loved everything about space. On Saturdays, before I became an Adventist, I would go to the movies. I would wait in line with my friends for the weekly serial. Fascinated by the future, the movie hero, Flash Gordon, would always end with each segment a cliff-hanger. He could solve the problems of the world in one brief half hour every single week, right on schedule. I would watch his space ship, wire suspended, match burning engines, smoke trailing, ready to visit outer space. "Wow, starship beyond," I knew.

When I got older and became a church member, I realized that those movies were, in essence, a microcosm of the world. And when I finally learned about the Great Controversy story, I understood that the macrocosm of the battle between good and evil was really only resolved by the good grace of God through Christ. I realized that the problems of this world were negated only through the actions of God, and that there never would be enough time for Flash Gordon to solve anything at all. That hero was good, but not really that great. If problems needed fixing, I would have to make some choices. Good change would only happen if I implemented God's plan in my life and made my own choices to follow Him. Change in general happens anyway, but good change is an intentional activity. God proved that by His coming and will guarantee it again at His next appearance. And even if we sit still and do nothing, that change will happen.

CHANGE, REAL CHANGE

But of course, the real crunch comes when you try to make *good change* occur. Change that makes life better. Change that doesn't go away. Change that lasts. Change that survives. Change that is maintained. Change that perdures. This book, after all, is about change, good change, made by combining the gifts of God's presence with the energy of stable parenting, quality schools and relevant spiritual life, mixed with a blend of interesting and meaningful worship and clear, messaged Adventism in our homes, schools and churches.

Long before *Valuegenesis* research began in the 1990s, we had decades of excellent research studies that identified which change strategies might work and which would probably fail. We have all seen the folly of bandwagons, reactions, and technological panaceas, and we should have learned by now about making change that persists. All too often, we haven't.

BEEN THERE, DONE THAT

S adly, much of the research on making good change has been widely ignored during the current rush to get on with the "real" work or to install the best evangelistic technology, or build new buildings rather than focusing on the people and attitudes and procedures where change can happen best, and when done, makes a difference in the lives of everyone. We've often ignored the concept of Christian nurture. And while bringing new people into the fold is a biblical command, caring for the sheep is equally central for the church. Here is a fictitious story that illustrates this very point

The superintendent and board chair are wandering the halls of Millennium Elementary School with the principal. They are looking for signs that their investment in computer network technology has paid off. In September, each classroom was equipped with three computers tied to the main frame. Millennium is a wired school.

"And you say the teachers were expecting us?" The superintendent queries, disbelief creeping into her tone. The principal had been around long enough to recognize more than disbelief in her voice.

"I told them not to launch anything out of the ordinary. I said that you would want to see a typical Wednesday afternoon."

The superintendent stops walking and turns to face him directly.

"But, Don. . .We have walked into more than a dozen classrooms so far without seeing significant use. In two of the classrooms, we saw students

doing drill and practice. In one room, we saw several students typing final drafts of papers from their handwritten work. In the other classrooms, we saw business as usual without anyone sitting near a computer. We saw no one using the Internet."

The board president, a tall women who usually wears a broad smile, is now frowning.

"Yes, Don. I have to add my own sense of disappointment. I expected to see more powerful things by now. After all, it is March. They have had the computers for seven months. Why isn't anybody using the Internet?"

Then the principal adds, "After all, we've been doing just fine, our scores are still pretty good, teaching is the best it has ever been. We don't want to do anything, I guess, that will undermine that performance."

The board president sighs and says, "You know, change doesn't happen in a school simply because you install new equipment." She continues thinking, disappointed, her tone quite serious now.[2]

Change doesn't happen anywhere simply because you upgrade equipment, grab onto the best technology, recommend the great books, do research projects, write this book, or just think about making change. Good change happens when we remember the past and begin to act on it for change. Wasn't it George Santayana who said, "Those who do not learn from the past are condemned to repeat it." Good change happens when we actually build on that foundation and stretch every institution, implement the baby steps to make something happen, and just get gutsy doing what we should to make something change.

Merton Strommen, religious educator and researcher who assisted us with the first *Valuegenesis* study, shares how change happens in his book, *Innovation in the Church.* His research-based approach, which was honed early on with the Adventist church, analyzes the need for change in congregations and shows why change is difficult. He offers a practical seven-step strategy for innovation. He calls it the *FUTURES* approach. And he says we all need to use it if we want something to happen. He says:

F = Free people to participate

U = Unite around needs

T = Tie in to mission and values

U = Use input of legitimizers

R = Rally broad ownership

E = Engage in action

S = Sustain the innovation long-term[3]

In his work he included inspiring stories of congregations that have managed change well and exercises that help congregational leaders clarify their vision, form task forces for change, overcome resistances, and develop a broad base of support. His book moves always towards action. That is his key for change.

RENEWING HOME, CHURCH, AND SCHOOL

Taking our cue from Strommen's work, much of what we have discovered this time in *Valuegenesis²* can be grouped around five main themes. Each of the themes can be identified with the first letter of these tasks too. If we would become involved in these issues, we would find ourselves beginning to move towards good change in our homes, schools, and churches. These themes provide us with a summary of just what we need to do to make a difference and begin the change process. For the sake of convenience and as a memory aid, let's group these under the heading of ways to *RENEW* our church based on the *Valuegenesis* research data sets.

R = Reunite with mission and message

E = Empower and involve

N = Nurture and sustain

E = Enrich relationships

W = Welcome innovation and change

Each of these statements summarizes a key research finding in *Valuegenesis*[2] and opens up discussion about what we might do to encourage change based on clear research.

R — REUNITE WITH MISSION AND MESSAGE

When we talk of the recommendations which target reuniting with our mission and unique message, we refer to a new appreciation of Adventism. The more conscious and central this understanding is in the minds of young people of the church, the

REUNITE WITH MISSION AND MESSAGE

more mature their faith becomes and the more committed to the church they grow. This theme can be divided into a number of significant concerns: Adventist identity; grace, love and works; and lifestyle choices.

While there are many, many recommendations that can be drawn from the data sets reviewed in this book, the following seem to us to both summarize and point out the most significant changes that can build a rich and growing religious experience, along with deep loyalty to the church. Here are the suggestions that we believe are central to making relevant change in the home, church, and school. Some of these suggestions are directed directly to specific venues; others are equally as relevant in all of the areas where we nurture our young people.

Refocusing Adventist identity

1. *Revision the Adventist church for family action and values, school mission and purpose, and church involvement and beliefs.* When we do this, we make the church relevant to each new generation. Doing so will both refocus what is central in each venue and clarify what is important to the young of the church.

2. *Find ways for the church to interpret its beliefs into relevant actions.* When we do this, youth will be changed because of the modeling and mentoring of parents, adults, and teachers in the church, and by becoming participants, they will build their own ideology that includes an understanding of the purpose and mission of Adventism. They will personalize their faith.

3. *Help young people with their witness to Christ and sort out their own reasons to be an Adventist in the midst of the Christian world through dialogue and critical skills.* Our unique contribution to holistic theology is central to both our identity with the Christian church in general and Adventism specifically. Framing this discussion in an intentional way brings positive results.

4. *Stress the unique Seventh-day Adventist beliefs with clear biblical explanations and relevant applications.* If we don't, young people won't understand those truths central to Adventist identity. That means

we must focus on the three least believed doctrines in Adventism —the doctrine of the remnant, Ellen G. White's unique role in Adventism, and the belief about the function of the heavenly sanctuary. Doing this will bring these doctrines into this new century and help them remain central for Adventist identity. If we fail here, this unique aspect of Adventist belief will perhaps disappear over the coming decades.

In the area of grace, love, and works

5. *Determine whether a grace-orientation is central and growing among our youth and in our church.* If so, it will permeate both our understanding about God's actions in the world and direct our methods of approach to parenting, school discipline, personal relationships, and the image of the church in the world. We will be biblically correct and have a reason to both believe and act in faith as we watch our lives change and grow. Our work teaching about God's grace is far from finished among this generation even though we have seen more general acceptance and understanding of God's actions in Christ for us.

6. *Continue to make central God's love and grace in all of our actions, institutions, and beliefs.* Through this focus we learn how to model and instruct young people to understand this crucial theological concept central to Adventist belief.

7. *Help young people to place their "works" (actions and choices) in proper perspective in constructing their personal theology.* This issue is always to be understood and taught as a response to God, an act of worship, never as a means of securing God's favor by actions and personal merit. This continues to be a critical misunder-

standing among Adventist young people.

Regarding lifestyle choices

8. *Reevaluate the three types of standards—Adventist Lifestyle, Substance Abuse, and Popular Cultural standards—with a view to understanding the values they express and the reasonableness of the logic which affirms them.* This is another call to look closely at the values and biblical reasons why we elect to do what we do and moves us to make personal commitment to make life-affirming choices and never to make life-denying ones.

9. *With a view to enforcement of Popular Cultural Standards in Adventism, we must strive for relevance and consistency in application, targeting the family as the proper place for these to be discerned and looking for creative ways to explain these contemporary choices to young people.* This research provides a clear challenge to parents especially as they instruct their young people in what is expected of them and what the family understands as important behaviors rather then looking solely to the school and church to do their job.

E — EMPOWER AND INVOLVE

We discovered the importance of involvement and handing over the faith to our children in our discussion of families and prosocial behavior and the family's importance and centrality in building a mature and intrinsic faith. While this is especially important in the teen years, we noticed that the transition between 8th and 10th grades

EMPOWER AND INVOLVE

to be a particularly troubling and trying time for young people. Of course, this is due to the powerful identity-forming aspects of life itself during these years. And because of this, empowering young people to believe and understand the reasons for that belief are important aspects of the faithing experience. Worship, service, and involvement provide the themes of this aspect of our research. So, what should we do?

Regarding worship

10. *Encourage meaningful and engaging family worship.* This is almost the same recommendation we made ten years ago, but little change occurred since. We can't stress enough the power of family involvement in religion as a means of fostering a life of faith in our young people. We hope we won't have to emphasize this again ten years from now.

11. *Help the church meet the worship needs of the young people in the congregation.* We can do this in many creative ways. Reevaluate the music style used in reaching young people, select relevant worship content, initiate regular ministry and exciting programming, along with an exploration into the practical implications of Adventist beliefs. Remember two sets of concepts. One is relevance, relevance, relevance. It is just as important for this generation as relationships, relationships, relationships.

12. *Encourage and provide help for young people in building a regular personal devotional life, rich in prayer, Bible reading, devotional practice, and family and personal worship.* Personal piety is crucial, according to our research, and young people need to be shown how to build a personal spiritual life. Show them how to have mean-

ingful Bible study with the use of inspirational materials, Christian music, and community service involvement. Use Ellen G. White to open up new concepts and discussions rather than to close them. Model and mentor your own spirituality as parents and adult church leaders. Be obvious and intentional about your own spirituality—pray out loud, have regular worships, care for others, mentor someone in need. Doing all those things with youth is best.

Encouraging involvement

13. *Provide regular congregational spiritual parenting seminars, and exciting and life-challenging programming.* Use all of the departments in the local church and conference and help them see how their speciality can include young people in their ministries. Practice involving children, youth, and young adults in the active life of the church and school, giving real responsibility when appropriate and encouraging personal involvement in social issues and church mission

14. *Identify the ways in which your young people can participate in the faith life of the religious education institution, family worship activities, and local congregational ministry and mission.* This involvement encourages exciting ministry which increases faith development, intrinsic faith life, and loyalty to the church.

15. *Don't neglect a strong pre-teen, youth, Pathfinders, youth, and young adult ministry through programming in schools and congregations.* These ministries create positive attitudes towards the church and religion in general and help to internalize Adventist identity. No church in the North American Division should be with-

out these targeted ministries. And not only should they exist, they should flourish through clear leadership, training, and exciting programming.

Empowering Service

16. *Provide an active ministry which includes children, families, youth, and young adults in service and community involvement to a greater extent.* These types of compassionate involvement empower young people to see the relevance and importance of religion in their lives. And adults who model this behavior share the meaningfulness of participation in community service. Doing is always more powerful than just thinking about doing.

17. *Involve youth in creative, up-to-date, mission-oriented activities and altruistic involvement in their church, school, family, and community.* Get your young people involved in short-term missions, local projects, home-based mission projects, and school helping tasks. All of these activities are important ways to encourage altruistic values.

N — NURTURE AND SUSTAIN

Nothing is more important than maintaining a relationship with God. There are a number of things that can be done which the research supports that make growth in faith a priority. Nurturing others is one of the ways people learn about God.

My wife has an herb garden. Judy spends as much time as possible grooming the garden, and Mother's Day is always a gardening day. My gift to her is a whole day of work. But if the garden could be planted in a day, it certainly can't be nurtured in one. My wife's daily visits to her plants helps them grow strong and tall, full and colorful. Nurture and sustenance go hand in hand. So as we reviewed the data and its findings, we recognized that we could not leave out this essential concern for schools, churches, and families. Here is what we suggest. The themes here are *nurture, modeling the Kingdom*, and *climate control.*

NURTURE AND SUSTAIN

Nurture

18. *Increase the time parents, teachers, pastors, and adult leaders talk to young people about their own faith.* When this happens, we encourage young people to begin to tell their own story about God in their lives, to share their commitment and love of God, and to model faith-talk.

19. *Create materials for those in the significant transition years between the 8th and 10th grade.* By building and providing this unique targeted ministry for this crucial time in your local congregation, you will help to reduce the negative effects that are so widespread in young people during this transition. Changing their attitudes will impact those that have not yet made clear decisions for God and the Adventist church.

20. *Nurture spiritual parents who see their lives as important in focusing and modeling the Kingdom of God.* While it is true that working with the children of the church builds long-term loyalty and commitment, a commitment best learned in the home, the church's responsibility to assist parents to build their own

spiritual life is important too. Churches that have never had parenting classes that stress spirituality in the home, and schools that have not seen it their responsibility to share these concepts with the parents of their students have neglected to nuture crucial aspect of spiritual growth in the homes of their members and constituency.[4]

Modeling the Kingdom

21. *Help teachers in the school to replicate the attitudes of the Kingdom of God and the power of guaranteeing the faith of young people.* This is best done in their classrooms by their involvement and personal behaviors, their focus on faith development issues of their students, and by increasing school spirit and altruistic involvement through community service. And, of course, don't forget exciting programming for spiritual growth and involved action-packed activities that illustrate God's grace and love.

22. *Stretch the curriculum to include a rich balance of materials that explore one's relationship with God and the world.* Being relevant is again the goal. Always include "response aims" in all of the lesson planning in every area of learning. Knowing the content is only part of the job of education; remember that the whole person includes the spiritual side, and specific intentional ministry must be initiated.

Loving, caring climate

23. *An imperative for homes, schools, and churches is to change cold and unaccepting climates into warm and reinforcing ones by constant evaluation of those points where the home, congregation, and school and young people intersect.* And likewise, student-teacher, teacher-admin-

istration, administration-student, teacher/administrator-parent relationships must be open, accepting, grace-oriented, caring, and redemptive if students are to see the loving Jesus in the actions of those that are in charge of them during their growing years.

E = ENRICH RELATIONSHIPS

The last of our review topics, but certainly not the last of the insights this research brings, is that of the relationships between all of the entities and individuals we studied. People are ultimately the most important area of growth. Building a personal faith is central to building loyalty and commitment. So it is both logical and clear from the research that we bring again to the front those issues that are all about people and their relationships. Making a difference here can make all of the difference in the long run when we talk of the enduring power of the Gospel and Christian parenting. Let's try to initiate the following changes in the home, church, and school. The areas to be targeted include *personal relationships* and *environmental relationships*.

Personal Relationships

24. *Stress building a close, personal relationship with Christ first, then explore doctrinal meaning and its implications in practice.* Encourage personal devotions, Bible reading, and involvement with religious

ENRICH RELATIONSHIPS

media—music, film, discussions, etc., but always with a view towards making Jesus first in your young person's life. Discussions about standards, doctrines, and behaviors should always be a result of this primary commitment.

We've talked a lot about building a personal faith experience. Building a relationship with God is an important developmental task for young people, especially those in their teens. Encouraging these personal aspects of religious life cannot help but aid in faith maturity and intrinsic faith experience. When the church takes seriously the task of providing situations where faith can be seen as personal, the ministry to adolescents in the church may take on a new sense of urgency and relevance. "It will do so because the experience of God has become personal and the choice to follow God's call has been personally experienced."[5]

Environmental relationships

25. *Rethink the climate issues in churches and schools to ensure an accepting, open, and warm environment in all areas of student contact, discipline, and learning.* Attitudes about relationships are communicated through the environments we build and the climates and attitudes that are perceived by young people. Why would anyone want to become a member of any church or a student in any school that seemed to be gruff, critical, nonsupportive, or angry. It would be wise to institute some kind of climate control in each venue. One could regularly evaluate the openness to new ideas and critical thinking skills that were at work here. The church could spend time seeing

just how user-friendly their church was to visitors, teens, and young adults. All these types of changes make a clear difference when it comes to perceptions. And remember, "perceptions are the rule" for young people. They govern their responses. And if the climate issues are negative in this perception, then the message of the good news of the Kingdom of God is never modeled and good change does not happen.

26. *Reevaluate the climate in the home as to its representation of the Kingdom of God.* Those who care about this in the home could spend time working on building friendly relationships, governing the language and anger that is often found in family relationships. After all building a model of the Kingdom is the first of all the tasks of the home. The New Testament shares this concern in Ephesians 5:22-6:4 where counsel is provided for fathers, mothers, and children as to their role in representing Christ to the world.

27. *Work with churches who are not friendly to young people to find ways to involve, empower, and accept youth.* Finally, something must be shared about the perceptions of the Adventist church by the students of our study. All too often the picture of the church is a negative one. Not all, of course, feel this way, but if any do, then we must deal with this challenge. Evaluate the points of contact a local congregation has with children, pre-teens, youth, and young adults. Build positive relationships through analysis of the acceptance of young people in your church. Usually we see a rather complete ministry at the children's level, with some decrease of ministry as the child moves through the

pre-teen age and then to a small degree, as we have seen, we have some youth ministry. But building a balanced ministry to ALL the young people is our target.

W — Welcome Innovation and Change

Welcome home. One of the primary biblical concepts of Adventism is that of conversion. The biblical use of this term is all about coming home—returning. It is the Great Controversy theme in verity. The whole purpose of our living for Christ is to eventually return to become the people of God. The story of Enoch is a beautiful one in the Old Testament. Here is a picture of a believer who walks with God. I picture this as if Enoch and God were so close that one day God said, "Don't go back to the world. Just keep walking with me." And so together they left this earth to spend eternity together. Enoch had gone home.

Is your church and school a place where people feel at home? A place where innovation is central and people are so comfortable with it that it is their nature to encourage it and initiate it? Welcoming innovation and change is about being comfortable with it, not threatened by it, but seeing it as an opportunity to do something right. It's about making the old new again. There is central issue in

this area of concern—*creating Kingdom environments.* Some research findings suggest these innovative welcoming activities.

28. *Schools must encourage the value of critical thinking.* Teachers need to assist students in developing the skills necessary to think by using evaluation, logic, and choosing wisely after reviewing sound evidence. These skills will go a long way to building a good thinking climate in the schools and increasing the understanding of Adventism. Pastors, youth leaders, youth ministry professionals can only be benefited those who come from families, schools, and churches who spend time working on critical thinking as a Christian skill.

The beliefs students hold will be personalized more clearly and the concomitant commitment will build loyalty and clarity regarding difficult Scriptural passages as well as go a long way in helping young people develop the basis for their witness. Parents will benefit too. When they spend the time needed to clarify the families values and standards, help their young people choose wisely regarding popular cultural standards, and open dialogue in a clear, nonthreatening fashion, everyone benefits.

29. *Students must become more involved helping the school make necessary changes.* Ownership always increases loyalty to the church and commitment to Adventism. As involvement in change becomes a way of life for students, they often become more interested in the school, and thus, school spirit grows. All in all, this process of involved change makes for a community that begins to care about each other.

30. *Faculty must be seen as open and accessible, interested in the deepest*

problems of their students, and willing to initiate dialogue and faith-talk in order to increase the intrinsic quality of the student's religious life. This attitude change is crucial if the school is to be seen as a place where caring, grace, and constraint are equally provided. Parents can use the same model in building a Christian home. As faculty are available to their students and begin a regular time for faith-talk and discussion about religion and sharing of their own personal experience with God, the young people become more interested in the other members of the school family. The returns for the home and the church are great also when this attitude is in evidence in the home.

31. *Everyone—faculty, school board members, pastors and local congregational leaders, church board members, mothers, fathers, family members—everyone could evaluate both the warmth and thinking character of the climates they create, their grace-orientation and attitudes, and their own support for Christian standards to see if those who come into their purview see God's love permeating the relationships and environment.* This, along with clear biblical guidelines for discipline and service opportunities will begin to provide the basis for mature faith and intrinsic religious life. In short, doing what we know is best does work.

These recommendations will move us toward renewing the home, church, and school, we believe.

THE POWER OF HOME, CHURCH, AND SCHOOL

We cannot stress enough the accumulative power of the three venues that have been highlighted in this book.

The home—loving, caring, full of affection and grace, disciplined with reasoned constraint, and committed to the Adventist way of life and ready to talk about faith, as well as model clear popular cultural standards.

The church—an involved and nurturing place where grace dwells in all of the attitudes of adult leaders and the openness of members in general, filled with faith-talk, ready to be warm and to build a place where issues can be discussed clearly and with logical and critical expertise, a true model of the Kingdom of God.

The Adventist school—a safe place to grow, open about faith and the reasons to believe, ready to guarantee the heritage of Adventism, clearly a place of love and warmth, with programming and school spirit and involvement that stretches youth to become what they can become.

Ten years ago Roger Dudley concluded that the three venues above were key to building a rich and growing faith as well as loyalty to the church. We wanted to see if things had changed, and if so, how much. Well, they have.

We used some of the scales discussed in this book. We built a measure of positive influences for each of the three locales and decided that an effective environment is one that combines support and warmth, along with a high quality of religious heritage. Each of these issues were treated as "yes/no" variables. A student had to report a 'yes" for all three for that environment to be considered supportive: Here are the questions we used to determine the scales used in this report.

EFFECTIVE ENVIRONMENT SCALE

() *Family support*—Parents often helped with homework.
() *Family caring*—A loving, caring family based on scoring "High" on the Family Climate Scale reported on in this book.
() *Family religious education*—Family worship interesting, meaningful, and family worship rated as both.

() *Church support*—Adult leaders are seen as caring and supportive.
() *Church caring*—There is a warm climate with scores marked as "High" on the Warmth Scale.
() *Church religious education*—Programs at church are thought-provoking with ratings on this statement as "True" or "Very true."

() *School support*—Students "agree" or "strongly agree" that teachers don't put them down while in class.
() *School caring*—There are caring, supportive teachers with ratings as "Agree" or "Strongly agree."
() *School religious education*—Students talk to their teachers about faith "Often" or "Sometimes."

The number of students that can claim an effective and supportive environment are shown in the next graph on the following page. It is most interesting to see that in the high school some 54% of the students do not experience any significant supportive environments. While this number is lower for those in the 6th to the 8th grades, it is disappointing to see such a high percentage here.

While these numbers are disappointing, the flip side of this discussion is very important. Ten years ago to see how many environments young people actually participated in we only looked at the sum of the effective environments using concepts such as support, caring, and religious education. This time we wanted a more detailed portrait. So for example, when we look simply at faith maturity, students with no exposure to supportive environments, only 35% reach a high faith maturity. With one environment, say the home, church, or school, that number increases to 55%; with two supportive environments, the percentage is 69%; and with three, it jumps to 75% of the students who would develop a mature faith.

The integration of the three environments is important for denominational loyalty too. For example, with no environments, our research shows that the possibility exists that only 48% will develop loyalty to the Adventist church. That is an impressive number with no significant support; however, when that is increased by only one rich environment the probability of loyalty jumps to 64%; with two environments it increases significantly to 82%; and with involvement with three, some 88% will develop loyalty to the Adventist church.

Let's look more closely at this data. We wondered what exposure to effective environments would have on the possibility of staying an Adventist at 40 years of age. With no environments, only 22% felt they would remain in the church, while with one some 36% said they would. With two positive environments, however, that number increased to 55%; and with all three working together to support the youth, 62% saw themselves as Adventists down the road.

And if you look at the concept of intrinsic religious orientation, even though our numbers are high for everyone, with all three working together there is a 99% chance that intrinsic faith will be achieved. And in contrast, if we look at the other end of the spectrum, that of an extrinsic religiousness with no environments, 53% seem to develop that type of religion, while with three environments working together, only 3% shared this negative type of religion.

What can we say? It is obvious, the power of these three environments is positive. But look at the graph below and notice just how many students experience a significant number of these effective, positive environments. Families that elect not to send their children to Adventist schools do so at some risk, it seems. Their children will not have all of the advantages they could have to build a rich and growing faith, intrinsic in nature, and loyal to the church. And the same could be said with any of the three. For example, without a clear ministry to

SUM OF SUPPORTIVE AND EFFECTIVE ENVIRONMENTS

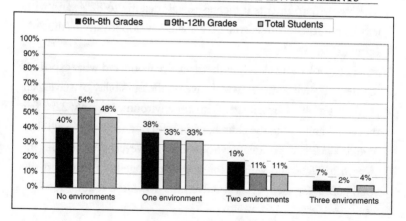

children, youth, and young adults, the church fails. And without a home lead by parents, warm, loving, clear in their understanding of Adventist beliefs and behaviors, and willing to share these concepts, values, and principles with their children in regular and meaningful worship and discussions, the percentages decrease as to mature faith and loyalty. As we said ten years ago, "The results were amazing."[6]

So we conclude

Our summary above does not target everything that can or should be done. It is meant as only a beginning. It is not a conclusion or the end of it all. We provide this work now because we must begin somewhere.

We wish we had more information about older youth—young adults. Our research at the Hancock Center does have some responses from college-age students and young adults. And over the past ten years we have over fifteen studies that target this age group. These older youth are equally critical of the ministry that is often absent for them. We must look closely at their needs, their musical tastes, their modes of worship which are more focused, for their need for a caring church is even more crucial because relationships are the utmost center of their religious experience. The local church is important to these young people too, and the local congregation needs to take their needs seriously as they build a warm, accepting, open, and disciplined culture targeted at building faith in this age group. After all, ministry is never done in the Kingdom of God on earth. So there is much to begin and much to encourage in all of the venues we have mentioned.

And ten years later how are we doing? All in all, we have wonderful young people. Our schools are strong schools and many of them, who are implementing *Valuegenesis* insights along with their own prayer and leadership innovations, are more healthy in a spiritual sense then ever before. Faith maturity has grown. Intrinsic faith is high. Young people are good people. For the most part, they represent the church well, and the products of Christian education come from safer environments, and clearly their schools are healthy Adventist Christian schools working to help young people make better choices and grow in the faith.

Surely there are exceptions. We all know of some. But the thousands of young people that responded to our questionnaires said clearly that things are going well. And the problems, well, they have been with us for a long time, and some of them have not yet been cleared up and in their place creative, innovative change, good change has not yet occurred. So there is still much to do.

What would be a proper conclusion for this book? If we would plan good change, in ways that are true to these principles and insights, we need to

---

SOME CONCLUSIONS

Faith maturity has grown, Intrinsic faith is high. Young people are good people. For the most part, they represent the church well, and the products of Christian education come from safer environments, and clearly their schools are healthy Adventist Christian schools working to help young people make better choices and grow in the faith.

think of ourselves primarily as artists and only "secondarily, if at all, as technicians, and programmers."[7] And because building a church that represents Christ means we must give form by reordering and recreation of experience in order to give it meaning, this means we have to continually strive to reform and recreate as we give new meaning to the old forms and staid ways that served older generations but are not seen as relevant now. We must become more and more committed to comprehensive models of ministry, new shapes of church, clear sculptors of relationships that build and never tear down. Our work is one of fashioning, and it is an artistic work, I believe. So it is appropriate to provide some direction to those who craft the lives of young people.

A FEW WORDS FOR PARENTS

George Barna says, "Teens crave the mind and heart of their parents, but it all starts with a parent's willingness to listen."[8] We have our children for so few years, a dozen or more. But as they grow up, they believe they have the right to talk and perhaps we should listen. That is what has happened with the *Valuegenesis* research responses. We've tried to listen. This book paints a portrait of what they have said. But if we must direct specific comments to those responsible for nurture and care, the first words must be directed to the parents who are the key ingredient in any mix about budding spiritual life.

"We are looking for meaning and purpose," they seem to be saying. We cannot just demand that they follow our ways, nor can we tell them to become what they are not quite sure they want to become. Instead we, as parents, provide the key ingredients to the mix of spirituality and commitment. We've seen that they are experimenting. They do so with beliefs, commitments, values, and behaviors. The parental role is to provide key examples, close communication, and clear purpose coupled with truth in life. Reinforcement is to always be seen through the gracefulness of Christ, and in loving acceptance, while at the same time exampling standards and values that are important for each family. And so we will define appropriate values that are important and worthwhile. We will do it by discussions, our faith-talk, with consistent Christian values, in living our faith in a family that loves and constrains, but always in the context of grace and goodness.

A FEW WORDS FOR THE CHURCH

Ministry to children, youth, and young adults becomes your daily task. The mission of the local church must include consistent, active, exciting, and regular programming for these age groups. The leaders must be clear that marketing to youth is not the same as ministry with and for them. And while the by-word for our church as it grows up in this world is contextualization, at the local level we must try to individualize the ministry directly to the needs of the young people. We have to do research too—find out the needs, discover the leadership gift, build mission, message, and practice into every program and activity. Don't let the church forget such a valuable resource as the young in the church. And while building ministry in the local congregation, don't forget how to talk to the young in the church. They are not passive observers. The best learning is done when they are involved and can see results. Think big, think about God in the world, and help the young of the church see the activity of God in their daily lives and in the mission and ministry of the local congregation.

What we've said implies leadership training by pastoral experts, and targets time spent with young people. And on the practical level, If the membership does not know the youth in your church by name, then they don't know their young people.

A FEW WORDS FOR SCHOOLS

Keep it up. The work you have begun, try to finish. Schools must be a key place where professionals know the world of young people, and know how to enter that worldview patiently, with love and acceptance. Continue to build on the quality that private educaton provides. And for those in charge, teach your teachers how to talk to young people and think how you can share your own faith experience more clearly and more equally among all of the students in the school.

Administrators, spend time building ministry into your whole school program—involvement in the community, with parents, with local churches—and provide models of ministry for parents to implement at home and at work. Teach young people how to pray and grow in their daily walk with God. Be creative in the curriculum of the school, trying to integrate faith with the learning of every discipline. That way you model God's grace and care in a real way with every class. And while you are building a spirit-filled, grace-oriented school, work on experiential learning which is the most effective way to teach young people. Engage them in the learning process as you discuss values, standards, involvement with others lives, and as they try to understand the adult world. Your eyes can help them see clearly. Your lives teach.

We would like to get you involved in this process, a process that has the Kingdom of God as its model, has Christ as the example, one that is caring, loving, graceful, and careful in a world that is filled with distractions and traps. After all, our children are worth it.

REFERENCES

1. Sydney Lewis, *A Totally Alien Life-Form—Teenagers* (New York, NY: The New Press, 1996), 17.

2. See the complete story in Jamie Mckenzie, "Making Good Change Happen," *The Educational Technology Journal* (Vol. 9., No. 10, June 2000).

3. For a complete discussion of how churches change see Merton P. Strommen, *Innovation in the Church* (Minneapolis, MN: Augsburg Press, 2001).

4. See V. Bailey Gillespie, Judith Gillespie, Timothy Gillespie with Cheryl Webster, *Keeping the Faith: A Guidebook for Spiritual Parenting* (Lincoln, NE: AdventSource, 2002). This guidebook contains hundreds of ideas for family spiritual growth, age-graded, and organized into presentation for pastors, teachers, home and school leaders, and young families.

5. V. Bailey Gillespie, *The Experience of Faith* (Birmingham, AL: Religious Education Press, 1988), 149.

6. Roger L. Dudley with V. Bailey Gillespie, *Valuegenesis: Faith in the Balance* (Loma Linda University Press, 1992), 294.

7. Maria Harris, *Fashion Me A People* (Louisville, KY: Westminister/John Knox Press, 1989), 171.

8. George Barna, *Real Teens: A Contemporary Snapshot of Youth Culture* (Ventura, CA: Regal Books, 2001), 146.

For centuries prior to our Modern Era, the church viewed the gospel as a romance, a cosmic drama whose themes permeated our own stories and drew together all the random scenes in a redemptive wholeness. But our rationalistic approach to life, which has dominated Western culture for hundreds of years, has stripped us of that, leaving a faith that is barely more than mere fact-telling. Modern Evangelicalism reads like an IRS 1040 form: it's true, all the data is there, but it doesn't take your breath away.

— *Brent Curtis & John Eldredge*

History must be learned in pieces. This is partly because we have only pieces of the past, shards, ostraca, palimpsests, crumbling codices with missing pages, newsreel clips, snatches of song, faces of idols whose bodies have long since turned to dust—which gives us glimpses of what has been but never the whole reality. How could they? We cannot encompass the whole reality even of the times in which we live. Human beings never know more than part, as "through a glass darkly"; and all knowledge comes to us in pieces. That said, it is often easier to encompass the past than the present, for it is past; and its pieces may be set beside one another, examined, contrasted and compared, till one attains an overivew.

—*Thomas Cahill*

CHAPTER 14

()

FROM THE STATISTICIAN'S DESK
What do the numbers say?

14

FROM THE STATISTICIAN'S DESK

What do the numbers say?

"Divers weights, and divers measures, both of them are alike abomination to the Lord."

— Proverbs 20: 10

It has been my great honor and pleasure to have been lead statistician for the *Valuegenesis* Project almost from its inception. Since my published research has been in the area of the definition and measurement of Christian religiousness specifically, and in the empirical psychology of religion more generally, the project has been of very great interest to me. Here is an opportunity to gather huge amounts of data—both in terms of the number of people involved and the amount of information per person.

At the same time, I have also found it a very humbling experience. This is no academic exercise, no "journal article" to create a line on my vitae and then be archived in a bound journal volume on a library shelf. This is the real thing. Important policy decisions would be made on the basis of this information, by a national denominational body, and one of which I am not a member.[1] So before having my say, I thought it would be appropriate to mention my "Philosophy of Analysis" for approaching topics as delicate as the present one has been.

WHY IS **THAT** IN THE SURVEY, OR WHERE'S **MY** FAVORITE QUESTION?

The first issue is to distinguish between data which are useful and data which are interesting. I read about this distinction in an article by Richard Gorsuch[2], an expert statistician, a prominent psychologist of religion, and a member of the faculty at Fuller Theological Seminary. Whenever a survey of this type is being put together, a large number of people will come forward with a list of things they would like to investigate. In both *Valuegenesis* and *Valuegenesis²*, the steering committee wrestled (some might say not very successfully) with the dialectic of wanting to include everything that was important, while keeping the survey at a manageable length. Frequently, when a given item or series of items was being considered for inclusion or exclusion, the deciding question was whether it (or they) were *interesting* or *useful*. When asked why a particular item was to be included, frequently the rationale would be-

> *"To distinguish between data which are useful and data which are helpful."*

gin, "Well, I've always wondered..." or, "Some people say," or, most tellingly, "I think it would be *interesting* to know..." This would then be followed by, "OK, but if you knew that, how could we change what we do to improve things for our students? How is that information *useful* to our students or to the people who teach and guide them?" While a fair analysis of the items in the survey will indicate that this test did not prevail in every instance, it was helpful in many instances.

WHY USE SCALES?

The concept of usefulness also comes in when deciding *how* certain questions should be asked. The length of the *Valuegenesis* surveys has been due largely to the inclusion of a number of scales: groups of items, closely related to one another, all measuring the same "thing"—an underlying concept or content area. But why use multiple items? Wouldn't a fewer number of questions, or even a single well-worded item, make it clearer what was being measured?

The analysis of individual items is often important. For example, while a particular group may obtain a high score on the Adventist Orthodoxy Scale, it is nonetheless of interest to see whether particular items are persistently low, or whether particular items tend to be lower among

DO YOUR OWN SURVEY

One way to evaluate and periodically measure faith maturity, values shifts, and attitudes regarding Adventist lifestyle practices is by using the Valuegnesis[2] Short Form survey. If you or your group would like to do your own survey of young people in your school or church, contact the Hancock Center at hcyfm@lasierra.edu.

some groups. One might expect, for example, that items that uniquely reflect the understanding of the Adventist heritage might increase in endorsement over time as students become more familiar with them.

And yet the use of multiple items does provide unique benefits. For example, it might seem a simple matter to ask, "How old are you?" And yet, one quickly discovers that young people will tend to hedge their age upwards, as their birthdays approach; older people might do the opposite, or be more vague and respond only in ranges. Perhaps greater precision should be sought: "What is your date of birth?" My experience in survey research, however, has taught me that, from force of habit, approximately 5% of the respondents will indicate the current year as their year of birth, for example, 10/21/03 rather than 10/21/54. If the respondents' ages are particularly important, one would be advised to ask both questions.

In a broader sense, the purpose of using scales is to avoid the sort of misreading, misunderstanding, and idiosyncratic interpretation errors that can accrue when individual survey items are used. While one question may be misread or read idiosyncratically, statistics tell us that over a series of items these errors will cancel each other out. Put another way, a misunderstanding on one item out of ten will have far less effect on one's measured opinion on that topic than it would if that were the only question that was asked.

But that presumes, of course, that the respondents are attempting to answer the questions honestly. What if they aren't?

"CLEANING" THE DATA

When one presents the results of a survey such as this, someone who doesn't like the results (either because they are
"too good" or "too bad") will invariably ask, "How do you know
they are telling the truth? What if students choose to answer delib-
erately 'better' or 'worse' than their actual opinion. What if they
answer at random?" When asked this question, I often have to grab
the leash on my inner "Bad Statistician" that attempts to leap out
and bark, "What makes you think Adventists are more likely to lie
than other teenagers?" While I put Bad Stat back in his cage, I
conceal my initial reaction by saying "That's a very good question,"
and then go on to talk about issues of what statisticians call *validity*
and *reliability*.

First, how do we know that the students weren't just trying to
"look good," or perhaps were paying no attention at all? The process of prudently reducing the likelihood of such occurrences is
called "cleaning" the data, and for the *Valuegenesis* project, this is
how it was done. Beginning with sending out over 22,000 surveys
and building the data set of 16,020 scanned surveys, a series of
criteria was applied to delete surveys from the data set. (The number of surveys that were omitted for the reason cited is in parentheses.) First, those who had not reported their grade, gender,
school, conference, denomination, or school type (a total of 1,661
surveys) were excluded from all further analyses, since the reports
use each of these characteristics extensively. Those who did not
complete all 12 of the first 12 items on the survey were omitted

(995), inasmuch missing data so early in the survey was considered a bad sign.

Then some "believeability" criteria were applied. Anyone who claimed to have attended parties at which drinking occurred (332), dance clubs (94) or movies in movie theaters (314) *more than once a day* were omitted. These behaviors were included in a list of other behaviors (e.g., smoking) that were possible to engage in more the once a day, but since these behaviors were barely possible more than once a day, they were taken as evidence of either inattentive responding or deliberate misresponding. Similarly, those who claimed to have engaged in *all* the possible "at-risk" behaviors (e.g., drug, alcohol, and tobacco use, shoplifting, fighting) 40 or more times in the previous year (26) were also deleted. Lastly, those who said they were not attending an Adventist day or boarding school (60) or who were not Adventists (1762) were excluded from the present data set. This left 10,832. Thus 3,387, or some 21% of the original surveys were excluded because of missing or inaccurate data; the reminder because they were not "Adventist students in Adventist schools."

As another way of ensuring valid data, many of the scales we used have extensive pedigrees.

() The items measuring drug use and other "at-risk" behaviors are the same as those used in the annual *Monitoring the Future*[3] surveys which are reported annually as the national data on such topics. The University of Michigan Institute for Survey Research has conducted "reality checks" on the information these questions produce by doing blood tests and checking school records, and report they are reasonably accurate.

() The Faith Maturity Scale was first developed in a nationwide survey of five Protestant denominations[4] and then later involved in testing and refinement for Adventists.[5]

() The Intrinsic-Extrinsic scales, new to *Valuegenesis²*, are probably the most extensively used scale of religiousness in the English language, as well as having been translated into Dutch, German, Korean, Norwegian, Polish, Swedish, and Vietnamese. It has been used in some 800 published articles and doctoral dissertations.

MARGIN OF ERROR

The pervasive—some would say obnoxious—presence of polling in American society has created an awareness concerning "margins of error," or sampling error, and I expect people are interested in the margin of error in the *Valuegenesis* data. There is none. There is no sampling error, because these data are not based upon a sample.

The purpose of "sampling error" is to tell how likely it is that if someone did a poll over again, getting their sample the same way, and asking the same questions, they would get the same answer. A margin of error of 3% means that there is a 95% chance that the answers they would get would be ± 3% of those reported the first time. The *Valuegenesis* surveys

VALUEGENESIS ²

In the case of the Valuegenesis *surveys, there was no sample; they were both done as a census. Effort was made to obtain responses from the entire population of Adventist students in Adventist schools, grade 6 through 12.*

were not samples but, in both cases, a census. Effort was made to obtain responses from the entire population of Adventist students in Adventist schools, grade 6 through 12. Thus there is very little point indeed in "doing it again"; we have everyone's answers, and aside mismarkings (or frustration over having to take "that survey" again), we would get the same answers. But like all things human, our efforts were not perfect. Some people chose not to answer, or answered in a way that made their answers invalid, as discussed above. Not all schools chose to participate. But this is a question of nonresponse, rather than sampling. Rather than reflecting random factors, the main question in addressing nonresponse is: "Is there something different about the people who chose not to respond, as a group?" At the present time, we have no evidence of that. Thus, the percentages reported can be treated as accurate (at least to the nearest whole percent) reflections of the opinions of the students in Adventist schools.

MY MOST IMPORTANT FINDING IN TEN WORDS OR LESS

Unfortunately, this is very easy, and I can do it in six words: *Watch out if they smoke cigarettes.*

It is, of course, illegal for the vast majority of the students who took the survey. But among 11th and 12th graders, it has frightening strength in predicting a host of bad outcomes. It is correlated -.31 with intrinsic religiousness; -.27 with faith maturity; +.22 with dissatisfaction with Adventist standards, -.22 with both denominational loyalty and personal piety, and an astounding +.56

with the "At-Risk" index. The items on that index are in the Appendix, but it measures the number of times the student has engaged in a wide variety of self- and other-abusive behaviors. Its relation to other "at-risk" behaviors is consistent with other research that suggests the existence of an "at-risk syndrome"[6] The marked negative relation to the religiousness and denominational variable also indicates a more general rejection of right living.

This is not the first time in my research I have seen this outcome, but it is frankly stronger that I have noted in other settings. Apparently, tobacco is the true "gateway drug."

GENDER DIFFERENCES

One of the notable findings in the present data are the differences between the boys and the girls. Even when there is almost no room for difference, as on the Grace Scale, boys score an average of 4.81 on a five point scale, and girls score 4.84. But this should not be a cause of concern. In a recent article, Rodney Stark[7], one of the premiere sociologists of religion, presented both a literature review and current international data to indicate that, regardless of culture or religion, re-

---

GIRL'S RELIGIOUSNESS

Research shares the differences in religiousness between girls and boys. Girsl are more religiously committed than boys at all ages. Girls in almost all grades experienced God's nearness and guidance more often than the boys did. As children age, religious experiences decline in number and importance, with the greatest decline at puberty (13-15) — Kalevi Tammnen, "Religious Expereinces in Childood and Adolescence: A Viewpoint of Religious Development between the Ages of 7 and 20", *International Journal fo rthe Psychology of Religion 2,* 61-85.

gardless of controls for any number of other variables, women are, on average, invariably more religious than men. This finding is so strong, in fact, that he has thrown down the gauntlet to challenge his fellow social scientists to attempt to prove that the difference is not a function of physiological or biological differences. So the finding that, even among Adventists in Adventist schools, girls are more religious than boys comes as no surprise. In turn, when we find that variables like "at-risk" behaviors and negative attitudes to the church, which are in turn related to religious, also show gender differences, this is simply the direct result of the religiousness difference.

So, ARE OUR SCHOOLS WORKING?

It is a curious fact that repeated attempts to demonstrate a "school effect" for religious schools have failed. The reason is that the most important aspects of any religious tradition are conveyed to children by parents. Religious parents send their children to church-affiliated schools. If they cannot afford that, they see to it that the child is more involved than average in church-related events, and make a point of conveying their faith in a thousand ways. After accounting for the influence of parents, studies have failed to find value differences between religious students in church-supported schools and those in secular schools. Although the present study did not

A look at public or private schools

include an "Adventists in public school" sample, I have little doubt that the same findings would be manifest here.

But we do have *Valuegenesis* data to compare with *Valuegenesis²*. There are areas in which there has been little change. To the extent that these areas are important, it indicates that either intensification or change of approach is in order. But the tables throughout the book have shown that there have been real, meaningful differences in many areas that have been specifically targeted. It is these sorts of areas, the deepening and enriching of Adventist identification, that would be expected to show effects "down the road" when choices of marriage and child-raising are made (and long after parent-child-school studies are feasible). It is these areas that may be involved in inculcating a mature, intrinsic religious faith.

SO WHAT IS INTRINSIC RELIGIOUSNESS?

Several of the analyses described above concluded that something called "intrinsic religiousness" was important in bringing about the sort of faith outcomes that were most desirable. Fine, but then how do we bring about intrinsic religiousness?

An attentive reader will have noticed that I am quite familiar with the research studies involving that scale. (For example, knowing that there are 800 of them, including dissertations, which are unpublished and must be specifically tracked down, probably indicates a

What is intrinsic religiousness?

higher than average interest in the topic.) So I can say with some authority that there is very little actual research on how this type of religiousness develops. But an examination of the scale itself is fairly enlightening. The Intrinsic Scale is in the Appendix. As used in *Valuegenesis²*, the scale has seven items. Six are answered with the standard "strongly agree/strongly disagree" format, and the one about church attendance is answered with a "how many times per month" format.

I think it is clear that four of the items (*"I enjoy reading about my religion"; "It is important to me to spend time in private thought and prayer"; "I have often had a strong sense of God's presence"; "I would prefer to go to church. . ."*) describe the *effects* of an intrinsic religious orientation. But the remaining three (*"I try hard to live all my life according to my religious beliefs"; "My religion is important because it answers many questions about the meaning of life"; "My whole approach to life is based on my religion"*) describe how to get there.

> *One should not follow standards to be Adventist, but follow standards because they are Adventist; standards, like works, should be effects, not causes.*

Adventism in particular has always made a point of being very clear about carrying its convictions about the nature of the godly life into day-to-day activities; the Adventist lifestyle choices and standards make that clear. But such standards should not be defining but guiding. One should not follow standards to be Adventist, but follow standards because they are Adventist; standards, like works, should be effects, not causes.

Thus, at least some complaints about how standards are enforced are grounded in exactly this intrinsic religiousness. The complaint that standards are enforced in such a way that "behaviors are more important than beliefs" may reflect either that the student rejects the underlying moral theology that produced those standards, or may reflect a complaint that they have not been lead to (to educate, is from the Latin *e-ducere*, to lead forth) such an

> *"It is this idea, that the committed Christian life can be—should be— reflected in every waking moment, that underlies the intrinsic religious motivation."*

understanding. The goal is that young people will be able to say, *"My whole approach to life is based on my Adventism."*

There are certain areas in which the Adventist heritage points toward very specific behaviors or abstentions. But it is important to show that these were not created in isolation, and reflect a larger theological underpinning.

In some theological traditions, some form of service for others is required prior to full adult commitment to the faith (for example, "confirmation"). Others point toward some form of service mission. But both are little more than what has come to be called "service learning" unless such experiences are clearly grounded in the Christian life. "We don't do nice things so we will feel nice about ourselves, or even to make other people feel nice. We do this because our faith demands it of us." The following illustration may help clarify:

> ### It is sometimes easier to "act our way into a new way of thinking than think our way into a new way of acting."

> *You are writing to me in the kitchen, by the stove . . . By your side your younger sister—the last one to discover the divine folly of living her Christian vocation to the full—is peeling potatoes. To all appearances, you think, her work is the same as before. And yet, what a difference there is!*
>
> *It is true: before she only peeled potatoes, now, she is sanctifying herself peeling potatoes.*[8]

It is this idea, that the committed Christian life can be—should be—reflected in every waking moment, that underlies the intrinsic religious motivation. Thus, the more deeply grounded such an all-encompassing approach to the faith is, the more likely its specific demands can be seen as disciplines rather than burdens.

This is no simple matter: its most important aspects can only be modeled, and thus require an unwavering commitment by those who wish to imbue the tradition in the young. And it is true, it is sometimes easier to "act our way into a new way of thinking than think our way into a new way of acting." But latter must only supplement the former, not vice versa.

SO WHAT DOES IT ALL MEAN?

In any study of this type, people will pull out a particular finding or number that interests them and feed it to their pet theory, which will inevitably grow stronger as a result. But in interpreting this information fairly, we must apply one of the central questions of social scientific analysis: *As compared to what?*

Information such as that presented here can be treated in at least two ways: *normatively* and *comparatively*. On the normative side, the standard is clear. No amount of drug abuse or nonmarital sexuality is acceptable; any deviation from this is a type of failure. How can there be an "acceptable level" of sin or of violation of standards?

On the other hand, there is a comparative approach. The levels of at-risk behavior shown in the latest research are lower than that in the population at large, lower, in some cases, than the corresponding numbers in *Valuegenesis[1]*. It is true there is no "acceptable level" of failure, but in a fallen world, much can be said for protecting Adventist youth from behavior patterns that have come to be considered "normative" in the wider culture. In a world of finite resources, particular attention can be turned to those areas in which current efforts have been shown not to be effective, and the only real way to judge that is through "numbers."

Every youth lost or gone astray is a tragedy. No parent can be comforted in the face of a shoplifting charge, or a teenage pregnancy, with the knowledge that "Adventists are less likely to do that than other youth." It is in such situations that the pastoral resources of the church must be brought to bear, to comfort the sorrowing and counsel the angry. At the same time, none can say that

DOCUMENTATION OF SCALES

A complete copy of the documentation of the scales and indices prepared by Michael J. Donahue, Ph.D. is available from the Hancock Center. E-mail us at hcyfm@lasierra.edu and we will send you a PDF file of the detailed listing of all of the survey questions and the related scales and reliabilities used in this research.

> **"No more prizes for predicting rain; prizes only for building arks."**

news that the efforts of the church have been successful, either in contrast to the larger society or in comparison to previous information about Adventist youth, is to be ignored. *"No more prizes for predicting rain; prizes only for building arks."* They are doing God's work who strive to bring about his kingdom the best they know how, or who seek ways to do better still.

REFERENCES

1. I am a practicing Roman Catholic. I was taught by, among others, nuns in grammar school, priests and brothers in high school, and Jesuits at Loyola of Chicago. During graduate school at Purdue, I found myself surrounded by Hoosiers. I did a two year postdoctoral fellowship at Brigham Young University, where less than 4% of the staff and students are "Gentiles" (non-Mormons). Then off to Minnesota, to live among Garrison Keillor's Norwegian Lutherans for some 15 years. Most recently I have been teaching in a graduate clinical psychology program (although I am a social, or research, psychologist, and not a clinician or any kind of health care professional) at Azusa Pacific University, which sees itself grounded in a Wesleyan, evangelical background.

2. R. L. Gorsuch, "Research and evaluation: Their role in decision making in the religious setting." *Review of Religious Research,* (17. 1976), 93-101.

3. J. G. Bachman, L. D. Johnston, & P. M. O'Malley, (1993). "Monitoring the future: Questionnaire responses from the nation's high school seniors" Ann Arbor: Institute for Social Research, University of Michigan (1992).

4. Peter. L. Benson, Michael J. Donahue, & J. A. Erickson, "The Faith Maturity Scale: Conceptualization, measurement, and empirical validation" *Research in the Social Scientific Study of Religion,* (5, 1993), 1-26.

5. Michael J. Donahue, & J. Kijai, "Researching faith maturity: Questions on methods and findings of Valuegenesis," *Journal of Research on Christian Education,* (2.1 1993), 85-92; Michael J. Donahue, "Reply to Jerome Thayer. [Reply to "Measuring faith maturity: Reevaluating Valuegenesis and development of a denomination-specific scale,"(2.1, 1993), 93-113, same issue]. *Journal of Research on Christian Education,* (2. 1, 1993), 115-118.

6. R. Jessor, "Risk behavior in adolescence: A psychosocial framework for understanding and action," *Journal of Adolescent Health,* (12, 1991), 597-605.

7. R. Stark, "Physiology and faith: Addressing the 'universal' gender difference in religious commitment," *Journal for the Scientific Study of Religion,* (41, 2002), 495-507.

8. J. Escriva, *Furrow,* #498. (New York, NY: Scepter Publications, 1986).

Ephesians says it. Christ's "gifts unto men" were varied. Some he made his messengers, some prophets, some preachers of the gospel; to some he gave the power to guide and teach his people. His gifts were made that Christians might be properly equipped for their service, that the whole body might be built up until the time comes when, in the unity of common faith and common knowledge of the Son of God, we arrive at real maturity—that measure of development which is meant by "the fullness of Christ."

We are not meant to remain as children at the mercy of every change wind of teaching and the jockeying of men who are expert in the crafty presentation of lies. But we are meant to hold firmly to the truth in love, and to grow up in every way into Christ, the head . . . For it is from the head that the whole body, as a harmonious structure knit together by the joints with which it is provided, grows by the proper functioning of individual parts to its full maturity in love.

(Ephesians 4:11-16, Phillips Translation)

Yes, Ephesians says it. The product, and the goal, of youth ministry is growth, together, to maturity.

— Lawrence O. Richards

APPENDIX

()

SCALES AND INDICES
Valuegenesis²

APPENDIX

SCALES AND OTHER INDICES
BY MICHAEL DONAHUE, PH.D.

VALUEGENESIS²—SCALES EMPLOYED IN THE REPORTS

This appendix provides the item wordings for the scales and indices most extensively discussed in the text. Some of the "stems" (questions) have been abbreviated for space considerations. A fuller copy of this appendix, including the full wording of all items in the survey and additional analytical information is available on request from the John Hancock Center.

Reliability coefficients were calculated separately by gender at each grade level; the range of the resulting 14 coefficients are listed after the name of each scale. The range of response options for questions are shown in italics before the items. Numbers in front of questions indicate the item's location in the original survey.

Adventism as Life Value (.63 to .79)

For each of these, indicate how important the goal is to you.
(1) Not at all important — (4) Extremely important

100. To live my life according to Adventist standards.

104. To be active in the Adventist church.

Adventist Standards: Enforcement

Indicate how strictly it is enforced by (1) your family, and (2) your Adventist school (1) Not at all strictly enforced—(4) Very strictly enforced

Drug Standards Strictness Scale (for families .78 to .88; for schools .76 to .90)

148. Not smoking tobacco.

149. Not drinking beer and alcohol.

154. Not using illegal drugs.

Popular Culture Strictness Scale (for families .81 to .88; for schools .76 to .90)

150. Not wearing jewelry.

151. Not listening to rock music.

152. Not dancing.

153. Not attending movie theaters.

159. Not doing competitive sports.

161. Not wearing a wedding ring.

162. Not using drinks that contain caffeine

Adventist Lifestyle Strictness Scale (for families .63 to .74; for schools .51 to .69)

155. Having sex only in marriage.

156. Not eating unclean meat.

157. Observing the Sabbath.

158. Wearing modest clothing.

160. Exercising daily.

ADVENTIST STANDARDS: PERSONAL ENDORSEMENT

How much do you personally agree or disagree with each of these standards of behavior? (1) I definitely disagree—(5) I definitely agree

DRUG STANDARDS SCALE (.80 to .86)

129. One should not use tobacco.

130. One should not drink beer or liquor.

135. One should not use illegal drugs.

POPULAR CULTURE STANDARDS SCALE (.83 to .87.)

131. One should not wear jewelry.

132. One should not listen to rock music.

133. One should not watch movies in movie theaters.

134. One should not dance.

140. One should not engage in competitive sports.

142. Married persons should not wear a wedding ring.

143. One should not use drinks with caffeine.

ADVENTIST LIFESTYLE SCALE (.57 TO .72)

136. Sex should only occur in marriage.

137. One should not eat unclean meats.

138. One should observe the Sabbath.

139. One should wear modest clothes.

141. One should exercise daily.

ALTRUISM (.61 to .73)

How many hours do you do following each month? (1)
0 hours—(6) More than 20 hours

21. Helping people who are poor, hungry, sick, or unable to care for themselves.
22. Helping friends or neighbors with problems they have.
23. Promoting social equality or world peace.
24. Making your own town or city a better place to live.

AT-RISK BEHAVIORS (For most analyses, this was simply used to count how many times the student reported ever having done these things.

How many times, if ever, during the last 12 months did you do each of the following? (1) Never—(7) 40 or more times

221. Drink alcohol while alone or with a friend.
222. Use marijuana.
223. Use cocaine.
224. Have five drinks or more in a row.
225. Hit or beat up someone.
226. Take something from a store without paying for it.
227. Get into trouble at school.
112. Have you ever had sexual intercourse? (1) No—(5) 4 or more times
202. How often have you felt sad or depressed during the last month? (1) Not at all—(5) All the time

203. Have you ever tried to kill yourself? (1) No—(4) Yes, more than two times

DENOMINATIONAL LOYALTY (.68 to .95)
110. How satisfied are you with the denomination of the church you now attend? (1) Very dissatisfied—(5) Very satisfied
111. If you moved to another city that has many churches from which to choose, would you attend a church of the same denomination as the church you now attend? (1) No—(5) Yes, absolutely
145. When you are 40 years old, do you think you will be active in the Adventist church? (1) No chance—(5) Excellent chance

DISSATISFACTION WITH ADVENTIST STANDARDS ENFORCEMENT (.82 to .86)
(1) No opinion; (2) Never true—(8) Always true
121. Students breaking a school standard or rule in Adventist schools are punished too harshly.
122. Some adults insist on certain rules or standards for younger Adventists that they do not observe themselves.
123. The feeling is conveyed in the Adventist church that how one behaves is more important than what one believes.
124. Emphasis on Adventist rules and standards is so strong that the message of Christianity gets lost.
127. Adventists are loaded down with too many restrictions.
128. Adventist rules and standards just don't make sense.

EVANGELIZATION (.72 to .81)

> (1) 1-2 times—(6) 40 or more times.

18. How often have you tried to directly encourage someone to believe in Jesus Christ during the last year?

19. How often have you told others about the work of God in your life during the last year?

FAITH MATURITY SCALE (.81 to .88.)

> (1) never—(5) often

1. I help others with their religious questions and struggles.
2. I seek out opportunities to help me grow spiritually.
3. I feel a deep sense of responsibility for reducing pain and suffering in the world.
4. I give significant portions of time and money to help other people.
5. I feel God's presence in my relationships with other people.
6. I feel my life is filled with meaning and purpose.
7. I show that I care a great deal about reducing poverty in my country and throughout the world.
8. I apply my faith to political and social issues.
9. The things I do reflect a commitment to Jesus Christ.
10. I talk with other people about my faith.
11. I have a real sense that God is guiding me.
12. I am spiritually moved by the beauty of God's creation.

FAMILY CLIMATE (.85 to .90)

> Response options: (1) No opinion; (2) I definitely disagree—

(6) I definitely agree

174. My family life is happy.

175. There is a lot of love in my family.

176. I get along well with my parents.

177. My parents give me help and support when I need it.

178. My parents often tell me they love me.

GRACE (.75 to .85)

41. There is nothing I can do to earn salvation.

53. Salvation is God's free gift to us that we don't deserve and cannot earn.

54. We can do nothing to deserve God's gift of salvation.

INTRINSIC/EXTRINSIC RELIGIOUS ORIENTATION

(1) I strongly disagree—(5) I strongly agree

INTRINSIC (.78 to .85)

311. I enjoy reading about my religion.

315. It is important to me to spend time in private thought and prayer.

316. I have often had a strong sense of God's presence.

318. I try hard to live all my life according to my religious beliefs.

320. My religion is important because it answers many questions about the meaning of life.

325. My whole approach to life is based on my religion.

338. I would prefer to go to church: (1) A few times a year or less—(5) More than once a week.

EXTRINSIC (.70 to .78)

312. I go to church because it helps me to make friends.

313. It doesn't much matter what I believe so long as I am good.

314. Sometimes I have to ignore my religious beliefs because of what people might think of me.

323. Although I am religious, I don't let it affect my daily life.

324. I go to church mostly to spend time with my friends.

326. I go to church mainly because I enjoy seeing people I know there.

327. I pray mainly because I have been taught to pray.

MATERIALISM AS LIFE VALUE (.73 to .85)

For each of these, indicate how important the goal is to you.
(1) Not at all important—(4) Extremely important

101. To have lots of nice things.

103. To have lots of money.

ORTHODOXY

How strongly do you believe each of the following? (1) I have never heard of this; (2) I definitely do not believe this—(6) I definitely believe this.

ORTHODOXY I (.61 TO .86)

60. God created the world in six 24-hour days.

61. Jesus will come back to earth again and take the righteous to heaven.

62. The Ten Commandments still apply to us today.

63. The true Sabbath is the seventh day Saturday.

64. The investigative or pre-advent judgment in heaven began in 1844.

65. When people die, they remain in the grave until the resurrection.

66. The wicked will not burn forever but will be totally destroyed.

67. Ellen G. White fulfilled Bible predictions that God would speak through the gift of prophecy in the last days.

68. The Seventh-day Adventist Church is God's true last-day church with a message to prepare the world for the Second Coming of Christ.

69. The body is the temple of God, and we are responsible in every area of life for its care.

ORTHODOXY II (.73 to .90)

70. There is one God: Father, Son, and Spirit, a unity of three eternal Persons.

71. God, our Heavenly Father, is the Source, Sustainer, and Ruler of the universe.

72. Jesus is truly and eternally God.

73. Jesus became truly and fully human.

74. God, the Holy Spirit, teaches us how much we need Jesus in our lives, draws us to Jesus, and makes us like Him.

75. The first man and woman, created as free beings in the image of God, chose to rebel against God. We have inherited their fallen nature along with all its consequences.

76. There is a great controversy taking place between God and Satan. It began in heaven with the rebellion of Lucifer and will continue until the end of time.

77. The church is God's family on earth, a community of faith in which many members, all equal in Christ, join for worship, instruction and service.

78. Baptism is a public testimony that we have accepted Jesus and want to be involved in His church.

79. Taking part in the Communion Service expresses thanks to Jesus for saving us.

80. God has given spiritual gifts to each of us that we can use in ministry.

81. We acknowledge God's ownership of the earth and all its resources by returning tithes and giving offerings.

82. Marriage is a loving union that should be entered into only by people who share a common faith.

83. The end-time millennium (1,000 years) begins with the Second Coming when the righteous are taken to heaven, and ends with the final destruction of the wicked.

84. After the millennium, God will recreate the earth as a perfect, eternal home of the redeemed. Sin will never exist again.

PARENTAL MONITORING (.75 to .85)

If you live with your parents or guardian, how often do they do the following? (1) Never—(4) Often

182. Limit the amount of time you can spend watching television.

183. Limit the amount of time for going out with friends on school nights.
184. Limit the amount of time for going out with friends on weekends.
185. Limit the types of music you listen to.
186. Limit time spent playing video games.
187. Limit time spent on the Internet.

PARENTING STYLE

First Mother and then Father: (1) very unlike this—(4) very like this. Some of the items are "reversed scored"; agreeing with them produces a low score toward the total of the corresponding index, while disagreeing with them produces a high score. These item are indicated by an "R"

CARING PARENTING STYLE SCALE (for Fathers, .88 to .93.; for Mothers, .88 to .92)

346. Spoke to me with a warm and friendly voice.
347. Did not help me as much as I needed.
348. Let me do those things I liked doing.
349. Seemed emotionally cold to me.
350. Appeared to understand my problems and worries.
351. Was affectionate to me.
356. Enjoyed talking things over with me.
357. Frequently smiled at me.
359. Did not seem to understand what I needed or wanted.
361. Made me feel I wasn't wanted.

362. Could make me feel better when I was upset.

363. Did not talk with me very much.

369. Did not praise me.

OVERPROTECTIVE PARENTING STYLE SCALE (for Fathers, .75 to .85; for Mothers .80 to .85)

352. Liked me to make my own decisions.

353. Did not want me to grow up.

354. Tried to control everything I did.

355. Invaded my privacy.

358. Tended to baby me.

360. Let me decide things for myself.

364. Tried to make me dependent on her/him.

365. Felt I could not look after myself unless she/he was around.

366. Gave me as much freedom as I wanted.

367. Let me go out as often as I wanted.

368. Was overprotective of me.

370. Let me dress in any way I pleased.

PERSONAL DEVOTION (.60 to .72)

How often do you do each of the following: (1) Never—(8). More than once a day

35. Pray other than at church or before meals.

36. Watch religious programs on television or listen to religious radio programs.

37. Read the Bible on my own.

38. Read the writings of Ellen White.

Religious Education Quality (.87 to .90)

Think about your experience with religious education at your church. For each of these statements, tell how true it is for you. (1) Does not apply; (2) Not at all true—(6) Very true

213. Programs at my church are interesting.

214. Programs at my church make me think.

215. My teachers or adult leaders know me well.

216. My teachers or adult leaders are warm and friendly.

218. My teachers or adult leaders care about me.

219. I look forward to going to things at my church.

220. I go to things at church because I want to.

School Climate (.78 to .85)

How much do you agree or disagree with each of the following statements concerning the school you now attend? (1) Strongly disagree—(4) Strongly agree

204. Students often feel put down by teachers.

205. There is real school spirit.

206. Discipline is fair.

207. The teaching is good.

208. Teachers are interested in students.

209. When students work hard on schoolwork, teachers praise their efforts.

210. Teachers listen to what their students say.

211. Students have a say in how the school is run.

212. I like my school.

SERVICE AS LIFE VALUE (.70 to .80)

For each of these, indicate how important the goal is to you.
(1) Not at all important—(4) Extremely important
99. To spend time helping people.
102. To help people who are poor or hungry.
105. To show love to other people.
106. To help promote social equality.

THINKING CONGREGATION (.82 to .92)

Think about the local church that you attend. (1) I do not attend church; (2) Not all the time—(6) Very true
88. I learn a lot.
90. Most members want to be challenged to think about religious issues and ideas.
92. It challenges my thinking.
93. It encourages me to ask questions.
95. It expects people to learn and think.
96. It stretches me in worship.

WARM CONGREGATION (.80 to .92)

Think about the local church that you attend. (1) I do not attend church; (2) Not all the time—(6) Very true
87. It feels warm.
89. It accepts people who are different.
91. It is friendly.
94. Strangers feel welcome.
97. It provides fellowship.

WORKS (.80 to .88)

(1) I definitely disagree—(5) I definitely agree

39. I know that to be saved I have to live by God's rules.
42. Following Adventist standards and practices will cause me to be saved.
43. The way to be accepted by God is to try sincerely to live a good life.
44. The main emphasis of the gospel is on God's rules for right living.
47. Salvation is the way God rewards us for obeying Him.
48. Salvation is God's way of saying thank you for our good behavior.
49. We show we are worthy of being saved by doing good to others.
51. My salvation depends on whether I keep the law perfectly.

True education is the inculcation of those ideas that will impress the mind and heart with the knowledge of God the Creator and Jesus Christ the Redeemer. Such an education will renew the mind and transform the character. It will strengthen and fortify the mind against the deceptive whispering of the adversary of souls, and enable us to understand the voice of God. It will fit the learned to become a co-worker with Christ.

Those who are seeking to acquire knowledge in the schools of earth should remember that another school also claims them as students—the school of Christ. From this school the students are never graduated. Among the pupils are both old and young. Those who give heed to the instructions of the divine Teacher are constantly gaining more wisdom and nobility of soul, and thus they are prepared to enter that higher school, where advancement will continue throughout eternity.

— Ellen G. White

INDEX

( )

HOW DO I FIND THAT?
Valuegenesis²

INDEX

HOW DO I FIND THAT?
Valuegenesis²

Abuse, drug(s), 64; substance, 83; 117; 248

Academic performance, (see Performance, academic)

Acceptance, 85; 130-131; 135; 145; 154; 200; 206; 215; 226; 234; 264

Activity(ies), religious, 64

Addison, Joseph, 35

Administrator(s), 15; 32; 318

Adolescent(s), iii; 18; 29; 54; 94; 151; 175; 184; 204; 223; 255; 291; 339

Adult(s), 48; 85; 94; 97; 120; 132; 183; 209-210; 223; 236; 325; 345; 397

Adventism as a Life Value, 394

Adventism, 61-63; 95; 160; 303; 327; 340; 344-346; 356-357; 385

Adventist Attitude Scale, (see Scale, Adventist Attitude)

Adventist Christian education, (see Education, Adventist Christian)

Adventist Lifestyle Standards, (See Standards, Adventist Lifestyle)

Adventist Lifestyle Strictness Scale, (see Scale, Adventist Lifestyle Strictness)

Adventist Lifestyle, (see Lifestyle, Adventist)

Adventist Orthodoxy Scale, (see Scale, Adventist Orthodoxy)

Adventist schools, (see Schools, Adventist)

Adventist standards, (see Standards, Adventist)

Adventist theology, (see Theology, Adventist)

Adventist Way-of-Life standards, (see Standards, Adventist Way-of-Life)

Adventist young people, (See Young people, Adventist)

Adventist Youth (AY) 208;

Adventist youth, (see Youth, Adventist)

Adventist Youth, 14; 49; 51

African American, 328-332; 335

Alcohol, 61; 73-74; 83; 118; 181; 286; 303; 306; 378; 396

Aleshire, Daniel, 29; 43

Alienation, 50; 179

Allport, Gordon, 80

Altruism, 133; 331; 396

Anderson, Amber, 64
Anderson, Neil, 144; 147
Anthony, John, vi; 21
Apathy, 52
Asian, 328-332; 335
Atonement, 54
At-risk behaviors, 66; 73-74; 117; 181; 211; 306-307; 332; 378; 381-382; 296 Index, (see Index, At-Risk); indicator(s), 234; Scale, (see Scale, At-Risk)
Attendance patterns, church (see Church attendance patterns)
Attitude Scale, Seventh-day Adventist, 57
Attitude(s), 31; 47; 65; 66; 180-181; 198; 221-222; 236; 248; 301; 341; 358
Audiocassettes, 115
AY meetings, (see Adventist Youth)

Baby Boomers, 14; 17; 27; 51; 66
Bachman, J. G., 389
Baptism, 52; 68; 164-165; 211-213; 402
Baptismal statement, 243
Barna Research Group, 66; 95; 115
Barna, George, 47; 75; 88-89; 95; 117 123; 365; 369
Bartlett, Kellie, 274
Basler, Ed, 27
Battery, 60
Beaudoin, Tom, 43; 147
Beck, M., 23
Beer, 72; 181; 225; 240; 394-395
Behavior(s), 50; 64; 93; 105-106; 119; 130; 136; 175; 186; 188; 214; 222; 227; 229; 234-235; 242; 284; 354; 363; 385 at-risk, (see At-risk behaviors); life-affirming, 130; 243; life-denying, 73; 130; religious, 64-65; 176; 225

Belief system, (see System, belief)
Belief(s), 65; 68-69; 71; 112; 153; 156-157; 159; 168-169; 180-181; 189; 203-204; 234-235; 279; 345-346; 348; 357; 363; 399-400
Believing, 154; 184
Belonging, 154; 184; 195; 203
Benson, Peter, 191; 278; 389
Benson, Reggie, 64
Berry, Dave, 31
Bible(s), 61; 95; 111-113; 127; 139; 189; 211; 229-230-231; 247; 303; 401; class(es), 303; reading, 109; 113; 348; 353; 404; study, 79; 106; 154; 164; 349
Bietz, Reinhold Reinhardt, 43
Binge drinking, (see Drinking, binge)
Black, Wesley, 89
Blazen, Ivan, 248; 251
Blech, Rabbi Benjamin, 218
Boomers, (see Baby Boomers)
Boyatt, Ed, v; 19
Brokaw, Tom, 108
Brown, L.d. B., 273
Burns, Jim, 87; 89;124; 192

Caffeinated, drinks, (see Drinks, caffeinated)
Cahill, Thomas, 370
Caring Parenting Style Scale, (see Scale, Caring Parenting Style)
Case, Steve, 71
Chamberlain, Gary L., 335
Change(s), 15; 42; 51; 127; 214; 333-334; 340-342; 344-345; 356; 358
Charry, Ellen, 291; 293
Child, iii; 78
Children, 14; 23; 29-30; 36-37; 42; 64-66; 106; 112; 145-146; 175; 189; 230; 247; 249; 252; 255; 262; 265; 268;

270; 274; 317-318; 320; 328; 347; 349-350; 355; 362-363; 366; 382; God's, 54

Choice(s), 50; 129; 143; 178; 222; 227-228-229; 235-237; 247; 249-250; 287 320; 340; life-affirming, 66; 72; 122; 184; 225; 229-230; 286; 347; life-denying, 72; 122; 225; 347; lifestyle, 40; 71-72; 235; 241; 344

Choonghoon, Lim 23

Christ, Jesus, (see Jesus Christ)

Christian life, 56-57

Christian(s), iii; 31-32; 94-95; 98; 127; 131; 176; 184

Christianity, 84; 151

Church(es), iii; 16; 22; 34; 36; 38-39; 50-51; 60; 61; 64-65; 85-86; 93-94; 117; 119; 121; 129; 130l 132; 139;146; 151; 155; 159; 165; 183; 186-187-188; 192; 195; 198; 201; 208; 211; 215; 221; 223; 226; 228; 236; 247; 249-250; 279-281; 284-285; 290; 292; 318; 340-341; 345; 348-349; 354-355; 358-360; 363; 366-367; 397; 399-400; 402; 405; Adventist, Seventh-day, 56-57; 72; 98; attendance (patterns), 63-65-66; 106; 188-189; 195; growth, 35; loyalty, (see Loyalty, church); positive influences, (see Influences, church positive); services, (see Services, church); Remnant, 67; 70; 159; 346

Cigarette(s), 380

Clark, Chap, 89

Climate(s), 50; 80; 82; 180; 183; 199; 321; 352; 354-355; 358; church, 85; congregational thinking, 201; 324; congregational, 323-324; family, 145; 233; 320-321; 398; school, 304; 405;

thinking, 201; 204; 239; warm church, 199; 239; 248

Cobble, James, 169; 203

Cocaine, 73-74; 306; 396

Commitment(s), 15; 55-56; 60; 67; 73; 80; 96; 100; 103; 10-108; 110; 114; 143; 155; 157; 166; 183; 185; 192; 211; 213-215; 223-224; 235; 320; 344; 351; 353-354; 357; 366

Communion, 68; 165; 402

Community, 104; 132; 154; 231

Compact discs, 115

Computer(s), 89; 115

Congregation(s), local, 51; 62; 80; 84; 190; 197-198; 201; 205; 208; 289; 367; warm, 406

Congregational climate, (see Climate, congregational)

Constraint, loving, 321

Contextualization, 214; 366

Conversion, 151; 356

Core dimensions, 98

Correlation(s), 166-167; 202; 232; 239

Coupland, Douglas, 13

Covenant, 96

Cox, Harvey, 28-29; 43

Crime, 52

Critical thinking, (see Thinking, critical)

Culture(s), 15; 49; 61; 182; 192; 235; 303; 317

Curtis, Brent, 370

Dai, Yong, 217

Dance, dancing, 72; 118; 221; 225; 227; 239-240-241; 245; 250; 287; 394-395

Death, 95

Decision making, 250;

Decision(s), 122; 222; 231; 235; 250; life-affirming, 250

Demographics, 52

Denominational Loyalty Scale, (see Scale, Denominational Loyalty)

Development, faith, 67; 168; 171; 200; 204; 239; 247; 256; 285; 291; 349; mental, 54; physical, 54; spiritual, 54; 87; 197

Devotion(s), 97; 187; family, 53; 97; 267; personal, 56; 302; 353; 404

DeVries, Mike, 89

Discipline, 40; 145; 303-304; 327; 405

Disciplines, 185; 386

Disorders, eating, (see Eating disorders)

Dissatisfaction with Adventist Standards Enforcement, 397

Diversity, 155; 222

Doctrinal questions, (see Questions, doctrinal)

Doctrine(s), 40; 68; 165; 167-169; 214-215; 255; 346; 353

Donahue, Michael J., v; 19; 135; 147; 387; 389; 393

Downs, Perry, 127-128

Drinking, binge, 73; 239; 396

Drinks, caffeinated, 118; 225

Drug abuse, (see Abuse, drug)

Drug Standards Strictness Scale, (see Scale, Drug Standards Strictness)

Drug(s), 52; 60; 72; 83; 181; 211; 225; 240-241; 243; 250; 263; 286; 303; 378; 394-395

Dudley, Roger, 20-21; 31; 40; 43; 61; 84; 96; 102; 114; 123; 132; 141; 147; 156; 171; 195; 198; 216-217; 221; 223; 245; 251; 287; 293; 359; 369

Dulles, Avery, 154; 171

Eating disorders, 73-74; 306

Ecclesiology, 84

Education, Adventist Christian, 33; 75; 177; 307; Adventist, 31-32; 35-37; 85; 164; 190; 298; 306; 326; Christian, 31; 35; 37; 71; 83; 242; 278; 333; 364; higher, 32; public, 36-37; 83-83; 168; 307; 383; religious, (see Religious education)

Educators, 16; 109; 127

Effective Environment Scale, (see Scale, Effective Environment)

Ekind, David, 255

Elder, Jr., Glen, 64; 89

Eldredge, John, 370

Empower, 344; 347

Endorsement of Standards Scale, (see Scale, Endorsement of Standards)

Environment(s), 184; 361-362

Erickson, J. A., 389

Escriva, J., 389

Ethnic group(s), (see Group(s), ethnic)

Ethnicity, 53

Evangelism, 35; 56; 151; 154-155; 398

Exercise, 72; 225; 241; 250; 394; 396

Experience, iii; 13; 319; religious, 78; 95; 110; 154-155; 198; 345; 363

Extrinsic, 81; 191; 362; 400; faith, (see Faith, extrinsic); Religious Scale, (see Scale, Extrinsic, Religious)

Factor analysis, 280

Faculty, 357-358

Faith, iii; 15; 38; 61; 78-79; 96; 100; 105; 109; 127; 130; 132; 147; 154-155 165-166; 168-170; 184-185; 197; 204; 207; 211; 230-231; 249; 255; 265; 268; 277; 302-303; 309; 320; 344-345; 347;

351-352; 354; 359; 363; 369; 386; 398; and life, 98; Christian, 95; concerns, 15; crisis, 175; development, (see Development, faith); experience(s), 97-98; 204; 303; extrinsic, 82; horizontal, 79; 99; 101-103; integrated, 101-103; intrinsic, 82; 206; 347; 364; mature, 96; 321; Maturity Index, (FMI), 80; 98; 101; 166; Maturity Scale (FMS), (see Scale, Faith Maturity) maturity, 66; 79-80; 97; 99-101; 109; 175-176; 206; 233; 249; 328; 361; 364; 380; personal, 107; 207; 262; 353-354; religious, 54-55; 187; 302; 314; situations, 203; undeveloped, 101-103; vertical, 79; 99; 101-103

Faith-stage theory, 98

Faith-talk, 78; 268; 271; 321; 351; 358

Family(ies), iii; 22; 33; 41-42; 51; 66; 75-77; 88; 119; 181; 233; 240-242; 247; 249-250; 255; 270-271; 317; 322; 330; 347-348; 350; 357; 360; 366; 394; 399; 402; Climate Scale, (see Scale, Family Climate); climate, (see Climate, family); devotions, (see Devotions, family); life, 75; 252; 255; ministry, 23; positive influences, (see Influences, family positive); Seventh-day Adventist, 76-78; standard enforcement, 329-330; styles, 40; worship, (see Worship, family)

Father(s), 48; 52; 97; 180; 157; 257; 259; 265; 269-270; 321; 355; 403

Feelings, 15

Fellowship, 199-200; 406

Forgiveness, 153

Fowler, James, 98

Friedman, Thomas, 123; 251; 336

Friend(s), 61; 95; 119; 178-179; 190; 214; 286; 303; 396; 403

Furrow, James L. 191

Future, 49; 94; 120; 178; 215; 221-222

Gallup, Jr., George, 123; 314

Gane, Barry, v-vi; 19; 84; 280; 293

Gen Xer(s), 28; 51

Gender, 381; 393

Generation X, 14; 17; 20

Generation Y, 14; 17-18; 27-28; 49; 63; 103; 129; 214

Generation(s), 27; Millennial, 123

GenX, 107; 117; 129

GenY, 117; 129

Gillespie, Judith, 251; 273-274; 369

Gillespie, Tim, 251; 273; 369

Gillespie, V. Bailey, iii; v-vi; 19; 43; 123; 147; 171; 217; 251; 273-274; 293-294; 305; 335; 369

Gilligan, Carol, 251

Glasser, William, 313

Goal(s), 51; 105

God, iii; 13; 36; 49-50; 56-57; 59-60; 93; 100; 106-107; 113-114; 127; 139-140; 145-146; 151; 169; 162; 166; 179; 183; 186; 207; 211; 214; 221; 245; 255; 299; 303; 350; 354; 356; 358; 367; 398

God's will, (see Will, God's)

Goldman, Ronald, 151; 171

Gorsuch, Richard. L., 374; 389

Grace Scale, (see Scale, Grace)

Grace, iii; 95; 98; 103-106; 121; 127-129; 131-139; 144-146; 185; 212; 215; 250; 327; 340; 346; 352; 366-367; 399; God's, 22; 57; 223; orientation, 143; saving, 98

GraceLink, 104

Grace-oriented (orientation,) 59; 121; 129; 132; 346; 358

Great Advent Movement, 13

Great Controversy, 68; 163; 340; 356; 402

Griffin, Em, 152

Groome, Thomas, 184; 191

Group(s), ethnic, 61

Growth, iii; 111; 122; 197; spiritual, 98; 314; 317; 319; 351

Halpern, Diane, 217

Hancock Center, (see John Hancock Center for Youth and Family Ministry)

Harris, Maria, 172; 369

Health, 239

Hernandez, Edwin, 19; 335

Hesiod, 44; 47; 88

Hispanic, 328-332; 335

Holy Spirit, 162

Home(s), 16; 18; 38-39; 51; 75; 121; 132; 145; 159; 183; 255; 280; 318; 340; 345; 351-352; 356; 358-359

Homework, 81

Horizontal Faith Scale, (see Scale, Horizontal Faith)

Horizontal faith, (see Faith, horizontal)

Horizontal, 96; theme, 102

Howe, Neil, 88

Hypocrisy, 183

Identity, 30; 49; 71; 169; 176; 179; 182; 203-204; 344-346; quest(ing), 15; 30; 203; formation, 202; negative, 181

Ideology, 71; 155; 167; 202; 345

Inclusiveness, 83

Index, At-Risk, 381; Warmth, 200

Influences, church positive, 323-324; family positive, 320-323; school climate, 326; school positive, 325-327;

Innovation, 344; 356

Integrated faith, (see Faith, integrated)

Intercourse, 120; 396

Internet, 115; 119; 342; 403

Intrinsic faith, (see Faith, intrinsic)

Intrinsic Religious Orientation Measure, 167

Intrinsic Religious Scale, (see Scale, Intrinsic Religious)

Intrinsic, 81; 166; 191; 224; 232-233; 267; 362; 383; 399

Intrinsic/Extrinsic Religious Orientation, (see Orientation, Intrinsic/Extrinsic Religious)

Intrinsic-Extrinsic scale(s), (see Scales, Intrinsic-Extrinsic)

Investigative Judgment, 70; 401

Involve, 344; 347

Jersild, Paul, 251

Jessor, R., 389

Jesus, Christ, 54-56; 78; 93; 177; 179; 196; 212-213; 229; 340; 398; 400-401

Jesus, divinity, 70; 162; humanity, 70; 162

Jewelry, 118; 225; 240; 287; 394-395

John Hancock Center, for Youth and Family Ministry, iii; 18-19; 21-22; 40; 223; 235; 317; 332; 335; 363; 393

Johnson, Amber Anderson, 89

Johnson, Greg, 252; 273; 335

Johnston, L. D., 389

Jones, John, 21

Jones, Karen, 87; 89; 217

Jones, Tony, 93; 148; 151;171

Kijai, J., 389

Kimball, Dan, 171

Kimbrough-Melton, Robin, 89; 191

King, Pamela Ebstyne, 191

Kingdom of God, 22; 103; 106; 119; 121; 196; 198; 200; 263; 284; 291; 327; 330; 351-352; 355; 363; 367

Knight, George, 297

Kohlberg, Lawrence, 223; 251

La Sierra University, 19; 21; 29; 40; 223; 235; 317

Latino, 328

Law orientation, 59; 132; 135

Law Scale, (see Scale, Law)

Law, 127; 137; 250; 407

Lay leader, 49

Leader(s), 41; 65; 83; 189; 248; adult, 85; 210; 325; 405; local church, 16; 208; religious, 95; volunteer, 87

Lee, James Michael, 256; 273

Lee, Jerry, 19

Leffert, Nancy, 191

Legalism, 135; 229

Lewis, Sydney, 317; 335; 369

Life cycle, 103; 127

Life, spiritual, 60; 112; 175-176; 178; 184; 188; 340; 348; 352; 365

Life-affirming choices, (see Choices, life-affirming); decisions, (see Decisions, life-affirming); values, (see Values, life-affirming)

Life-denying behaviors, (see, Behaviors, life-denying); values, (see Values, life-denying

Lifestyle choices, (see Choices, lifestyle)

Lifestyle(s), 37; 71; 116; 131; 165; 228; 248-249; 320; 347; Adventist, 167

Liquor, 72; 181; 225; 240; 394-395

Local congregation, (see Congregation, local)

Loma Linda Academy, 104

Loma Linda Elementary School, 31

Loma Linda University, 244; 248

Love Index, 132; orientation, 57

Love Scale, (see Scale, Love)

Love, iii; 77; 105; 121; 127; 130-132; 146; 155; 185; 196-197; 271; 327; 344; 346; 352; 399; 406

Loving constraint, (see Constraint, loving)

Loyalty, iii; 40; 63; 108; 151; 176; 345; 349; 353; 361; church, 62; denominational, 167; 203; 206; 232-233; 248; 267; 361; 380; 397

Magazine(s), 115

Mallery, Janet, 19

Mallery, Lynn, 19

Marijuana, 73-74; 68; 73; 165-166; 306; 396

Marriage, 225; 227; 240; 395

Marzano, Robert J., 313

Materialism as Life Value, 400

Maternal Parenting Style, (see Style, Maternal Parenting)

Mature faith, 96; 120; 205; 235

Maturity, faith, (see Faith maturity)

Maturity, iii; 200; 278

Mckenzie, Jamie, 369

Meaning, 100; 107; 179; 181-182; 195; 365; 398

Meat(s), unclean, 225; 240; 244; 295

Media, 48; 115; 221; 227-228; 235; 354

Meditation, 56; 79; 152

Mentoring, 121; 345

Millennial generation, 38; 107; kids, 28

Millennial(s), 49

Millennium, 68-69; 163; 402

Milne, A.A., 191

Ministry, 47; 183; 350; 355; 363; 365; 367; pastoral, 71; preteen, 87; 209
Mission, 344; 349; projects, (see Projects, mission); statement(s), 87; 298
Missionary Volunteers, 13
Modesty, 118; 239; 241; 250; 326
Money, 100; 398
Mosaic, generation, 117
Mother(s), 53; 97; 180; 257; 260; 269; 321; 355; 403
Movie(s), 71; 118; 221; 224; 226-228; 240-241; 243; 250; 394-395
MTV, 27; 184
Music, 95; 107; 109; 115; 118; 182; 215; 349; 354; 403; Christian, 106; hip-hop, 116; R&B, 116; rock, 117; 225; 239-240; 287; 394-395

Narcotics, 243
Nel, Malan, 89
Nolan, Rebecca, F., 217
Norris, Stephen P., 217
North American Division, iii; 16; 21-22; 33-34; 110; 136; 318; 328; 349; Office of Education, 21; 38; 81; 158
Nurture, 341; 344; 350-351

O'Malley, P. M., 389
Obedience, 57; 59; 73; 104; 130; 212
Office of Education, North American Division, (see North American Division, Office of Education)
Once-saved-always-saved, 60
One-parent families, 52
Orientation, Intrinsic/Extrinsic Religious, 399

Ortho I, or Orthodoxy I Scale, (see Scale, Orthodoxy I)
Orthodoxy I, (see Scale, Orthodoxy I)
Ortho I, or Orthodoxy II Scale, (see Scale, Orthodoxy II)
Orthodoxy II, (see Scale, Orthodoxy II)
Orthodoxy Scale(s), (see Scale, Orthodoxy)
Orthodoxy, 66; 68; 160; 166; 224; 233; 400;
Overprotective Parenting Style Scale, (see Scale, Overprotective Parenting Style)

Pacific Island(ers), 328-332; 335
Parent(s), (ing), 16; 27-28-29; 34; 37; 49-50; 64-65; 71; 76-78; 95; 145; 160; 168; 175; 180; 189; 203; 221-222; 228; 255; 263-264; 268; 317-318; 322-323; 345-346; 349; 351-352; 365-367; 382; 399; divorced, 52; single, 262
Parental Bonding Instrument (PBI), 256
Parental Monitoring, 402
Parenting Style, (see Style, parenting)
Parenting, positive, 320
Parenting, spiritual, 320; 322; 349; 351; 369
Park, Dave, 147
Parker, Gordon, 260; 273
Parousia, 68
Parsons, Richard, 339
Participation, religious, 65
Pastor(s), 13; 15-16; 28; 41; 47; 49; 95; 164; 168; 208; 262-263-264; 284-285; 318; 357

Pastoral ministry, (see Ministry, pastoral)

Paternal Parenting Style, (see Style, Paternal parenting)

Paterson, Katherine, 90

Pathfinder(s), 14; 289-290; 349

Peace, 155; 187

Peer pressure, 178; 181

Peer(s), 204; 223; 317; 325

Perception(s), 94-95

Performance, academic, 64

Personal devotions (see Devotions, personal)

Personal piety, (see Piety, personal)

Personal religion, (see Religion, personal)

Peterson, Eugene, 54; 89; 176; 191

Pickering, Debra J., 313

Piece of the Pie Ministries, 71

Piety Scale, (see Scale, Piety)

Piety, 60; 105-107; 109; 121; 152; 175-176; personal, 203; 232-233; 380

Pluralism, 214

Pollock, Jane E., 313

Popular Cultural Standards, (see Standards, Popular Cultural)

Popular Culture Strictness Scale, (see Scale, Popular Culture Strictness)

Positive Parenting, (see Parenting, Positive)

Postmodern, 93; 129; 151; 160

Poverty, 64; 398

Practice(s), 51; 65; 109; 167; 179

Pray, 55; 108; 349; 400

Prayer(s), 66; 79; 98; 106; 109-110-111; 175-176; 185-187; 197; 348; 399; practice of, 56

Pre-Advent judgment, 157; 159

Preteen ministry, (see Ministry, preteen)

Princeton Religious Research Center, 95

Program(s), youth ministry, 85; 209; 405

Programming, 109; 209-210; 324; 349-350

Project Affirmation, 15

Projects, mission, 66; 189

Prophetic role, 67

Public schools, (see Education, public)

Puech, Henri Charles, 14

Purity, 326

Purpose, 100; 106-107; 179; 195; 345; 365; 398

Quality of Religious Education Scale, (see Scale, Quality of Religious Education)

Quality teaching, (see Teaching, quality)

Quality, Religious Education, 405

Questionnaire, 20; 51

Questions, 202; doctrinal, 67; religious, 100; spiritual, 95

Racism, 64

Rahn, Dave, 87; 89

Rasi, Humberto, 32

Rebellion, 181

Reese, S, 23

Reflection, 88; 98

Regnerus, Mark, 65; 89

Relationship(s), 49; 61; 96-97; 100; 121; 137; 139; 144; 146; 154; 166; 178; 180; 185-186; 212-214; 236; 239; 248; 255; 300; 303; 328; 339; 344; 352-355; 358; 365; 398

Relevance, 180

Reliability, 377

Religion, 49; 80; 95; 106; 115; 130; 156; 197-198; 204; 208; 239; 322; 399; personal, 54; 79

Religious, 50; 107-109; activities, (see Activities, religious); behavior, (see Behavior(s), religious); Education Press, 256; Education Quality, (see Quality, Religious Education); education, 65; 171; 189; 202; 208; 232-233; 248; 283; 360-361; experience, (see Experience, religious); faith, (see Faith, religious); participation, (see Participation, religious); educators, 49; issues, 50; worker, 49

Remnant church, (See Church, remnant)

Rice, Gail, 19

Rice, Richard, 19; 154

Thayer, Jerome, 389

Richards, Lawrence, O., 390

Righteousness, 105; 213

Ring(s), 118; 226-227;241; 394-395

Rockwell, Norman, 41

Roehikepartain, Eugene C., 292

Rosenthal, N., 23

Rule(s), 72-73; 131; 134; 142; 183; 223; 236-237; 397; 407

Sabbath School(s), 14; 189; 208; 290;

Sabbath, 62; 70; 73; 118; 157; 225; 240-241; 326; 395; 401

Sahlin, Monte, 89

Sahlin, Norma, 89

Salvation, 57; 60; 127; 130-132; 134-136; 138; 144; 170; 398; 407

Salvation, process of, 60

Sanctification, 142

Sanctuary (message), 67; 346

Santayana, George, 342

Scale, Adventist Attitude, 237-238

Scale, Adventist Lifestyle Strictness, 394

Scale, Adventist Orthodoxy, 375

Scale, At-Risk, 75

Scale, Caring Parenting Style, 403

Scale, Denominational Loyalty, 224; 397

Scale, Drug Standards Strictness, 394

Scale, Effective Environment, 360

Scale, Endorsement of Standards, 232

Scale, Extrinsic Religious, 80

Scale, Faith Maturity, (FMS) 166; 237-238; 379; 398

Scale, Family Climate, 360

Scale, Grace, 58-59; 167; 381

Scale, Horizontal, Faith, 102

Scale, Intrinsic Religious 80; 167; 238; 384

Scale, Law Orientation, 141

Scale, Law, 59

Scale, Love, 58-59; 134-135

Scale, Orthodoxy I; 69; 167-168; 400

Scale, Orthodoxy II, 68-69; 161; 165; 167; 401

Scale, Orthodoxy, 66-67; 156

Scale, Overprotective Parenting Style, 404

Scale, Piety, 109; 111;

Scale, Popular Culture Strictness, 394

Scale, Quality of Religious Education, 206

Scale, Spiritual-Influences, 166

Scale, Thinking Church Climate, 206

Scale, Thinking Climate, 202

Scale, Thinking, 206

Scale, Warm, Church Climate, 199; 206; 224

Scale, Warmth, 201

Scales, Intrinsic-Extrinsic, 379
School climate influences, (see Influences, school climate)
School climate, (see Climate, school)
School positive influences, (see Influences, school positive)
School spirit, 304; 327; 405
School(s), 14; 16; 22; 38-39; 51; 81; 86; 121; 132; 210; 240-241; 247; 250; 279-280; 292; 297; 299; 302; 309; 318; 340; 345; 349; 352; 356-357; 359-360; 364; 367; 396; Adventist, 19; 38; 66; 70; 82-83-84; 94; 103; 121; 146; 159; 137; 297-298; 378; 380; 382; 394; Christian, 33; Private, 31; Public, 31; 82
Scripture(s), 18; 111-112; 127; 170; 185; 214; 230-231; 255
Search Institute, 39; 55; 97
Second Coming, 67; 140; 157; 401
Self-esteem, 195
Selflessness, 52
Self-worth, 189
Senter, Mark, 89
Sermon(s), 201; 215
Service, 14; 104; 132-133; 155; 165; 197; 233; 348-349-350
Service, as a Life Value, 406
Services, church, 66; 215
Services, worship, 14; 65; 85; 182
Sex, 52; 73; 211; 225; 255; 263;
Sexuality, 60; 211
Shelton, Charles, 175; 178; 191; 222; 251
Shoplift(ing), 74; 306; 378; 396
Silent Generation, 14
Simmons, Ella, 19; 335
Sin(s), 131; 136; 145

Sisters, 95
Smith, Charles T., 19
Socialization, religious, 64
Socrates, 44
South Africa, 16
Southern Baptist Church, 79; 103
Spiritual gifts, 68; 165; 184-185
Spiritual life, (See Life, spiritual)
Spiritual Parenting, (see Parenting, Spiritual)
Spiritual values, (see Values, spiritual)
Spiritual, 56; 106; 120; 181
Spiritual-Influences Scale, (see Scale, Spiritual-Influences)
Spirituality, 28; 54; 61; 106-107; 176-177-178; 222; 349; 351; 366
Sport(s), 118; 226-227; 239-240; 287; 394-395
Standard(s), 223-225; 227-228; 232; 234; 236-237; 239; 240-241; 247-248; 287; 331; 354; 357-358; 368; 397; Adventist, 40; 66; 71-73; 83; 104; 117-118; 131; 141; 183; 206; 226; 235-236; 240; 242; 244; 380; 384; 394; 407; Adventist Lifestyle, 71; 167; 225; 232; 234; 249; Adventist Way-of-Life, 72; 117-118-119; 226; 233; 322; 326; 347; Popular Cultural, 73; 117-118-119; 122; 167; 182; 227; 232-234; 249; 267; 322; 347; 357; Substance abuse, 72; 118; 122; 226; 232-233; 322
Stark, R., 389
Steinberg, Paul M., 294
Stewardship, 68; 165-166
Storm Co., 14
Strahan, Bradley, 256; 273
Strauss, William, 88

Strommen, Merton, 87; 89; 342-343; 369

Stronge, James H., 313

Student(s), Adventist, 84; 115; 147

Style, Caring Parent, 256

Style, Caring Parenting Style, 257-258

Style, Maternal Parenting, 259

Style, Overprotective Parenting, 257

Style, Parenting, 403

Style, Paternal Parenting, 260

Substance abuse, (see Abuse, substance)

Suffering, 100

Suicide, 48; 396

Sujansky, Joanne, 43

Sullivan, Randall, 88

Surveys, *Valuegenesis*, 69; 375-376; 393

Sustain, 344; 350

Symbol(s), 27; 154; 169; 330

System, belief, 182

System, theological, 67

Tammnen, Kalevi, 381

Teacher(s), 13; 27-29; 32; 49; 82; 85; 95; 146; 160; 168; 175; 209; 248-249; 263; 278; 299; 301; 317-318; 325-326; 345; 405

Teaching, quality, 325

Teen(s), Teenagers, 17; 29-31; 42; 47-49; 58; 75; 93-95; 97; 107; 119; 123; 152-153; 166; 169; 176; 179; 182-183; 206; 221; 230; 255; 355

Teenager (see teen(s))

Television, 95; 115; 404

Temperance, 72

Ten Commandments, 67; 157; 230; 400

Thayer, Jane, 19

Theological system, (see System, theological)

Theology, 71; 169

Theology, Adventist, 57

Thinking Church Climate Scale, (see Scale, Thinking Church Climate)

Thinking Climate Scale, (see Scale, Thinking Climate)

Thinking Congregation, 406

Thinking Scale, (see Scale, Thinking)

Thinking, 203

Thinking, critical, 204-205; 235; 357

Third Angel's Message(s), 297

Thomas, Evan, 88

Tillich, Paul, 27

Time, 100; 398; 402

Tobacco, 72; 74; 83; 118; 225; 239-240-241; 243; 286; 378; 381; 394-395

Tradition(s,) 14; 72; 175; 189; 214; 230

Trinity, 68; 161; 163; 401

Trolley car, 60

Tuition, 34

Tupling, Hilary, 273

Turco, Douglas Michele, 23

Two-parent families, 52

Tyner, Stuart, 22

Unclean meats, (see Meat(s), unclean)

Undeveloped faith, (see Faith, undeveloped)

UPDATE, 21; 23

Validity, 377;

Value system(s), 38; 181

Value(s), 15; 37-38; 49-50; 64; 119; 127; 143; 145; 175; 180; 188-190; 204; 223; 224; 228; 243; 247; 326; 330; 333-334; 343; 345; 357; 363; 366-367; spiritual, 95; life-affirming, 99; life-denying

Values, parental religious, 65

Valuegenesis research, 15-16; 20; 38; 49-50; 96; 107; 109; 113; 340

Vertical, 96-97; 102; faith, (see Faith, vertical)

Video games, 118-119; 226-227; 241; 403

Violence, 52; 255

Volf, Miroslav, 221

Wagener, Linda Mans, 191

Walcker, Ottilia Bietz, 32

Warm Church Climate Scale, (see Scale, Warm Church)

Warm Congregation, (see Congregation(s), warm)

Warm(th), 85; 199

Warmth Index, (see Index, Warmth)

Warmth Scale, (see Scale, warmth)

Webster, Cheryl, 251; 273; 369

Weir, John, 123

West, Diana, 88

White, Ellen G., 33; 35-36; 43; 70; 96; 108-109; 113-115; 121; 123; 139; 147; 158-160; 188; 196; 205; 217; 255; 273; 277; 292-293; 297; 300; 313; 346; 349; 401; 404; 408

Wilcox, W. Bradford, 273

Wilde, Oscar, 319; 335

Will, God's, 96; 106; 127; 169; 180; 204

Williams, William Carlos, vii

Wine, 181

Wisdom, 54; 113

Work(s), 57; 105; 129; 135-136; 138; 140; 223; 331; 344; 346; 407

Works-oriented, 129; 131-132; 136; 142

Works-righteousness, 229

World Trade Center, 245

World-view, 179

Worship(s), 59; 66; 105; 132; 154; 165; 179; 182; 185; 199; 201; 207; 215; 222; 247; 267; 271; 340; 348; 363; 406; services, (see Services, worship) family, 79; 248; 265-268; 323; 348-349

Yaconelli, Mike, 195

Yoon, Won Kil, 19; 207; 335

Yorkey, Mike, 273; 335

Young adult(s), 16-17; 23; 46; 107; 146; 182; 221; 247; 318-319; 328; 349-350; 355; 363; 366

Young people, 13; 20; 27; 29; 49-50; 56; 60; 73; 79; 87; 94; 116; 130; 157; 167; 184; 190; 195; 198-199; 201; 213; 227; 248; 250; 280-281; 291; 344-345; 348-349; 351; 357; 364-365; 367

Young people, Adventist, 51; 54; 71; 186

Young person, iii; 35; 204; 269

Youth, 17; 23; 35-36; 40; 47; 64; 71-72; 94-96; 107; 119-120; 130-132; 135; 139; 146; 160; 164; 170; 165; 177; 181; 183; 188-189; 202; 210-212; 221; 235; 247; 255; 264; 277; 318; 320; 328; 345; 349-350; 355; 363; 366; , Adventist, 67; 100; 117; 121; 162; 181; 229; 319; 387; culture, 22; group, 208; leader, 50; ministry programs, (see Programs, youth ministry); ministry, 16-17; 39; 80; 84-85; 88; 171; 210; 274; 277-290; 292; 356; pastor(s), 27; 49; 208; 339; worker(s), 28; 41

Zeng, Qing, 217

Zoba, Wendy Murray, 17; 23; 24; 88; 147